THE NEW DACHSHUND

Smooth Dachshund

Longhaired Dachshund

Wirehaired Dachshund

The New
DACHSHUND

by
LOIS MEISTRELL

With Special Chapters by
DR. C. WILLIAM NIXON
JEANNETTE W. CROSS and PEGGY WESTPHAL

First Edition

HOWELL
BOOK HOUSE
New York

Howell Book House
Macmillan Publishing Company
866 Third Avenue, New York, NY 10022

Collier Macmillan Canada, Inc.
1200 Eglinton Avenue East, Suite 200
Don Mills, Ontario M3C 3N1

Library of Congress Catalog Card No. 75-30419
ISBN 0-87605-107-7

Macmillan books are available at special discounts for bulk purchases for sales promotions, premiums, fund-raising, or educational use. For details, contact:

Special Sales Director
Macmillan Publishing Company
866 Third Avenue
New York, NY 10022

10   9   8

Printed in the United States of America

To Harland,

and to the many happy memories
of the times when we owned and
showed our Dachshunds.

Photo: Harland Meistrell with Can. & Am. Ch. Frederick
v.d. Isar, CD, Best of Breed at the 1955 Dachshund Association
of Long Island (DALI) Specialty.

The Name:

DACHSHUND is of German derivation (*dachs*: badger; *hund*: dog) and is pronounced *Doxhoont*. The breed has been in America since before the first stud books. In the period of anti-German fervor following World War I, its name was changed to "Badger Dog." The name Dachshund was restored in 1923, and in line with American Kennel Club practice at the time of retaining the native spelling for plurals of foreign breeds, *Dachshunde* was used for the plural. This was Americanized to Dachshunds in 1941.

Contents

Acknowledgments

For THEIR HELP in the research and writing of this book, I am especially indebted to: John Carson, John Hutchinson Cook, Mrs. Jeannette W. Cross, Mrs. William B. Hill, Jr., Laurence Alden Horswell and his sister Mrs. G.E. Johnson, Mrs. John Marshall Jones, Miss Louise Magary, Mrs. Elizabeth Weller McNeill, Mrs. Dorothy Mullen, Patricia Davis and the Gaines Dog Research Center, Dr. C. William Nixon, Mrs. Sara Peterman, Dr. and Mrs. George Pickett, Mrs. Pierce Onthank, Maxwell Riddle, Sanford Roberts, Michael Triefus, George Wanner and Mrs. Alan Westphal.

My thanks also to Mr. and Mrs. Franklin Frantz, for their help in the translation of German books and documents, old and new; to Miss Beverly Petrelis, who made the drawing of the St. Hubert stag pin reproduced in the first chapter; to the many who contributed pictures of their dogs; and to all, named or unnamed, who by their encouragement and cooperation have helped make this book possible.

I have tried to properly acknowledge sources throughout the text. Important references included: *The Complete Dachshund*, Wm. Denlinger, 1954; *The Complete Dog Book*, copyright by The American Kennel Club, 1975; *Der Dachshund*, R. Corneli, 1885; *Der Dachshund*, Dr. Fritz Engelmann, 1925 and 1958 editions; *Der Dachshund*, Emil Ilgner, 1896; *The Dachshund or Teckel*, Herbert Sanborn, 1949; *The Dachshund*, Grayce Greenburg, 1955; *Dachshund Pedigrees* (complete to December 1896), compiled by E. Sydney Woodwiss and E. Watlock Allen; *25th Edition Teckel Stambuch*, 1890–1914; *The Pet Dachshund*, Laurence and Dorothy Horswell, 1958; *The Popular Dachshund*, E. Fitch Daglish, 1960; *This Is The Dachshund*, Leonore Loeb Adler, 1964; *Report of the United States Dachshund Field Trial Club*, 1935; *Origin, Structure and Movement of the Scent Hound*, Dr. Braxton Sawyer.

Back issues of the following magazines were most helpful: *The American Dachshund* (from 1949 to 1975); *The American Miniature Dachshund As-*

Author Lois Meistrell has long been identified in all three aspects of Dachshund interest—show, Obedience and field trial. She is pictured handling Ch. DeSangpur's Traveler's Trix to win of the Group at Westbury, L.I. in May 1960. —*Shafer*

sociation News; Popular Dogs; The American Kennel Gazette — Pure Bred Dogs; Dog World; and Dogs.

It has not been my aim to include long lists of champions or kennels in this book. Instead, the emphasis has been on capturing the essence of the Dachshund — its tradition, its physical makeup, its character — and to explore the many interests and pleasures it offers owners. The story of a breed is very much tied up in the people who have owned it — the breeders, exhibitors, judges — and I have tried to highlight some of the personalities that have most influenced the development of the breed. Through their stories, I hope that you — the reader — will gain a fuller understanding and appreciation of why and how the Dachshund has come to its place as one of the world's most popular breeds.

— *Lois Meistrell*

International Champion De Sangpur Traveling Man, C.D., a show-field-and-Obedience competitor of the '50s, owned by the author.—
Tauskey

Dachs 16, black and tan, the pillar of the breed. Descent and breeder unknown. Owner, Freiherr von Knigge.

Mordax, pioneer wirehair. Owner, Capt. v. Wardenburg.

Mann, chocolate, pillar of the longhairs. Whelped 1868. Breeder, von Kalisch. Owner, von Alversleven.

The Beginning

A SINNER turned saint, a poor Emperor who wed a Duke's daughter, the hunting habits of the Pharoahs and a theory that Dachshunds may not be of German origin after all, are among the tales told of the breed's history. Sorted out from among these legends and ancient tales are facts that warrant serious consideration as to how the Dachshund came into being.

There is more fancy than fact in many of these stories, but real or imagined, they make interesting reading. Actually, no one really knows the origin of the Dachshund, or for that matter the origin of a large number of breeds as we know them today. It remains that Dachshunds did arrive and judging from the current registration figures (about 50,000 a year—fifth ranking of all AKC-approved breeds) they are here to stay.

Dachs 16, in the first Dachshund studbook, and Figure, the first and founding sire of the Morgan breed of horse, have in common that their ancestries have never been proven and that their offspring have been a reproduction of their own images for centuries.

All dogs, Dachshunds included, are descended from a small, prehistoric animal, the *Tomarctus,* that lived on the earth fifteen million years ago. The only present day animal that resembles it in any way is the civet cat, a mammal that lives in the warmer regions of the Old World and has been described as a weasel-cat, since it displays the characteristics of both. From the Tomarctus came four distinct varieties of the *Canis Familiaris* and it is from the *Canis Familiaris Leinere* that the hound family (of which the Dachshund is a member) is descended.

Archeological evidence points to the Saluki, the Afghan, the Greyhound and possibly the Borzoi as being the oldest of the hound breeds. These dogs were the ancestors of the Sleuth hound, a large, early version of the Bloodhound which, in time, was the progenitor of the St. Hubert hound, a breed of fine scenting and hunting ability that was bred by the monks of the monastery of St. Hubert in the Ardennes section of Belgium. It is from the St. Hubert hound that authorities believe that the Basset Hound, the Beagle and the Dachshund are descended. The St. Hubert hound also had a strong influence on many other hound breeds.

These hounds derive their name from the patron saint of hounds and hunting, St. Hubert, who lived from 656 A.D. to 727 A.D. A Duke's son, as a young man he had led a completely dissolute life. One Good Friday, the cynical, irreverent young fellow—at the peak of his wayward ways—scoffed at worship on the holy day and took to the forest with his horse and hounds to hunt. Luck was with him, for he had not penetrated the woodlands very far when he sighted a magnificent stag. Raising his bow to take aim, he got the fright of his life when, between the stag's antlers, there appeared a cross. (To this day, the stag with a cross between its antlers is the emblem of St. Hubert.) Hubert left the forest and went straight to church, where he confessed his many sins, received absolution and from that time on led a life of such exemplary piety that he became Bishop of Liege. He founded the monastery that bears his name and, some time later, was beatified by the Roman Catholic Church.

The religious life did not dull his enthusiasm for hunting. From the time of its founding, St. Hubert's monastery maintained a pack of hunting hounds.

The St. Hubert hound is mentioned in the writings of Charles IX (1550–1574) and by Du Fouilloux in his book *La Venerie* (The Hunt) written in 1585. The hounds are described as low-set, medium-sized, long in body, not very speedy but possessed of exceptionally accurate scenting powers and pleasingly mellow voices.

Accepting the premise that the Basset Hound and the Dachshund have a common ancestor in the St. Hubert hound, one then wonders how the Basset and the Dachshund became two separate but related breeds and which was developed first.

The relationship between the Dachshund and the Basset is a highly acceptable concept. Sir John Buchanan-Jardine, in his book *Hounds of the World*, describes four varieties of Bassets known in France. They were the Artois Basset, the Vendée Basset, the Basset Bleu de Gascogne and the Basset Faune de Bretagne. Of the Basset Bleu, he has this to say, "At first sight, these Gascogne Bassets remind one very strongly of German Dachshunds; the general build is very similar, which, with the rather pointed nose, helps increase the resemblance."

The first edition of *British Dogs* by Hugh Dalziel, published in London in 1897, quotes a Basset hound fancier, who wrote under the pen name of "Wildfowler". After first explaining that the French and Belgian Bassets are divided into three main classes — Bassets *a jambes droites* (straight-legged), Bassets *a jambes demi-torses* (forelegs half crooked) and Bassets *a jambes torses* (fully crooked) — Wildfowler says ". . . a black and tan or a red Basset *a jambes torses* cannot by any possible use of one's eyes be distinguished

The vision of St. Hubert made into jewelry. Drawing of a pin owned by Mrs. Jeannette W. Cross.

TONHUNDE aus COLIMA.

MITGEBRACHT von PROF. D? SELER.

Clay models of dogs from Colina, Mexico, according to Stiebel.

from a Dachshund of the same colour, although some German writers assert that the breeds are quite distinct." E. Fitch Daglish, the English author and Dachshund breeder, also supported this concept and used the same quotation in his book, *The Popular Dachshund*, published in London in 1960.

Assuming that the Dachshund and the Basset Hound were once one and the same, which came first? Probably the Basset, or at least a Basset-like type of short-legged hound. A dog very similar to a Basset could be produced by several generations of selective breeding that utilized low-stationed individuals from one of the larger hound breeds such as the Bloodhound, which is considered to be a leggier replica of the St. Hubert hound.

How these short-legged Basset-like descendants of the hounds of St. Hubert developed into Dachshunds is explained by John Hutchinson Cook, Dachshund breeder, judge and a serious student of all hound breeds. He presents a credible theory and one that also raises a question as to whether the Dachshund might have originated in Austria and later migrated to Germany.

It would appear that there is a link between the history of the Dachshund and that of the imperial Hapsburg family who ruled Austria until 1918. In 1477, the eighteen-year-old Hapsburg heir, the Holy Roman Emperor Maximillian I, journeyed west from Vienna to Burgundy to become the husband of Marie of Burgundy, daughter and heiress of Charles the Bold, Duke of Burgundy. Maximillian knew he was marrying into a family of great power and wealth but this knowledge did not prepare him for the awesome magnificence of the Burgundian court. Having grown up in war-torn, impoverished Austria, in his family's cold and barren castle, the young emperor was bedazzled by the opulence and beauty of his father-in-law's palaces. He wrote letters to relatives in Austria describing the wonders of the Burgundian ducal establishment and made particular mention of what impressed him most of all the marvels he found there—Marie's father kept for his hunting pleasure three thousand trained falcons and *four thousand trained hunting hounds*.

At first thought, four thousand seems an incredible number of hounds for anyone to keep, be he duke, prince, king or emperor; however, when some of the circumstances are considered, perhaps it isn't. For one thing, Charles the Bold was richer than most kings and his lands more extensive. Today one thinks of Burgundy as a French province or, perhaps, a red wine, but in the fifteenth century the Duchy of Burgundy embraced the larger part of present-day Belgium, the Netherlands, Luxembourg, and huge areas of northern and northeastern France. Charles could probably have supported twice as many hounds had he so chosen.

A second factor was the absolute passion for hunting possessed by royalty and the nobility of that period. They seem to have hunted to the exclusion of just about all other activities. The Austrian nobles who had accompanied Maximillian to Burgundy were apparently favorably impressed with the hounds, for when they returned to Austria, they took some Burgundian hounds home with them where they hunted them in packs. From these

16

Some of the old type of Dachshunds were much more
of Terrier type than those of today, and many resembled the Basset Hound.

hounds, by selective breeding, Mr. Cook theorizes that the Dachshund was evolved.

Later in this book, we shall read of the *Dachskrieger*, the *Huhnerhund* and the *Wachtelhund*, all now extinct German breeds. These breeds have also been credited as being sources of Dachshund origin. It is quite possible that either the St. Hubert hounds or the Burgundian ones, lost during an extended hunt or given as gifts to German princes, were mated with these native German dogs and possibly produced the Dachshund simultaneously with those that were bred in Austria.

Another theory is one proposed by Major Emil Ilgner, the first president of the German Dachshund Club in 1888. It is one that was widely accepted at that time and still has many adherents today.

Major Ilgner was apparently convinced that it enhanced a breed's status if it could be shown to be of great antiquity. This obsession, to depict their breed as the most ancient and therefore the most honorable, seems to have afflicted many of those in the past who have written about the origin of various breeds. One finds such phrases as "comrade of the Vikings," "origin lost in the mists of time," "of considerable antiquity," "of very ancient lineage," and so on. In his book, published in 1896, Ilgner declared that the Dachshund's history could be traced back through 35 centuries.

Ilgner's conclusions are founded on somewhat shaky evidence. Carvings, murals, and inscriptions discovered in ancient Egyptian tombs do show short-legged dogs, but likening them to Dachshunds requires a vivid imagination. The dogs so portrayed are prick-eared and snipy-nosed. Furthermore, drawing conclusions from Egyptian works of art as to the actual size of the object depicted is impossible. Artists of that period ignored relative proportions altogether. For instance, in a painting showing Pharoah in the company of other people, the Pharoah figure would be drawn larger than any of the other people to demonstrate the ruler's importance. Secondly, the work of these artists was so highly stylized as to be distorted and cannot be taken seriously.

Much ado has been made over an inscription on a monument to Thutmose III. The hieroglyphics of the inscription were wrongly translated as "teckal," or "teckar," and the fact that the word "teckel" is synonymous with "Dachshund" in Germany was seized upon as evidence of the breed's existence 4000 years ago. This in spite of the fact that the dog shown in connection with the inscription does not bear the slightest resemblance to a Dachshund and looks, in fact, to be more of a Mastiff-type animal.

Further claims as to the breed's antiquity are based on stone, wood, clay models of short-legged animals found in Peru, Mexico, Greece and China. Judging from photographs and sketches of these animals, it would take a wild flight of fancy to seriously identify them as Dachshunds. Some look more like pigs.

Mrs. Jeannette W. Cross, Dachshund breeder, exhibitor and judge, who is

Illustrations from *The Complete German Hunter* by Flemming, 1719.

19

Detail from a linen and wool wall-hanging (V Century A. D.) depicting an Egyptian horseman with dog, and another hunting a lion.—*Reproduced by permission, The Metropolitan Museum of Art, Gift of George F. Baker, 1890.*

also an authority on needlework, past and present, called to my attention a wall-hanging in the Metropolitan Museum of Art, made of linen and embroidered in wool and classified by the museum as Coptic (Egyptian) V–VI Century. The left panel of the hanging shows a horseman, accompanied by a dog which Mrs. Cross considers to be a fair likeness of a Basset or a Dachshund. Mrs. Cross does not subscribe to the "Egyptian" theory of Dachshund origin, but she did point out the hanging as the only Egyptian work that shows anything like a Dachshund.

With all due respect to the ancient, unknown hunter, I doubt if he bagged much game. I have my own experience with Dachshunds and horses. I used to take my two longhairs and my Dalmatians with me when I exercised my horse on an unused polo field in Manhasset, Long Island. The only way the Dachshunds could keep up with the horse, at a collected canter, was to cut across the field and meet the horse and the Dalmatians at the corners. Although they were hunting hard from preparation for field trials and dog shows, both Dachshunds lay down under a shady tree long before the hour's exercise was over, and waited for me to finish my ride. This procedure had some funny results too. On the way home, crossing a main thoroughfare, Valley Road, I was sometimes stopped by passing motorists who after looking at this odd collection of a horse with big and little hounds inquired, "Are they part of a circus?"

So much for tales of the breed's origin. Whatever has been the Dachshund's past, his future seems happily assured.

Crooked and straight legged Dachshunds, according to Georges de Buffon, French naturalist, 1793.

The Way They Were

IT HAS BEEN generally assumed that the smooth Dachshund was the original one and that the longhaired and wirehaired varieties came later as the result of outcrossings with other breeds. Most historians and researchers in Dachshunds do not agree with this. While the origin of any given breed as we know it today is largely guesswork, the opinions of these experts are educated ones and there are enough facts to make their findings appear valid.

What does appear to be true is that the smooth Dachshund was the first to appear *in public*. Its coat may have been the reason why it was the first of the three varieties to leave the forests for the show ring and urban living. The short, sleek hair made it more vulnerable to bites from its prey and from brambles and thorns. The longhairs, who followed next, were found wanting in underground hunting, since mud frequently matted their soft coats and slowed their progress. The wirehaired was the least glamorous and the most versatile; his coat gave him ample protection, so he remained the last to join his cousins, the smooths and longhairs, in coming to public notice.

The appearance of long and wirehaired puppies among litters of smooth Dachshunds long before Mendel provided a scientific explanation for these occurrences, and the variety of coats, colors, sizes and shapes of the progenitors of modern breeds as we know them today, strongly suggests that all three varieties of Dachshunds began at about the same time. The separation into three distinct varieties came later through selective breeding by hunters who wanted dogs with the particular type of coat to suit their needs in the pursuit of game.

The description of dogs which appear most likely to be the ancestor of the modern Dachshund was given by Holmberg in *Georgica Curiosa*, written in 1700. The dogs were referred to as badger dogs. The French called them Bas-

Dachshunds, from work by Dr. Reichenbach, 1836.

sets because they were low to the ground (*bas* meaning low). They had long slender bodies and appeared in all sorts of colors. *The Complete German Hunter,* written by Flemming in 1719, contains illustrations that show dogs very much like today's Dachshunds. Other authors of that time, Parsons, Dobel and Buffon (a French authority on natural history), write of low-stationed dogs with either straight or crooked legs that occur in all colors, including white and dapple. They are described as "small, sharp dogs that like to trail," or "sharp dogs that work in the burrows of badger and fox," or "snappish and often cunning, brave but pugnacious animals which are tenacious of life and will engage with any dog, be he ever so big."

From 1820 to 1893, wirehaired and longhaired Dachshunds were mentioned, although they were seldom seen until 1900. Two writers of that time, Dietrich aus dem Winckell (1820) and Dr. Reichenbach (1836), mention all three coats as being in existence prior to their writings and describe the colors common to all three varieties as "yellow, brown, black, dapple, brindle" and the legs as "short and either crooked or straight."

By this time "Dachshund " (*dachs* meaning badger, and *hund* meaning dog) was the name being more and more given to these dogs, not only in Germany but in other countries where they were located.

The revolution in Germany in 1848 caused a national political struggle. All other activities, including dog breeding, were almost at a standstill. A certain amount of breeding continued but it was carried on by people isolated from each other by occupation and distance. They were mostly national foresters. There was no unified plan and each breeder pursued his own ideas as to the type of Dachshund that best suited his hunting requirements. Enough dogs were bred during this period to make possible a larger and better breeding program, once hostilities ended and communications were restored.

Early Development in Germany

Possibly it was the revolution that held back the establishment of the German Dachshund Club until 1888 and the writing of a Dachshund standard of points until 1889. The English had already established their Dachshund Club and their own breed standard in 1881.

This does not mean that the Germans did not keep records of their breedings. The first German stud book was published in 1879. It contained 54 entries and also included the names of breeders of that time. Some of the best known were: G. Barnewitz, Ludwig Backmann, Prince Solms-Braunfels, v Podewils, Lt. Fink, Emil Meyer, Wilhelm von Daacke, M. v Nathusius, Count von Waldersee, and Baron von Knigge. In 1883 von Knigge's dogs received the highest award at the Berlin show, the Kaiser Wilhelm I gold medal.

Wilhelm von Daacke of Osterode specialized in breeding red Dachshunds. He wanted to get better trailing ability in his Dachshunds so he introduced the German Bloodhound, a smaller and much different dog than the Bloodhound

An all-white Dachshund. From German book by Emil Ilgner, 1902.

Tiger-Reinecke, dapple Dachshund, c. 1890. (Extract from *Journal Der Hunde-Sport*.)

of today, into his Dachshund breeding. He got the trailing ability but he also got an unexpected bonus, the red color that made his kennels famous. He was so pleased that from then on (1868) he bred particularly for red Dachshunds. He wanted dogs that would hunt both above and below ground. The weights he felt to be most practical were 17 to 18 pounds for males and 14 to 15 pounds for bitches. His most popular sire and greatest show winner was Monsieur Schneidig.

In black and tan Dachshunds, Hundesport Waldmann, bred by R. Stech and owned by Ernst von Otto-Kreckwitz, and Schlupfer-Euskirchen, owned by Albert Latz, were shown at Cologne in 1889. Breeders had divided opinions as to which was the better of the two, but one thing is clear — they were both outstanding Dachshunds and influential sires in both color and type. Both traced their ancestry back to Dachs 16, registered in the first Stud book.

Some of the early breeders of all three varieties include: G. Barnewitz of Berlin, who bred the outstanding black and tan dogs: Berolina Frigga, Berolina Waldmann-Mako, Berolina Waldhexe and Berolina Waldteufel; R. Benda, who bred the black and tans, Schlaula-Reinecke and Altremlin-Reinecke; and Isermann of Sonderhausen who bred Junker Racker vom Jagerhaus and Junker Schlupfer vom Jagerhaus.

Chocolates were usually bred by chance but Boeckelman's Erda and Pucher's Traudel deserve mention.

The tiger dogs, which were also referred to as dapples, were bred by von Daacke whose Holle was noteworthy, and by Emil Ilgner — some of whose best were Hexe Erdmannsheim, Janke Erdmannsheim and Hannemann Erdmannsheim.

A fairly large number of white Dachshunds existed about that time. Among these were Berolina Wanda, Sylva Brunonia, and Waldemar Brunonia. Breeders of whites were W. Muller, of Steudel; Hampe, of Braunschweig and Siefert, of Plauen. Apparently they all encountered difficulties in their attempts to produce a strain of pure whites and eventually gave up. No modern breeder has yet been able to produce such a strain.

Captain Brunau of Bernberg was an active breeder of longhaired Dachshunds. His Schnipp set the standard for the variety. Baron v Cramm was another breeder whose dogs won consistently from 1883 to 1890. Other longhaired breeders were: Wilhelmi, of Strehlen; E. Schaper, of Rohrsheim; Franz Fischer, of Zwieselmuhle; Denner, of Erfurt; Herding, of Gelsenkirchen; Ph. Kramer, of Hochst; Schmitt, of Jena and Dr. Fritz Engelmann, of Gera.

One of the first breeders of wirehaired Dachshunds was Captain v Wardenburg of Hamburg. His Mordax was exhibited at the Berlin show in 1883 and received a "prize of encouragement."

Count Claus Hahn was another breeder of the time. His dogs passed into the kennels of R. Benda, of Wurtenberg, where the best wires of that time were produced.

Feldmann, first Dachshund shown in England
(1870). Bred by Prince Edward of Saxe-Weimar
and imported by John Fisher.

Hundesports Waldmann, c. 1889. Breeder, Revierforst-
er Stech. Owner, Ernst von Otto-Kreckwitz.

Schlupfer-Euskirchen, a Waldmann contemporary. Owned
by Albert Latz.

Often these older breeders not only bred just one variety of Dachshund but also favored one particular color. Franz Hof, of Stuttgart, bred red wirehairs and Meinhold of Dornap bred black and tans. Th. Wittmaack of Hamburg — noted for his success with, and understanding of, inbreeding — produced fine wirehairs. His most famous were Mentor Ditmarsia, Quickborn Ditmarsia and Kleines Dirndl Ditmarsia. More on the Ditmarsia strain is contained later in this chapter.

The belief that the longhaired Dachshund is a cross between a smooth Dachshund and a Cocker Spaniel is denied by most authorities on the breed. Something did happen, centuries ago, which may have given rise to this theory.

In ancient Germany there were two native hunting breeds, the Dachskrieger and the Huhnerhund. Both were used to hunt birds. A crossing of these two, whether by accident or design, produced the Wachtelhund. Some of these were low-stationed, others longer in the leg. Their coats varied too. Some had smooth coats, others curly or wavy coats and still others a short but fairly harsh textured coat. However they looked, they were prized throughout Europe as matchless in their ability to hunt quail and to work with falcons in the pursuit of game birds.

The Wachtelhund was thought to be the progenitor of another now extinct breed, the old English Water Spaniel. The low-stationed Wachtelhund, and those with wavy or curly coats, were used as the beginnings of a strain of Dachshunds that would hunt both above and below ground by two foresters, the Wopkes, father and son. Along with accomplishing long-coated Dachshunds that did the work expected of them, the Wopkes' dogs were notably good in hunting birds.

The Wopkes began their program in earnest during the reign of Johann Georg III (1666–1693). They kept careful records of their dogs long before the advent of official stud books, and hunted with them in the forests of Anhalt. As early as the beginning of the 18th century there were longhaired Dachshunds at the court of Anhalt-Dessau. They were recognized as a pure-bred strain and were called "Wopke-sche Rasse" or the "Wopke" strain, after the two foresters. Hunters referred to them also as "Wachtelhund" and "Dachshund." They were used both above and below ground but showed an unusual ability for trailing and for work on birds. These special abilities are noted elsewhere in this book in our coverage of longhaired Dachshunds in the 1970s.

There was a chocolate colored longhaired Dachshund at the court of Duke Ernst II of Saxe-Coburg and Gotha during the 19th century. He had been bred by the royal Prussian chief forester, Reiff, whose father, chief forester of the Harz Mountains, had obtained his foundation stock from the royal Anhalt forester, Thiele of Reysen. Duke Ernst later made a present of this dog to the Fischers, another father-son team who were interested in breeding longhairs. Fischer, Jr., was the organizer and leader of the Longhaired Dachshund Klub.

From the two Wopke strains which represented much independent work by both father and son, came a series of longhairs which trace their descent from "Mann", a chocolate, born, in 1888. He looked more like the modern Dachshund than some of his smooth contemporaries of that time.

From Mann to Kitty-Hochst to Walfried Forstrevier there was an unbroken line of descent which, in the mating of Kitty-Hochst and Forstrevier, brought together the two Wopke lines. Kitty-Hochst came from a line of nothing but longhairs; Forstrevier had longhaired parents with six generations of smooth breeding behind them. One of Walfried's daughters was Mirzl v Sonnenstein, owned by Dr. Fritz Englemann. From Mirzl came eight generations of smooth dogs. The ninth generation produced Moritzl v Zollbruck, a longhaired chocolate and tan out of a smooth chocolate bitch and a smooth black and tan sire.

The emergence of Moritzl created more interest in the breeding of longhairs, which had been sparked by the Fischers and others who bred to whatever longhaired stock was available. Some of this stock came from smooth breeding where past history had shown no longhaired infusion. This was the pre-Mendelian period and smooth breeders were unable to account for these occasional longhairs in their smooth litters. However, since there were breeders ready to buy them, they found a ready market and the results have benefited the entire breed.

While the German nobility and the foresters were keeping their Dachshunds in the isolation of their hunting lodges and cottages, the English had taken them to their hearts, formed a Dachshund Club in 1881, the first in the world, and had written a standard for the breed. They launched their Dachshunds on a career as show dogs and house pets which has made them among the most popular of any breed in most parts of the world. The Germans did not form their Dachshund Club until 1888 when they too wrote a standard for the breed, one which differed considerably from that of the English. Despite this difference, German imports won in England and English dogs won in Germany and by 1907, the English, recognizing that they were actually breeding closer to the German than their own earlier standard, changed theirs to conform with that of the German breeders.

German Dachshund fanciers complained bitterly that the public was following the English example of making pets and show dogs out of their Dachshunds. Type, style and showmanship were the qualities being sought, rather than working ability. The general public had no interest in hunting. Perhaps the German breeders were themselves partly to blame for this. However beautiful, a dog that was not a keen hunter was sold or given away. City dwellers were happy to get them since they made ideal pets for small homes and apartments.

The later appearance of the longhaired and wirehaired varieties proved even more popular than the smooths and today in Germany the longhair heads the popularity poll, with the wirehaired a close second.

30

Wirehaired Dachshunds were noted by writers during the later part of the 18th century and the early part of the 19th. The first to make an appearance in the show ring was "Mordax", from the kennels of Captain v Wardenburg-Hamburg, one of the first to breed this variety. The show was held in Berlin in 1883.

In their attempts to standardize the type and coat, now that the wirehairs had made their show ring debut, German breeders used a number of other breeds to produce the modern wirehaired Dachshund. Many people with little knowledge of its past history believed that these outcrossings were the origin of the wirehair; actually, it was really a regeneration and improvement of the original, which was fully as old as the smooth and the longhair.

Among these crosses, which occurred during the 19th century, was one of the smooth Dachshund with the wirehaired Pinscher which produced good coats but short bodies and small heads. Another was the smooth Dachshund-Dandie Dinmont cross, which produced better type but soft coats with a noticeable topknot of soft hair. Modern breeders still have trouble with the appearance of this type of coat among wirehaired litters. Other crosses were with more of the English terriers, such as the Scottish Terrier, the Skye and the Wirehaired Fox Terrier.

Count Claus Hahn, who bred all three varieties produced some good dogs. His kennels were later acquired by R. Benda who did well at shows with Wally-Reinecke and Aberdie-Reineke. The blood of these dogs and that of some wirehairs with a background of Pinscher crossings, shown by Master Forester Hesse in 1889, went into the breeding of Herr Florstadt of Herdersleben. His stock was taken over by Count Wurmbrand of Steyersburg. Large kennels began to add wirehairs to their Dachshund breeding programs. One of these was that of Herr Schrofli, who kept both type and coat by frequent crosses with smooth Dachshunds. His Sieger (Champion) Krott von der Klaus sired some first class dogs.

Most wirehaired breeders believed that outcrossings with smooth Dachshunds were necessary since inbreeding invariably produced soft coats. One who did not agree with this was Captain Zuckschwerdt, president of the Club for Wirehaired Dachshunds. He had bought a smooth bitch in Austria but felt she was too heavy and too deep in chest. In searching for a stud to counter these defects he found a wirehair, Mentor Ditmarsia. He was so pleased with the results of this mating that he decided to breed only wirehairs and began eliminating all smooth blood from his kennels. By inbreeding with Mentor and his son, Klausner's Pan, Zuckschwerdt produced a strain that had excellent stance, a good hard coat and a good head.

Just as he was about to achieve his aim, the supreme naval command recalled him to active service in 1912. He spent seven years away from home, mainly in the South Seas and later as an American prisoner. When he returned home, his dogs had been dispersed and he had to start all over again.

By 1919 the Ditmarsia strain had moved to Sweden and the only wirehaired

Sieger Mentor-Ditmarsia, wirehair, bred by Th. Whittmaack and owned by Franziska Konigsberger.

Klausner-Ditmarsia, wirehair, bred and owned by Th. Wittmaack.

Quickborn-Ditmarsia, wirehair, bred and owned by Th. Wittmaack.

bitch that had some of its blood was Fiffli v Alsen, owned by a lighthouse keeper, Pabst, who lived on the island of Fehmarn. Fiffli had smooth blood in her background from the Lichtenstein strain. The only male that preserved Ditmarsia blood was Helios v Teckeltreu. He, too, had smooth blood but his sire, Quickborn Ditmarsia, had a strong infusion of Ditmarsia blood. The get from this mating was three wirehairs and three smooths.

Two of the males, Klausner's Bautz and Klausner's Blinda (both wirehairs) bred back to their dam, sired many good dogs. Bautz was the better sire of the two. He gave firm body, excellent coat, good muzzle and superb hunting quality to his offspring. But Zuckschwerdt's dream of pure wirehaired breeding without any smooths, never materialized. It is still accepted practice among wirehaired breeders today to occasionally introduce smooth blood to preserve type and coat.

Early Development in England

Smooth Dachshunds were the first variety to arrive in England. While the Germans saw this native breed infrequently, usually on holidays in the country or on trips to baronial hunting lodges, the British, from Queen to commoner, had discovered the Dachshund's virtues as a house pet. Queen Victoria had her "Dashy", Prince Albert and his Dachshund brace hunted woodcock in Windsor Forest and every Dachshund owner, from courtier to householder, enjoyed the same happy relationship with their dogs.

In 1870, at the Birmingham Dog Show, Feldmann, owned by J. Fisher was the first Dachshund to be shown in England. He was four years old and had been imported from the kennels of Prince Edward of Saxe-Weimar. For the next two years Feldmann and one or two other Dachshunds were shown occasionally, but there were no separate classes for Dachshunds and they did not do well when shown in the mixed classes.

The first separate class for Dachshunds, and there was only one class, was at the Crystal Palace in June 1873. It was not until five years later that there were classes for Dachshunds at German dog shows.

By 1873, there were enough Dachshunds being shown to warrant two classes. The Crystal Palace event listed a class for red Dachshunds and another for "any other color." The following year there were again two classes but this time they were for black and tan and "any other color". Apparently the black and tan Dachshunds had become more numerous. There were 13 black and tans and 17 "any other color".

The appearance of a ringful of royalty at this show, all with Dachshunds at the other end of the lead, sparked further interest which led to increased classes and popularity. The judge was Prince Solms; the owner of the winner was H.R.H., the Prince of Wales, later King Edward VII (who showed a homebred named Deurstich and two other dogs); and the winner in the "any other color class" was owned by the Duke of Hamilton. D. Elphinstone Seton's bitch, a daughter of a bitch bred by Queen Victoria, was second. Lady Spencer Churchill was another of the exhibitors. E. Fitch Daglish best expressed the British attitude toward Dachshunds past and present, when he wrote, ''All that need be said is that from the time the breed became generally known (in England) it has attracted an ever increasing number of devotees and has never lost its hold on the interests and affections of British dog lovers. For upwards of 120 years the Dachshund has retained its position among the most popular of dogs, despite competition from newer and, in some cases, more spectacular rivals and survived the impact of two World Wars though it was brought dangerously near extinction by the 1914–1918 conflict.''

To this I add the *History of the Dachshund Club in Great Britain* as provided by its secretary, Mr. Michael T. Triefus. As a history of the world's oldest breed club, and for its typically British phraseology, it is a treasure for Dachshund owners.

History of the Dachshund Club

Members will need no reminding that the English Dachshund Club is the oldest Club in the world devoted to the breed and indeed one of the very oldest breed clubs of any kind. It was founded on January 17th, 1881 at a meeting held at Cox's Hotel, Jermyn Street, London. Those present were: Mr. W. Arkwright, Maj. Harry Jones, the Rev. G.F. Lovell and Mr. Montague Wootten.

Very early on members were keen to provide the Club with Challenge Cups and Trophies, either by donation or subscription, so that over the years the Club has amassed a splendid collection ranging from the Champion Jackdaw Trophy (which was won outright by Maj. Jones in 1896 but evidently re-presented to the Club shortly afterwards) to the very artistic bronze presented by our Vice-President Miss K.M. Raine in 1972. In a further effort to promote the breed at shows, the Club from early on to the present day guaranteed classes and donated Specials.

In 1907 the Club adopted the revised standard of points as drawn up by a joint Committee with the comparatively recently formed Northern Dachshund Association, then the only other club devoted to Dachshunds in England. This standard was accepted by the Kennel Club and has remained substantially in force to the present day, though some alterations were made in 1937.

From early on, the Dachshund Club aimed to provide opportunities for members to get together socially on occasions apart from shows where the element of competition could be absent, notably at the annual Lunch preceding the A.G.M. now ably managed by Muriel Rhodes. Also other social events such as dances and wine and cheese parties have been put on at intervals. In 1971 the Ninetieth Anniversary celebrations culminating in the Banquet at the Painters Hall proved a high point of the Club's social activity; in the same way our Ninetieth Anniversary Show with its world record entry for the breed was a fitting climax to the Club's efforts in promoting the breed at Shows of all kinds.

The Club has, throughout its history, enjoyed very long service from its Officers and Committee Members. At our last A.G.M. we congratulated Ambrose Spong on his completion of 21 years unbroken service on the Committee. Though not quite unbroken, the record of our President, Mrs. E. Grosvenor-Workman, is as remarkable as she joined the Committee in 1946 and has continued to serve the Club in some capacity or other virtually ever since. The office of President seems to have been created only in 1909 when Maj. Harry Jones was elected, and that of Vice-President only in 1913 with the election of Capt. Byron. The holders of these offices from then on were as follows:

Presidents		Vice-Presidents	
1909–1945	Maj. Harry Jones	1913–1924	Capt. A.W. Byron
1945–1951	Maj. P.C.G. Hayward	1924–1945	Mr. J.F. Sayer
1951–1958	Miss D. Spurrier	1945–1946	Lt. Col. G.S. Spurrier
1958	Mrs. Leonard	1946–1951	Miss D. Spurrier
1958	Mr. A.G. Spong standing in	1951–1958	Mrs. P.E. Goodman
1959	Mrs. E. Grosvenor-Work-man	1958–1963	Mr. A.G. Spong
		1963–1967	Mrs. M. Howard
		1968–	Miss K.M. Raine

In 1951 Mrs. Gilligan was made Honorary Vice President for one year. The new rules approved in 1966 allowed the appointment to this office for life of people who had given special service to the Club. The late Nina Hill was honoured in this way. Today Lt. Col. Biss, Ted Cozens-Smith and Muriel Rhodes hold this appointment.

During the last War, there being no Championship Shows, the Club's activities were suspended. With the resumption of dog shows the Club was quick to support the Miniature varieties. The Club had started life mainly interested in the Standard Smooths for the simple reason that although there was an occasional wirehaired dog in England in the late 19th century, Wires and Long Hairs were not imported and bred in any numbers until the late '20s. Both these varieties, however, went right ahead during the '30s with the interest and support of the Club. After the War, when the Miniature varieties began to emerge, the Dachshund Club was quick to embrace their cause and has continued to seek its membership from owners and breeders of all varieties of Dachshund without any particular bias towards one coat, size or variety.

From 1883 to 1935 the Club ran Produce Stakes and Puppy Sweepstakes. They never gained the support that had been hoped for and were therefore discontinued. On two subsequent occasions the Club has attempted to restore something similar, notably at our Open Shows in the late '50s and early '60s and then once again with our Futurity Stakes and Puppy Sweepstakes. Unfortunately, the idea has never really caught on and it has continued to be something which though successful in other countries does not seem to be wanted in England.

Although the Club has such a long history, we pride ourselves on searching always for new ideas. The early Club Handbooks from 1923 to 1947 pointed the way for other breed clubs to bring out such works. In the '50s, instead of a Newsletter and Handbook, the Club published quarterly a magazine called *The*

Dachshund, a set of which some members are lucky enough to possess, which combines both ideas. These are of immense historical interest for students of the breed. After the discontinuation of *The Dachshund* magazine, the Club began to produce Handbooks more or less regularly, first at 5-year intervals and latterly at 3-year intervals. It is generally agreed that this series of Handbooks has been without equal by any other breed club. We are proud that they go all over the world and to most public libraries. In this way, too, a permanent record has been created of the breeding programmes of the exhibitors virtually since the last War. Our annual News, which has in the last few years been succeeded by a Newsletter issued three or four times a year, has always been popular with members, especially those who do not show and perhaps keep only one or two Dachshunds. The Club has also published booklets on the Standard, breeding to type, whelping and puppy rearing.

For England, at any rate, our series of judging trials to bring on and develop the skills and judgement of the newer breeders and exhibitors has also been quite an innovation which some clubs have paid us the compliment of copying. Although a good beginning has been made, there is still much room for improvement. We like such new ventures and are always on the look-out for others. The Club's Committee is a forward-looking and open-minded one drawn from all over the country; it is always prepared to listen to and consider new ideas and constructive suggestions of members in order to keep the Club what we feel it has been for most of its history — one in the forefront of breed clubs, energetic in supporting the development of the breed and its members.

— M. F. Triefus

Although longhaired Dachshunds are German in origin, it was the English who are largely responsible for having brought them to public attention. American breeders looking for longhaired breeding stock had a choice between good dogs from both Germany and England. One of the pioneers of English longhaired breeders was Mrs. Allingham. Her kennels were founded on Austrian stock and were maintained up to the start of World War I. However, Mrs. Allingham never showed her dogs and most of them were sold to private homes. The variety remained unknown to the English dog fancy.

E. Fitch Daglish, already identified as author of *The Popular Dachshund,* had been familiar with smooth Dachshunds since his boyhood days but he saw his first longhairs in Germany when he was a student at the University in Bonn, during 1912. He was so taken with them that he bought a pair and for the next two years spent much of his time at dog shows talking to breeders and exhibitors of longhairs.

The outbreak of the war in 1914 ended all this and he returned to England where, for the next six years, he was in military service. By 1920, the war had ended and Daglish was ready to start again with his breeding of longhaired Dachshunds.

It was not until 1922 that he made his start. A friend, Mrs. E.S. Quicke, a Scottish Terrier breeder whose Tattenham Kennels were well-known, was planning a trip to Germany. Daglish asked her to bring him back a pair of longhaired Dachshunds. She did. They were a deep red and not closely related. The male was Ratzmann von Habichtshof and the bitch German Ch. Gretel III von Lechtal. Daglish was delighted. He thought Ratzmann a little large (he was about 23 pounds) but he was an elegant dog with no sign of coarseness. Entered at Crufts in February 1923, he was the sole longhair, and appeared in the Open dog class with nothing but smooths as his competitors. The judge, Major P.C.G. Hayward, awarded him the challenge certificate over some of the best known smooths of that time.

The award created a sensation and brought the variety to public attention with a bang. The smooth exhibitors were angry at being defeated by what they said was not a Dachshund at all. To avoid further clashes, Ratzmann was shown only in variety competition until there were enough longhairs to warrant separate classes. Gretel III died before she could be bred in England, although she had produced litters sired by Ratzmann in Germany. She was replaced by another German import, Edeltrud von der Waldflur, a black and tan daughter of Ratzmann and Gretel III. She weighed about 15 pounds and her show career in Germany had been brilliant. Bred to Ratzmann, her puppies found ready buyers and many exhibitors were attracted to these elegant Dachshunds with coats like those of Irish Setters.

Since there was no other source in England for breeding, bitches had to be put back to their sires or mated with their brothers. For a while this produced good dogs but its continued practice caused overshot mouths. Accordingly, an outcross was found in Sepel of Combe, owned by Colonel E.J. Harrison. The results were not satisfactory and the need for new blood became critical.

In 1927 a waif from a dog shelter provided the needed help. Daglish received a letter from Lt. Col. W.G. Bedford saying he had found a longhaired Dachshund at the Battersea Dogs' Home and was so taken with the little fellow that he thought of starting a kennel. Daglish lost no time in reaching Bedford and between them they were able to identify the dog as a son of Ratzmann and Edeltrud, whose owner had gone to South Africa. How the dog had got to the Battersea Dogs' Home is still an unsolved mystery. Bedford registered him as Hengist of Armandale and asked Daglish to help him find a mate. When he was told that the only bitches available were his own sisters he agreed that it would be best to import one of unrelated stock. In 1928 he found Elfe von Fels in whelp to German Ch. Stropp von der Windberg. The litter was born in quarantine and included a dog and bitch that made history. They were Rufus and Rose of Armandale.

In 1929, the Longhaired Dachshund Club was formed. Colonel Harrison was its president, Lt. Col. Bedford its Committee Chairman and Daglish its secretary. Daglish drew up the standard of points which was almost a literal translation of the German. In 1930, the club received permission for a separate breed register from the Kennel Club and challenge certificates were allotted. In 1931, Rose of Armandale became the first English champion longhair and her brother Rufus the first male champion.

The infusion of this new blood into the homebreds was successful and, encouraged by the results of the outcrossing, Col. Harrison decided he wanted to import a dog that was a deep, Setter red. Good quality red longhairs were rare in Germany (black-and-tans were dominant), but finally Jesko von der Humbolshohe was located and brought to Harrison's Combe Kennels. His beautiful color and delightful disposition made him a champion and a popular stud dog. The most impressive of his get was Jager of Dillworth, bred by Mrs. Dillworth and sold as a puppy to Mrs. B. Franklyn. He finished his championship quickly and became one of the leading show winners of his day. Another was Canadian Ch. Bartonbury Vogue, bred by Mrs. V. Rycroft.

Col. Bedford imported a black-and-tan, Otter von Fels, in 1931. He showed the dog for the first time at the Windsor show and Daglish, who was the judge, was so impressed that he gave him the challenge certificate and Best of Breed. Otter was later sold to Mrs. J.M. Stuchbury, who brought over from Germany a black-and-tan bitch, Ursel von der Goldenen Perl, as a mate. Their progeny has somehow been lost from sight and Otter was only lightly used as a stud, and not often shown, after he left Armandale. But even his limited breeding has been enough to establish him as one of the pillars of the breed and his blood is carried by many modern champions.

Two other notable imports were Alma von der Glonn (in whelp to German Ch. Ebbo Krehwinkle) and one of Ch. Ebbo's daughters, Ilse von Jungfrauental. Another important bitch was Zola von Jungfrauental. Mrs. Smith Rewse of Primrose Patch Kennels, one of the largest and most successful in England, owned Ilse and Alma, who were both bred to her original Armandale stock. The last of the German imports before the start of World War II was a small red dog, Eberhard von Adlerstein, brought over by the Hon. Mrs. Still. The best of his offspring was Dandelion von Walder, bred by Daglish from Knowleton Madel, a Zola von Jungfrauental daughter.

The best known of the English longhaired Dachshund kennels that came into being from the 1920s through the 1940s, or who added the longhaired variety to their smooth kennels were Dillworth, Primrose Patch, Combe, Armandale, Stutton, von Walder, Brincliffe, Northanger, Hilltrees, Knowleton, Warstock, Buckmead, Longcroft, Robsvarl, Ferrens, Brochurst, Windgather, Rosteague, Fenlands, Seton, Karlenwood, Kitenor, Whipsderry, Reedscottage, and Imber.

The Dachshund
In America

DACHSHUNDS in America began with German and English imports, and while lesser numbers were brought in from other countries, it was the German dogs that predominated from the 1880s, when they first appeared at American dog shows, until the start of World War I.

The Early Years

One of the first to show Dachshunds in the United States was William Loeffler of Milwaukee, Wisconsin. Since Dachshunds were virtually unknown to most people in this country at that time, Mr. Loeffler had to write ahead to dog show committees when he wanted to enter his dogs, to be sure there were classes for them. Alas for the good old days when an exhibitor could tell the show committee what classes he wanted for his dogs.

Mr. Loeffler must have been a man of means and social prominence. In attempting to buy Dachshunds in Germany in 1879, he discovered that they were owned almost exclusively by German nobility. He seemed to have had no difficulty in entering this elite circle of breeders and bought a dog and bitch from the Duke of Coburg, the male Waldmann and the bitch, Helba bei Meiningen. This was his foundation stock and throughout the duration of his breeding program he took the Coburg type as his standard. The pair were all he had hoped for but, unfortunately, Waldmann met with a fatal accident and Loeffler began a nationwide search for a suitable mate for the bitch.

He finally found a red Dachshund, Unser Fritz, owned by Dr. L. Henry Tradell of Philadelphia. The dog had been a gift to Dr. Tradell from the Duke of Baden.

Loeffler used Dachshunds from breeders and owners Charles Keocke of Pittsburg, William Korbe of Milwaukee, and E.F. Setiner of Dayton, Ohio, but he sought further perfection in his Dachshunds. At that time Hundesport Waldmann was considered the best Dachshund in Germany. The dog was owned by Herr Ernst von Otto-Krekwitz. Mr. Loeffler arranged, through Herr Valois, German Ambassador to the United States and himself a Dachshund fancier, to breed one of his bitches to Waldmann. Just to make sure he had the bloodlines for future use, he purchased Hundesport Bergmann, a chocolate Dachshund who took "first prize and a special for best in show" at Chicago in 1891. He also bought Hundesport Zanker whom he later sold to E.G. Ausmus of Milwaukee. Hundesport Waldmann was a son of Dachs 16, the dog to whom all Dachshunds eventually trace their ancestry.

There is known to have been an American Teckel Club of Chicago as far back as 1895. Not much is known about it but Herbert Sanborn, a noted American breeder of the early 1900s and author of the book, *The Teckel in America*, from which much of this early history is researched, believed that it was the forerunner of the Western Dachshund Club of which he was a member from 1912 to 1914. The Western Dachshund Club held its meetings at the Berghoff restaurant, a famous Chicago eatery whose manager, Carl Boening, was a club member. Club members imported and bred good quality dogs and all seemed well until the outbreak of World War I in 1914.

War hysteria created a hatred and outright persecution of everything German. Even German food was not exempt. Sauerkraut became "Liberty Cabbage," Dachshunds, those that dared appear in public, became "Badger Dogs," and people of German extraction were looked upon with suspicion. In spite of their new name, Dachshunds and their owners were harassed and persecuted. Sanborn tells of one member of the Western Dachshund Club who was so victimized that he went out, one day, to his kennels and shot every one of his dogs.

Eastern Dachshund owners were active, too, during the 1800s. Maj. Emil Ilgner, one of Germany's foremost authorities on Dachshunds and himself a breeder of note, sold a red dog, Ch. Junker Schnapphahn, to Arthur Padelford of Philadelphia in 1888. Another Philadelphian, Robert Konigbauer, purchased Ilgner's Aegir Erdmannsheim in 1898. Padelford also bought at a later date Ilgner's Mädel, Felle and Junker Erdmann. No trace of these dogs is found in American pedigrees but it is believed that they found their way into the hands of hunters who crossed them with Beagles at that time. The "Bench-legged Beagles", highly prized for their hunting ability by Pennsylvania and Delaware sportsmen, are believed to have been the results of crossing the offspring of these German Dachshunds with Beagles.

About the same time, in New York City, three men, Harry Peters, Sr., G.

Hundesports Bergmann, a winner at Chicago show in 1891. Bred by Ernst von Otto-Kreckwitz and imported by William Loeffler.

Asbecks Drickes, red. Bred by Karl Asbeck and imported by George Semler of New York City.

Junker Schnapphahn. Bred by W. Falkenberg and owned by Emil Ilgner.

Muss-Arnolt, the artist, and Dr. Montebacher, a doctor and chemist who had a combination home and drug store on Eighth Avenue, were importing and breeding Dachshunds. They were the moving spirits in the organization of the Dachshund Club of America and Mr. Peters was its first president. Dr. Montebacher combined business with pleasure. His Dachshunds were kenneled under the shelves of his drug store and exercised in his back yard. Fortunately for the doctor and his Dachshunds, the Federal Food and Drug Administration was not then in existence. His dogs were good ones and, on his death, his dogs were taken over by Harry Peters. Among them were three dappled or, as they were then known, "tiger Dachshunds" about five months old, the first ever seen here. Mr. Peters' concern for his friend's dogs earned him the distinction of being the first exhibitor of dappled Dachshunds in America.

The man who had the greatest influence on Dachshund breeding in America during that era was George Semler of New York City. Starting in 1898 with a pair of Dachshunds purchased from Ilgner's kennels, Lutz Erdmannsheim and Nellie Erdmannsheim, Semler's "West End" Kennels reached their peak during the years 1906 to about 1910. Experts from Germany, Austria, England and the United States declared his kennels among the finest in the world. Semler bought up almost every first class Dachshund in Germany including the Asbecks' famous Drickes, Lechner's Ramsch vom Seelburg, Dr. Reichenbach's Tell vom Bergsteig, Gugeline Isarlust and especially the best specimens from the kennels of F. Widmann, whose dogs bore the kennel name of "vom Lichtenstein." To this, Semler added his own kennel name, "West End". One of his best dogs Lutz West End, a son of Drickes and Emmy von der Bergspitz was sold to William Bradley of Lake Villa, to form the foundation stock for his Allendale Kennels.

Semler's homebreds were as good as his imports. In the opinion of Herbert Sanborn, Peter West End was the best dog the kennels ever produced. The dog was literally faultless but he weighed 30 pounds and his kennelmate, Schnapps vom Lichtenstein weighed 38. Most of the Widmann dogs weighed about 25 pounds or less. Most breeders avoided using Peter because of his size, but Sanborn was convinced of his quality and considered the size an asset to improving his own stock. Sanborn had this to say regarding these extra large Dachshunds: "The importance of the heavyweight dog, such as Peter and the Lichtensteiner, consists in the ability of these dogs to impart bone, substance, stamina and good rigid backs to the lighter and lightest weight strains; and this probably cannot be compensated for by any dosing with calcium or calcium-producing chemicals, much as these may help when there is a good inheritance to work on."

Dr. Carl O. Folkens of Cleveland was considered the dean of American breeders by the Germans, although he was not widely known in America — probably because he rarely showed his dogs, even at local shows. Among his many importations were Austrian Ch. Bergmann vom Rudolfsheim, Edelrot vom Jägerhaus, Papageno Weidmannsfreud, Christel Schneid and the first wirehaired Dachshunds ever brought to this country.

Ramsch vom Seelberg, impressive early import to America.
Bred by Jacob Lechner and owned by George Semler.

Gib Hals Exzellenz, red, bred and owned by Paul Selchow.

Gib Hals Schrimm, red, bred and owned by Paul Selchow.

Brynhild vom Isartal. Bred by Johann Metka, and imported to America in 1909 by Herbert Sanborn.

Group from the Teckelheim Kennels of Mrs. Justus Erhardt, of Boston. Left to right: Mauschen von der Haide, Erna von der Haide, Rex von der Haide and Manne von Welfenhorst.

Ch. Tenor von der Haide, bred by Heinrich Salzer and owned by Herbert Sanborn.

William Bradley, who had earlier purchased two of Semler's dogs, now had his Allendale Kennels in full swing. Bradley was a commercial breeder. He was interested in getting the best possible stock in order to sell them for good prices. He used his profits to finance the Allendale Farms School, a charitable institution of which his brother was principal. Many of these dogs were sold in all parts of the country, so a partial list of them may be helpful to breeders whose dogs go back to them.

There was a bitch, Fraulein Pretzel of Allendale carrying through her dam, Gretel of Cleveland, the Folkens line and also that of Modell von der Haide; and an imported pure longhaired bitch, Lady of Frankenwald the daughter of Walfried vom Forstrevier. He then added Mr. Sanborn's Wodan vom Isartal, a son of a German import, Schlief-ein Ingo, and bred his bitches to Sanborn's Ch. Tenor von der Haide and Ch. Rex von der Haide. Inbreeding on Allendale dogs frequently brought out the recessive longhaired stock. Anthony Alt of Cincinnati, after nine generations, found a longhaired puppy in one of his litters. Another was Konrad of Allendale, who had a successful show career.

Herbert Sanborn reversed the order common to most American breeders by buying and showing his dogs in Germany first, then bringing them to America for further showing and breeding. He became acquainted with Dachshunds during his student days at Heidelberg in 1900. A few years later, attending the University of Munich, he bought his first Dachshund puppy whom he called Rex vom Isartal. Rex won twelve firsts, seven seconds and a number of special prizes at some of Germany's larger shows. For a mate, Sanborn bought a bitch that he named Brynhild vom Isartal. Her show career started at six months at Zwickau where she won four firsts and special prizes and the award for Best Bitch in Show. By the time Sanborn was ready to ship the pair to America, Brynhild had won 21 firsts, seven seconds, Best Dachshund Bitch and Best of Breed. Shortly after she came to this country in 1909, she was shown at the Boston show where she won Best of Breed. It was her only appearance at an American show. She died during a Caesarian operation but the two puppies were saved.

With this as a start, Sanborn bought not only German imports but American dogs that he liked. From Semler he bought the German import Schlief-ein Ingo who inherited the Lichtenstein strain. He bred to Peter West End, also an offspring of imported Lichtensteiners. He writes, "There was a continuous interbreeding between Dr. Folkens, William Bradley and myself, even during the war period when almost every Dachshund kennel in America went out of existence, so that 'from Cleveland,' 'from Allendale' and 'vom Isartal' dogs all carried the same bloodlines."

Dr. Fritz Engelmann, like Emil Ilgner, was one of the most respected breeders and judges of Dachshunds in Europe. Along with Ilgner, he was an important influence in the shaping of early American Dachshund breeding programs. Both men judged Dachshunds at American shows.

Engelmann was born in 1874 and died in 1935. He practiced medicine in Gera, Thuringia, about 1918. He was an enthusiastic hunter, not only with Dachshunds but with birds as well. His vom Sonnenstein Kennel, with its ferocious little hunters, had its parallel in his falcons. Here too he was considered an authority and his books *"Meine Lieblinge, die Falken,"* (My Darlings the Falcons) and *"Raubvogel Europas"* (European Birds of Prey) were as widely read as his *"Der Dachshund."*

In 1966, Dr. Leonore L. Adler of Jamaica, Long Island, wrote *"This Is The Dachshund."* While it is not a literal translation of Dr. Engelmann's book, it does give a good picture of his practices and theories.

As a hunter, Dr. Engelmann believed that too much emphasis was being placed on type and not enough thought was being given to develop the Dachshund as a hunter. While he admired the dogs of the Lichtenstein and Asbeck strains he felt that their large size was something of a disadvantage under certain hunting conditions. Also he felt that after a time, breeding for type became a boring repetition of a formula. His ideal was a versatile Dachshund, approximately twelve pounds more or less, coat and color unimportant, a dog that was a keen hunter and resistant to distemper.

His search for dogs meeting these requirements lead him to the Gib Hals Kennels of Paul Selchow, founded in 1906. Modern breeders would consider them as scrawny, underfed and Terrier-like in appearance. When Herbert Sanborn first saw the Gib Hals dogs in 1909, he found them "so high in the legs and so short in body and head that they seemed to be another breed of dog." Up to that time Sanborn had seen mainly dogs bred in south Germany. In northern Germany, with its sandy soil, the Gib Hals type had an advantage since their longer legs made for faster movement and their lighter weight made it easier for them to get deeper into sand banks after wild game. Further acquaintance with Selchow moderated Sanborn's opinion and in spite of what he considered their many faults he admired their vivacity and nimbleness. He made sure that the blood of Gib Hals Schrimm, Selchow's founding sire, was bred into his own vom Isartal stock. Selchow did not insist that his was the only acceptable type of Dachshund. He claimed only that he bred with the aim in view of an animal suited for the special type of hunting that was to be met in his own region.

Sanborn was not the only American to take advantage of Selchow's breeding program. Mrs. Charles Lester imported Fritz vom Berlin, AKC# 142692, a son of Gib Hals Schrimm whose name still appears in American pedigrees. Laurence Horswell's Henrietta von der Festigteit was strongly inbred on Gib Hals Schrimm.

Dr. Engelmann took a more kindly view of the dogs. He wrote of them "Where something could be saved and chiseled away of a hindering substance, unnecessary heavy bone, too large dangling ears, in fat, skin and feet, that was done." He admired the agility, fleet movement and aggressiveness of the dogs. Today we might consider it savagery. Dr. Engelmann commented that on receiving a photograph of Gib Hals Olaf, Selchow had written on the back "torn to bits alive by Gib Hals Excellenz."

Selchow used Schlupfer v Fehman, a red dog, as his founding sire. He was a very sharp dog and the smallest and sharpest of his offspring were selected for breeding . Gib Hals Schrimm was his son.

In establishing his own vom Sonnenstein Kennels, Engelmann believed he followed a middle-of-the-road policy. It is apparent, though, from his writings and observations, that he leaned toward the small, lightly built, sharp hunters. He began with a smooth bitch, Dinchen, and bred her to a longhaired stud. From this mating came Braune Hexe vom Sonnenstein. She weighed slightly more than twelve pounds and was a good hunter. He used Hexe as his foundation bitch. In selecting breeding stock, Engelmann bred, as much as possible, to dogs that had never had distemper but had been exposed to it. He mated Hexe with a very sharp longhaired stud, Etzel, the son of a trailing Sieger (champion) named Stromer. From among their progeny he took, without regard for looks, the sharpest pup, Erda v Sonnenstein. He said that before long he made the error of selecting for beauty and found that as the dogs' size increased their hunting ardor diminished. But he did admit that it might have been a coincidence. He looked for a longhaired stud that would restore the fire and small size to his strain. Finding none, he resorted to a smooth. The result was Selchen v Sonnenstein and she was all he had hoped for. But, since the smooth coat is dominant over the long, he lost the source of his longhairs which he had admired. Selchen was bred to Schwefelgezwerg v Niflheim. From this mating came the very small Herkules v Sonnenstein. When bred to Gib Hals Schrimm, Selchen produced the 13-pound Teckele v Sonnenstein. Bred to Raudl v Seelberg, she produced Raudl v Sonnenstein, whom Engelmann considered his best and most versatile worker.

Engelmann cared little whether he bred with smooth or wirehaired dogs. The tests he applied were performance in the field, freedom from distemper, sound structure and aggressive character. He followed a practice of what he called "transplanting" and did very little inbreeding. At times he bred to his own dogs, which he had sold to other kennels in different parts of Germany, or to the offspring of these dogs. He seemed to feel that his own strain, but raised under a different geographical environment, could contribute a refreshing element into his breedings.

One of the kennels that remained in operation during the trying times of World War I was the Voewood Kennels of Mrs. C. Davies Tainter. Mrs. Tainter was one of the staunchest supporters of Dachshunds and the Dachshund Club of America. Present day Dachshundists credit her with holding the breed and the Club together during its most difficult times. Her foundation stock came from Semler. Among the best known were Ch. Plum of West End, Ch. Voewood Gizzi — a black tiger later sold to Mrs. Justus Erhardt, Ch.

Voewood Frieda, Ch. Brunhilda von Lichtenstein, Ch. Teckelheim Kasperl of Voewood — bred by Mrs. Erhardt, Ch. Ego Assmannsheim and Ch. Ratzmann Muck of Voewood.

Mrs. Erhardt's Teckelheim Kennels of Boston and Berlin, Vermont, had some fine imports and homebreds. The imports were Sonja von der Haide, Rose van Leeuwarden from Holland, and Ch. Rex von der Haide, which Herbert Sanborn later purchased.

Rex was sired by Rex Rubrorum, a product of years of von Daacke breeding. Shown in Germany, Rex had won all classes at the Homburg and Hanau shows with the qualification of *Vorzuglich* (excellent). After further wins including the Sieger class at Frankfort, he was sold to the Leeuwarden Kennels in Holland in 1912. He promptly won his championship at Brussels and then, under Mrs. Erhardt's ownership, his American championship.

Ch. Rex v.d. Haide, bred by August Hohmann and owned by Herbert Sanborn.

THE SMOOTHS

Following World War I, the Dachshund slowly won his way back to strong popularity. For four years, until 1923, he had suffered the name-change to "Badger Dog". In that year, in which his name was restored to Dachshund, only 26 dogs of the breed were registered by the AKC. By the end of the 1930s it had climbed to over 3,000 a year.

Many returning service men brought Dachshunds home from Germany as pets. The war's end also made it possible for American breeders to once again buy German dogs of good quality, but the confusion over German registrations, due mainly to a very depleted staff of the German Teckelklub, was sometimes a deterrent. Many Americans looked to England for outcrosses for their own stock since the English had already well-established strains and there was no difficulty in getting English dogs registered with the American Kennel Club.

The Dachshund Club of America had survived due, in a great measure, to the efforts of Mrs. C. Davies Tainter of Voewood Kennels and had proved itself strong enough to control the activities of its membership, including a group of dissenters who felt that the hunting Dachshund should be the breeders' goal, and whose activities led to the split within the Club in the 1930s. Its final solution left the Club in full control of field trial activities with Dachshunds from then on. It seemed clear that breeders, owners and exhibitors preferred the show dog so the emphasis has been on the development of type, structure and temperament of a Dachshund breed capable of a brilliant performance in the show ring. It had to have enough fire and spirit to make it a standout and at the same time possess a disposition so outgoing and friendly that it could be easily handled. (This development of temperament in Dachshunds has, in my opinion, been the greatest achievement of American Dachshund breeders; they have bred out the savagery and retained the courage of this versatile breed.)

New people were being attracted to the breed and Hollywood stars, like their Eastern contemporaries of the theatre and opera, were buying them as pets. Richard Barthelmess, Carole Lombard and Clark Gable, Adolphe Menjou, John Gilbert, Judith Anderson — all owned Dachshunds. Writers Hendrik van Loon, Noël Coward and publisher William Randolph Hearst were also owners, although I don't think anyone but Mr. Hearst ever entered them at dog shows. Mr. Hearst had a good-sized kennel at San Simeon. At his death, when the dogs were dispersed, some of them went to Mrs. Grayce Greenburg who had, by that time, a well established kennel in the Los Angeles area.

Nestor von Stromberg, chocolate dapple, imported to America by Mrs. Justine Cellarius of California.

Fillip Cellarius and playmate. Fillip, son of Nestor von Stromberg, was owned by Fred Cellarius, Jr.

It had been in 1921 that Grayce Greenburg had moved to California and discovered Dachshunds. From that time on until her death in 1959 she was one of the most active and controversial figures in the breed. Mrs. Greenburg had a true Dachshund disposition — energetic, curious, determined and stubborn. She bought the best dogs she could find and was proud to show them off. Inevitably she bred some very good ones and, like others, her share of poor quality, too. While many disapproved of her, Dachshund breeders recognized the quality of her imports and the good dogs she bred, and the results of this energetic dedication to the breed has been very beneficial.

Mrs. Greenburg met her first Dachshund at the home of her son-in-law on her arrival in California. She embarked on her career as a Dachshund breeder with all the enthusiasm of a swimmer diving into a pool on a hot day. In 1923 she set out to buy, not puppies, but proven winners and found two, Pottraut and Aladar v Boris at the greatly curtailed Astarte Kennels of Mrs. Marie Fuchs on Long Island. Wartime hardships and failing health had all but ended Mrs. Fuchs' ability to continue the famous kennel. She ceased to breed entirely shortly after Mrs. Greenburg's purchase.

Rottraut and Aladar had both won at Westminster and Mrs. Greenburg lost no time in completing their championships.

Her approach to the sport of showing dogs was unorthodox to say the least. At the Hollywood Kennel Club show that same year, she sailed into the Dachshund ring where Alva Rosenberg was judging. She joined the other exhibitors in circling the ring clutching the leads of both dogs in her hand. Mr. Rosenberg stopped the class and asked her if she intended to show both dogs herself. "Yes," she replied. "If you do, you're a better man than I am," said the astonished Alva and proceeded to judge the class. Mrs. Greenburg won it with Aladar.

Not satisfied with her initial triumphs, Mrs. Greenburg contacted Mrs. F. Nixon in England and asked her to buy her a good dog. Mrs. Nixon found her Int. Ch. Kensal's Call Boy, bred by E. W. Ricks. He was indeed a good one. Anton Rost, judging him at his first American show gave him Best of Breed. Enno Meyer, who was judging the Group (it was the Working Group in which Dachshunds were shown in those days) placed him second in the Group. A Great Dane was first. What a sight it must have been when the ribbons were handed out!

In 1926 Aladar won the Working Group at a West Coast show defeating the area's top German Shepherd Dog. On the same day at the Philadelphia Sesqui-Centennial Dog Show, the only show ever given by the American Kennel Club, Mrs. Greenburg's import, Dunner v Lichtenstein was Best of Breed. Because of a missing name in Dunner's German pedigree, he could never be registered with the American Kennel Club but Mrs. Greenburg showed him anyway and rolled up 90 championship points before he was retired.

After a two year span in which Dachshunds were shown in the Sporting Group, the AKC instituted the Hound Group in 1931. The first show to have

A quartet of the White Gables Kennels, owned by Albert and Miriam Van Court: Ch. Cid, Jr. of Lakelands, Ch. White Gables Goldilocks, Ch. Cornhill Goldie and Ch. Eric v Stahlhaus.

An early photo of
Albert Van Court.

this new group judged was the one at Long Beach, California that same year. Call Boy was the winner.

Call Boy finished his show career as brilliantly as he had begun it. At the first separate Dachshund Specialty show ever held in the United States — the Dachshund Club of California in 1932 — he took Best of Breed. It was his last and 31st victory. During his years of competition he had been defeated only once — by his own son, Ch. Boventor of Greenburg.

Dapple Dachshunds, a rarity then, caught Mrs. Greenburg's fancy and she bred them with the same vigor that she displayed in her other efforts.

During her early years in Dachshunds Mrs. Greenburg had persuaded Mrs. Harriet C. Preede, whose von Jagerhaus Kennels had gone out of existence during the war, to revive her interest in the breed. With the help of another Dachshundist, Mrs. Britomarte de Wein, Mrs. Preede was able to locate some of the dogs which she had placed with friends. Soon the von Jagerhaus prefix was again appearing in newly registered litters and the three ladies had formed the West Coast Dachshund Club with Mrs. Preede as president, Mrs. De Wein as secretary and Mrs. Greenburg treasurer. An outgrowth of this club was a members' newsletter put out by Mrs. Greenburg, which later developed into *The American Dachshund*. Mrs. Greenburg, aided by her daughter Alverna and Kaye Dore, was its editor and publisher from its inception until her death in 1959. In the same tradition, its succeeding editors have all been Dachshund breeders as well as journalists: Mr. and Mrs. Stanley Orne had wirehairs; Mrs. Jeannette W. Cross, whose smooth champions are well known, filled the spot briefly while the Ornes vacationed one winter; and Mr. and Mrs. Sanford Roberts, its present editorial team, have their Robdachs Kennels of champion longhairs.

But it was her interest in miniature Dachshunds that turned Mrs. Greenburg into a crusader. She battled the American Kennel Club in behalf of recognition for the tiny ones, only to learn in the end that "you can't fight City Hall." In the process she marshalled the full power of the press as expressed in *The American Dachshund* to convince breeders of the righteousness of her cause.

I can think of only one other breeder who resorted so strongly to the public press to express her views. That was Miss Marie Leary, whose Cosalta Kennels of German Shepherd Dogs was one of the leading in the breed. Miss Leary, involved in an argument within the German Shepherd Dog Club, bought advertisements in the leading dog magazines and a full page in the *New York Times* to make her points. Mrs. Greenburg had the edge over Miss Leary's approach. She owned the magazine.

Many other breeders on the West Coast began their kennels in the 1920s, or — now that they were able to resume their breeding and showing activities — expanded small ones that had been started before the war. Among these was Mrs. Justine Cellarius, who began in 1926. She is noted chiefly for her importation of the first chocolate dapple Dachshund to America, Nestor vom

Ch. Heini Flottenberg.

Ch. Heidi Flottenberg.

Ch. Helmar Flottenberg.

Three of the many outstanding dogs of the Flottenberg line (bred by G. F. Muller of Munich) imported to America in the 1930s by the Ellenbert Farm Kennels of Mr. and Mrs. Herbert Bertrand, Greenwich, Connecticut.

Stromberg. She also had the first dapple champion, Uhlan v Cellarius. On his way to the championship title, Uhlan won Best of Breed at a Specialty show with an entry of 110 Dachshunds. Another notable of her breeding was Fillip Cellarius, a son of Nestor. In all, Mrs. Cellarius imported thirteen smooth Dachshunds and one longhair, including a black dappled Canadian import, Widbrook Onyz, and a red bitch from Germany — Ch. Pia v Plater Schulhaus.

Also in California, the Van Courts — Albert and Miriam — had begun their White Gables Kennels. Among their founding stock were Cid, Jr. (who brought them the von Werderhavelstrand strain through his sire, Ch. Cid von Werderhavelstrand) and his brother, Eric v Stahlhaus. Mrs. B. De` Wein, whose Budweiser was Best of Breed in 1922 at the Hollywood Kennel Club show, continued to breed, and the J.M. Campbells began their von Moruth Kennels. Also started in the 1920s, on a modest scale, was the Heying-Teckel Kennels of Mr. and Mrs. Fred Heying, of which we'll read more later in this chapter.

The demand for good Dachshunds from Germany increased, and the German breeders whose fortunes had been depleted by the war, were happy to sell their stock to people who appeared so interested in the breed, and so well able to care for them properly. Stock came from such well-known German kennels as Flottenberg, Luitpoldsheim, Lindenbuhl, Asbecks, Holzgarten, Werderhavelstrand, Falltor, Erlbachtal, and Assmannsheim.

Outstanding among the breeders of this era were Mr. and Mrs. Herbert Bertrand of Greenwich, Connecticut. Like George Semler, they had the means (Mr. and Mrs. Bertrand were hosts to the entire Dachshund Club of America membership at dinner before a club meeting in New York City) and the desire to buy and breed the best. Their Ellenbert kennel flourished throughout the 1930s, and its name may be found in many modern pedigrees.

The Bertrands bought practically every good Dachshund bred at the Flottenberg Kennels in the period, and it was said that they had the first refusal on every good dog offered by the kennels for sale. Ten Flottenberg imports were finished to American championship during the decade, two of the most notable of which were Heini and Feri, both top dogs in Germany *and* the United States.

Other importers and owners of fine German dogs were: Mrs. Joseph J. O'Donohue III, who imported Sieger Lenz Assmannsheim and Ch. Theo vom Lindenbuhl; Mrs. Lawrence Zimmerman, Asbecks Erich Cilly vom Plater Schulhaus; Dr. E. H. Marquardt, Ch. Hansel vom Lindenbuhl; Mrs. H.D. Sims, Ch. Schalk vom Werderhavelstrand, Yvonne vom Werderhavelstrand, Schummel vom Werderhavelstrand and Rea Flottenberg; Mr. H.H. Sachers, Ch. Cid vom Werderhavelstrand; Mrs. Gussie Held, Ch. Held vom Erlbachtal, Ch. Flink vom Teipelskrug; Mrs. Tom Ash, Lottie-Hildesheim and the decendants of Swartpiek-Schneid; Mrs. Tristian C. Colket, Asbecks Sabine, Ch. Lot vom Falltor; Miss Anne B. De Armond, Asbecks Klaus; Mrs. Grayce Greenburg, Grille aus der Neidhohle; Mr. William Horvay, Ch. Graf vom Luitpoldsheim; Dr. William F. Machle, Tasso vom Goseneck, Herma Flottenberg, Fax vom Herzogstand; Mr. John Rhode, Troll vom Lindenbuhl; Mr. Victor Moench, Achat vom Werderhavelstrand, Arno vom Luitpoldsheim; George M. Schieffelin, Field Ch. Amsel vom Holzgarten, Gauner vom Fleesensee. The P.B.A. Wideners chose two English dogs from von der Howitt Kennels. Other German dogs were Mrs. Edith Mangold's Asso vom Luitpoldsheim; Dr. Hans Kniepkamp's Ch. Krabbe-Assmannsheim and Ch. Nazi vom Fels; Hurlburt Johnson's Tack vom Falltor and Berndt vom Plater Schulhaus.

All of these were smooth Dachshunds; the importation of longs and wires had only just begun, but there was enough good stock in this country so that American kennels could interbreed successfully without such frequent infusion of German imports.

The 1930s marked the entry of two names that were to become very important in the history of the Dachshund in America — the Laurence A. Horswells and the Josef Mehrers. So important has been their impact, we have chosen to write of them separately in chapters that follow.

England had its Jackdaw, the dog that sparked a winning streak for British Dachshunds in all-breeds competition and for whom the famous Jackdaw trophy is named. An English import, Mrs. Greenburg's Int. Ch. Kensal Call Boy, was the first Dachshund ever to win a Best in Show in the United States but it was an American-bred dog from New Jersey that really broke the ice for Dachshund wins in all-breed competition.

The dog was Herman Rinkton. He was bred by Richard S. Heller and whelped in November of 1935. He was sired by Victor Moench's German import and American Champion, Achat v Werderhavelstrand. His dam was Ch. Anny Rinkton.

I have been unable to learn the name of his first owner but apparently he treated Herman as a pet dog — the dog was allowed to run loose on the streets as was, and still is, unfortunately, a habit of many pet dog owners.

This was no hardship for Herman. With true Dachshund enterprise he discovered that he could slip easily under the swinging doors of neighborhood saloons and by simply being pleasant and wagging his tail ingratiatingly he would not only get a pat on the head but his share of the free lunch too. It was this confidence in his own ability to handle people and a firm belief that everyone was his friend that made Herman a great showman once he was launched on his show career.

Victor Moench, seeing him on the streets and recognizing his quality, registered the dog, bought him back from his first owner and returned him to Mr.

Ch. Feri Ellenbert, a homebred of Ellenbert Farm.

Herbert Bertrand in 1938, returning from abroad on the S.S. Bremen with some new additions for the Ellenbert Farm Kennels.

Ch. Feri-Flottenberg, a 1934 champion, one of the most influential of the imports from Herr Muller's kennels.

Ch. Herman Rinkton. —*Tauskey*

Ch. Leutnant v Marienlust. —*Tauskey*

Heller. Heller, who also recognized the dog's quality, turned him over to Hans Sacher to show for him.

Sacher and the spectacular red Dachshund proved to be an unbeatable team. Between 1936 and 1940 he was shown from the East to the West coasts, with a detour on the way through Canada — where he picked up his Canadian championship. Along the way he was shown at the Delaware County Kennel Club show where the breed judge, Alfred M. Dick (later to become president of the American Kennel Club) placed him Best of Breed, and Joseph Quirk gave him the Hound Group.

During his show career Herman changed owners but not handlers. He was purchased by C. Hyland Jones, another New Jerseyite, and registered in Mrs. Jones name. Herman's winnings, still an all-time high for smooth Dachshunds, included 106 Best of Breed wins, 66 Hound Group firsts, three best American-bred in Show awards and 14 Bests in Show. Jones, who bought him at the height of his career, is reported to have paid $1000 for him—a whopping price for a dog in those days.

This attracted world-wide attention from the dog fancy and judges everywhere began to look more closely at Dachshunds who entered the ring in the Group and Best in Show competition. Apparently they liked what they saw and from then on it was a lot easier for a Dachshund to get into the finals at all-breed shows. Dachshund popularity took a big jump. By 1938 the breed had the fourth highest registration in the American Kennel Club records.

Herman's greatest triumph was Best of Variety (and second in the Hound Group) at the 1938 Morris and Essex Kennel Club show. The Dachshund Club of America held its annual specialty show in conjunction with the all-breed event and had invited Herr Gustav Alisch, a world famous authority on Dachshunds, to judge the breed. Word that this famous man was to judge Dachshunds in America brought entries from hundreds of Dachshund breeders anxious to have the great man's opinion of their dogs. The final total of the Dachshund entry was 311 dogs, the largest entry for any breed at that time. It was not only a tribute to Herr Alisch but a test of his endurance at the two day show.

The account of how the little red dog came to be selected by the breed's greatest authority as the best Dachshund in this impressive entry comes from Laurence Horswell. Horswell blamed the show committee for the loss of the drama and ceremony which should have accompanied this achievement, but however much was lost in the rush to complete the Dachshund judging and get the winner into the Group ring in time, the win was a legendary one for Herman and a giant step forward for the Dachshund breed. Here is Horswell's account as published in *Popular Dogs*:

> The judging of the special classes for best smooth, best wire-hair, and best longhair, Saturday afternoon was marred by the decision on the part of the officials at 4:45 p.m. to call the Hound Group as the third Group to be judged. This in spite of the fact that Herr Alisch had 185 Dachshunds to judge on Satur-

Herr Gustav Alisch, internationally distinguished Dachshund figure, pictured above in his record-setting assignment of judging 311 Dachshunds at the 1938 Dachshund Club of America Specialty, held with Morris and Essex, and below with his wirehaired 1936 Reichssieger Knast v Heiligersbrunn. The high esteem in which Alisch was held preserved despite the war, and after it was over he was influential in seeing that Germany's best purebred dogs reached other countries. Through mediation of Col F. D. Rossborough from the American Kennel Club and the DCA, the Examining Organization for Export was built up in Germany in the spring of 1948. Herr Alisch died at Born/Darss in December of that year.

day, a task not equalled by any individual judge in Groups three, four, five or six; even if no consideration is given to the time required to record notes and ratings, or to the interruption and delay caused by transferring the Dachshund judging to another ring shortly before, and the substitution of a rickety card table for the solid inspection bench just before the judging of Mrs. Dodge's special American-bred class.

With a megaphone bellowing "Last call for the Hound Group" like a fog horn every few seconds, and loud threats to judge the Group without the Dachshund unless Best of Breed were produced within ten minutes, the judge was faced by the necessity of studying and comparing 16 smooth champions with the four smooth survivors of class competition, for his best smooth Dachshund; and of judging the corresponding competition of two wirehairs and three longhairs for best of their respective coats.

Although Dachshund judging was more than an hour ahead of last year's schedule, no time was permitted for the A. K. C.-prescribed, exhibitor-satisfying, fair consideration of each of these contestants; or to justify the expensive pilgrimages of top flight dogs from distant kennels; or even to fulfill the premium list promise to exhibitors that every Dachshund would receive individual written comment by the judge. Letter ratings were based upon inspection so brief that a single misstep or an instantaneous faulty posture might contribute unduly to the decisive impression.

Instead of a fitting climax to a world record Dachshund judging accomplishment by a world authority, the rosette, envelope, medal, etc., for best Dachshund were handed to Hans Sachers like a concealed lateral pass in a football game, as his long legs hurdled cords and chairs with Herman Rinkton under his arm — to be brought down just short of a Hound Group touchdown for the breed by Louis Murr's Borzoi, Vigow of Romanoff. Mr. Jones collected the Best of Breed trophies about an hour later.

In New York, after the show Herr Alisch devoted three sessions to editing the transcriptions of his 251 ring notes, signing the certificates, and preparing general comments from which the following paragraphs are quoted:

"My general impression of the black-and-tan and of the red dogs and bitches was by far more favorable than at any show I ever have judged. There is only one point I take the liberty to criticise: The Dachshund being primarily a hunting breed, he should not exhibit evidence of over-feeding, but the animation and physical vitality for such forceful purpose. Too many dogs showed lack of systematic exercise necessary to develop well-muscled and closely knit forequarters and (literally) 'iron-hard' level backs, and to keep the feet properly compact. American Dachshund fanciers should pay more attention to the encouragement of true Dachshund character: A Dachshund should be self-reliant and bold, not timid or retiring. In his small body, he should suggest the courage and capacity of a giant.

"Teeth, heads, and eye-color in most cases were very good. It is important that backs be firm and level, this being the most important part of the body in all breeds. Chests must not extend too close to the ground, too great depth is a hindrance to freedom of action. The ribs should extend well back, and the breastbone must not stop abruptly at the deepest part of the chest, interrupting the smooth line under the chest and reducing space for lungs and heart. Most of the fronts were good. A few dogs showed skin excessively wrinkled on the forefeet and over the shoulders, and dewlaps — faults which are transmissible in breeding and should be avoided. Hindquarters were generally good, and some animals which had rather narrow stance appeared better when in motion.

"In addition to the excellence of the smooth entries, I was very favorably impressed by the quality of the longhairs. I was less satisfied with the wirehairs, whose coats were of better than average texture, but whose conformation and animation did not achieve the general level of the other two coat varieties.

"In judging, I have attempted to give the rating *Gut* only to animals worthy of being used as breeding stock. The rating *Sehr Gut* has been awarded to animals whose conformation is free from serious faults and which give evidence of proper disposition. The highest rating *Vorzuglich* signifies a Dachshund free from significant faults of structure, condition or temperament, and such a rating should be conferred only after the most exhausting examination and appraisal. Only by most conscientious, rigorous, and just criticism can service be rendered to a breed, and I ask the exhibitors to accept my ratings from this point of view.

"It would have been impossible for me to rate and judge this great number of dogs in so short a time without the efficient help of my assistant Mr. Horswell, my steward Mr. Ebeling and my ring secretary Miss Lustig. 311 Dachshund entries is a record figure of which the American Dachshund Club has every right to be proud. The kind reception I received from American Dachshund fanciers, and the beautiful show grounds placed at our disposal by the generous patroness and president of the Morris and Essex club, Mrs. M. Hartley Dodge, have rendered my work an unforgettable pleasure, for which I express my sincerest thanks."

(Signed) *Gustav Alisch.*

Following the lull of the World War II years, Mr. and Mrs. Fred Heying, who had begun with a small kennel during the early '20s, began to look around for some new stock for their Heying-Teckel Kennels in California. They bought carefully and selectively, and their operation remained small until a chance request to an old friend catapulted them into a prominence that continues even now.

In 1945, they wrote to Lt. Col. (then Captain) Norton S. Parker who had been stationed during World War II at Long Island City with the U.S. Signal Corps. He was coming back to his home in Los Angeles and the Heyings asked him to bring them a puppy from the Mehrers' kennels. Col. Parker went to Hempstead to see the Mehrers. They sat him down in their living room and brought in a five-months-old black-and-tan male puppy that had been whelped in April. His sire was Bruce v Marienlust and his dam Melinda v Marienlust. Col. Parker later described him as "an atom bomb of a dog". He bought him then and there and departed for California with the puppy, whom the Mehrers had named Favorite von Marienlust, tucked into the station wagon with his own family and his own Dachshunds.

Prior to Col. Parker's visit to the Mehrers, Laurence Horswell, working on plans for the Dachshund Club of America's Golden Jubilee show to be held in

Am. and Can. Ch. Favorite v Marienlust.

The story of this picture of Favorite with the Dachshund Club of America plaque is told in the accompanying text.

November of that same year, asked Josef Mehrer to take a good puppy into the Manhattan studio of Percy Jones, a well-known photographer of dogs. Laurence had sent Jones a model of a bronze plaque which was to be awarded the Best of Breed at the Jubilee show and wanted a Dachshund puppy photographed with it. He wanted to dramatize the past and future aspects of the breed; the bronze plaque to crown the past, the well-bred puppy to represent the future.

Josef brought in three puppies, one of which was Favorite. It was impossible to pose any one of the three lively pups so Jones, long used to animal photography, simply set the plaque in place, focused his camera on it and told Josef to let the puppies loose to explore. The puppies were instantly attracted to the large, shiny object. Favorite playing behind it, suddenly rose up and put his front paws on top of the plaque and gazed straight at the camera. Jones snapped the picture. It was to be prophetic not only of Favorite's future, but that of all Dachshunds.

The Heyings were delighted when they first saw Favorite. They waited impatiently for him to mature to the point where he could be shown. Against the advice of some others, they entered him, at the age of 10 months, at the Golden Gate Dachshund Specialty at San Francisco in 1946. Once on the show grounds they began to have some doubts about their decision. The puppy seemed very sleepy — would he wake up and show well when his class was called? As Favorite dozed comfortably on his bench, Fred Heying sought a handler. Perhaps a professional could bring out the fire and spirit which seemed to have gone out of the young dog. He encountered Nick Finn. Nicky, busy with other assignments, was reluctant but finally agreed to take him in for the class, Open dogs, black and tan.

The judge was Edward F. Hirschman, a Californian who had drawn a fine quality entry of 110 dogs. Favorite suddenly came to life as class time neared and Hirschman commented later, "I was impressed with the dog's superb soundness, movement and happy disposition." He gave him Winners Dog over the first place Open dogs. His Winners Bitch was White Gables Marjoram shown by her breeder, Albert Van Court. Hirschman described Marjoram as "one of the most perfect bitches I have ever judged", but nonetheless gave Best of Winners to Favorite, basing his decision on movement and perfect stance on a loose lead.

By this time Nicky Finn realized that he had a tiger by the tail and juggled his schedule around so that he could take the dog in for Best of Variety. Both Nicky and the dog faced their toughest competition. Albert Van Court would be handling his Ch. White Gables Basil, and the two other champions were Ch. Eric v. d. Daniels and Mrs. Cellarius' Ch. Uhlan v Cellarius.

Favorite had enjoyed another nap on his bench while the bitch classes were being judged. He now came into the ring full of pep, happy to be the center of attention once more. Hirschman's choice narrowed down to Ch. Basil and Favorite. Exhibitors and ringsiders were treated to an exhibition of superb han-

Ch. Falcon of Heying-Teckel, BIS winner and sire of 82 champions. Bred and owned by Mr. and Mrs. Fred Heying. —*Ludwig*

Ch. Herman VI, standout of the 1962–65 era in which he won 8 BIS and 52 Groups. Owned by Mr. and Mrs. Seward Webb, Jr. of California, and handled by Woody Dorward.

Ch. Gunther v Marienlust. —*Tauskey*

Ch. Cavalier v Marienlust, by Ch. Leutnant v Marienlust ex Moya v Marienlust. Owned by White Gables Kennels.

dling as the skilled professional and the equally skillful amateur moved their dogs before a judge lost in admiration for both dogs and having a hard time making up his mind between them. Finally the younger dog's energy gave him a slight edge and Hirschman gave him the Best of Variety. It was a five point major.

Favorite's show career lasted only four years but by the time he died in January of 1959, he had sired 95 champions and become the top producing sire of the Dachshund breed. It seems almost an anti-climax to say that the second and third top producing Dachshund sires, Ch. Falcon of Heying Teckel (sire of 82 champions), bred and owned by the Heyings and Ch. Dunkeldorf Falcon's Favorite (sire of 90 champions) bred and owned by Mr. and Mrs. Thomas R. Dunk's Dunkeldorf Kennels, were his son and grandson. Falcon died in 1964 and Falcon's Favorite in 1972.

While Am. and Can.Ch. Favorite von Marienlust has been the most widely known of the Marienlust dogs, the Mehrers themselves considered Ch. Leutnant von Marienlust, mentioned in another chapter of this book, as one of the best dogs that they had bred and his two sons, Ch. Gunther von Marienlust and Ch. Cavalier von Marienlust as of his caliber.

In line with the Mehrer philosophy on showing dogs, Leutnant was not shown extensively but when he did show, he made top wins. One of these was Best of Breed at the DCA Specialty in 1940, which was held then in conjunction with the Morris and Essex show. In the ten years that followed from 1940 to 1950, eight of the ten winners at the same Specialty were either first, second or third generations of Leutnant's get. His son, Gunther was the winner in 1942, 1943 and 1945; Ch. Superman v Marienlust was the 1944 winner; Ch. Bit O' Black of Tween Hills in 1946; Ch. Cynthia of Jo-Rene in 1947; Ch. Cinderella v Marienlust in 1949; and Ch. Aristo von Marienlust in 1950.

Ch. Gunther, owned by Mrs. Jeannette W. Cross, had a brilliant show career. Among his most noted wins was the Best of Breed at the Golden Jubilee Specialty of the DCA in 1945. His prize was the bronze plaque described earlier in this chapter. It was the only one of its size (fourteen inches) ever cast and it now hangs in the picture gallery of the American Kennel Club. Another win was the DCA Cup given to him at the Club's 40th anniversary for his three Best of Breed wins at the Specialties held with Morris and Essex.

Gunther sired 26 champions including Ch. Janet of Tenroc, Ch. Marlene of Tenroc, Ch. Donald of Tween Hills, Ch. Little Vicki of Tween Hills, Ch. Baron of Tween Hills, Ch. Blackie Dockie, Ch. Gunther Again, Ch. Cornhill Linda, Ch. Hexe v Waldhof, Ch. Blackbeauty of Tween Hills, Ch. Bit O' Black of Tween Hills, Ch. Bencelia's Candy, Ch. Cinderella v Sieghofen, Ch. Bavarian Mousi, Ch. Rotcod v Tenroc, Ch. Hardway Welcome Stranger (shown by Mrs. Cross to six Best in Show awards), Ch. Guntherette of Earldale, Ch. Donahue of Brentwald, Ch. Derresheim of Brentwald, and Ch. Ballerina von Marienlust.

The talented Mrs. Cross, writer, sportswoman and expert needlewoman is probably the most knowledgable person today on Dachshunds and their owners, unless it be Mrs. Grace Hill, still DCA secretary after 20 years in office. Much of the material and some of the writing in this book comes from Mrs. Cross. Through the years, circumstances have made it impractical to continue her Hardway Kennels. This denial, like Horswell's dismissal from his advertising job, has benefited the breed. For without dogs to show and kennels to clean, Mrs. Cross has been free to do more and more judging and to concern herself with problems which confront the maintenance of the standard in modern Dachshunds.

Never one to rest on past achievements, Mrs. Cross has been active in founding the Connecticut Yankee Dachshund Club along with Mrs. George (Dorothy) Pickett. Both women have filled its program with progressive and innovative ideas. The establishment of a third licensed Dachshund Field Trial to give competitors another chance for the Field Trial title, Dachshund Racing and improvements on the Club's annual show, are among these. Mrs. Cross still has her aging champion "Gina" (Ch. Dixie Dachs Kruschina) from the Wallace Alfords' kennels in Raleigh and a young red male whose ancestry goes back to Gunther, Ch. Rose Farm's Redcoat.

Gunther's brother Cavalier, went to the Van Courts' White Gables Kennels in California. He sired 13 champions, among them White Gables Basil and White Gables Marjoram. White Gables was among the best of a considerable number of fine Dachshund kennels in California during the '40s. Mr. Van Court's knowledge of Dachshunds and other breeds made him more and more in demand as a judge. During the late 1940s and early '50s, Mrs. Van Court's health began to fail. Kennel activities slowed down and all but ended when her illness proved fatal.

After her death, the kennels were kept up but on a much smaller scale. Mr. Van Court accepted more judging assignments; perhaps the constant travel and change helped to ease his sense of loss.

A few years later he married Mrs. Lancaster (Ramona) Andrews. She had known both Albert and Miriam and they had shared a common interest in Dachshunds and in judging. The new Mrs. Van Court was already coming up in the judging end of dog shows and her Ch. Aristo v Marienlust was the celebrated winner of 10 Bests in Show, 47 Hound Groups and 118 Best of Variety awards. Her knowledge of dogs was not confined to Dachshunds; her early years had been spent with her family's Airedales and Greyhounds.

For a while White Gables was again in the show ring. Ramona Van Court enjoyed showing her own dogs, although on occasion she used a handler (most often Jerry Rigden.) One of the dogs she showed at that time was Ch. White Gables Ristocrat, a son of Aristo.

Ristocrat, who was shown in the late '50s, won a Best in Show, ten Hound Groups, and one Dachshund Specialty.

Ch. White Gables Basil, by Ch. Cavalier v Marienlust ex Ch. White Gables Mehitabel. Owned by White Gables Kennels.

Am. & Can. Ch. Aristo v Marienlust. —*Tauskey*

There were other dogs and other champions but judging assignments of this talented husband and wife team increased and they had less and less time for their own dogs.

They were a great pair — Albert with his great knowledge and almost 19th century manners, and Ramona already skilled as a judge and acquiring more knowledge and ability from her husband. She had a gift for organization and along with judging she ran two successful all-breed shows, the Beverly Hills Kennel Club in the West and the Westbury Kennel Association in the East.

Her show committees were so well organized and functioned so well that business firms with branch offices would have turned green with envy. She is still active on both show committees. The Van Courts judged from London to Australia and exhibitors were happy to show under them.

In the '70s Mr. Van Court became a member of the Westminster Kennel Club's show committee and Ramona was one of two women invited to judge the Groups on the final night. Tuxedos were required dress for the men judges and the women usually wore short evening dresses. Ramona, like Laura Delano, was particular about what she wore in the judging ring. The difference was that Ramona's outfits were carefully planned to avoid anything which might distract or frighten a dog when she examined it. For Westminster, she had a designer make her a black and white dress that somehow resembled a tuxedo without being a duplicate. I thought it the most attractive and appropriate outfit I had ever seen for such an occasion. Mr. Van Court quipped ''my wife looks like a head waiter,'' but he was truly proud of her appearance and her good taste in clothes. Mr. Van Court died suddenly a day or two after the 1970 show. White Gables is no more. Ramona is now Mrs. John Marshall Jones, but still judging and still active in the clubs for which she worked so hard.

Earlier in this Chapter I mentioned the Bertrands' Ellenbert Kennels and its accumulation of Flottenberg stock. On Mr. Bertrand's death most of the dogs went to Mrs. Florence Keller whose Blue Key Kennels were already well established. By acquiring these dogs, Mrs. Keller achieved the greatest concentration of pure Flottenberg lines of any kennel either in Europe or America. Grayce Greenburg, in her book *The Dachshund* writes ''No other kennel in America carried on with the Flottenbergs although it would have been easy for any of us to have done this — it is thus that great strains are lost.''

The Gilbert Stewarts' Windyriver Kennels and Maude Daniel Smith's von Dachshafen Kennels were well-known at that time and Mrs. Charles Cline's Crespi Kennels began to put some good smooth Dachshunds in the ring, followed later by equally good longhairs and miniature Dachshunds.

Dorothy Pickett and her veterinarian husband, George, have the most direct breeding to Marienlust of any kennel. Their Herthwood Saffron is a good ex-

Ch. Wildfire of Blue Key, one of the last of the Flottenberg line, owned by Mrs. Florence Keller.

Ch. Carrot of Blue Key, owned by Mrs. Keller.

Eng. Ch. Dimas Earthstopper, imported in May 1940 by Mr. and Mrs. Bertrand's Ellenbert Farm Kennels (shortly before Mr. Bertrand's death.) Earthstopper quickly proved himself with Best in Show wins at Lenox KC in August 1940 and again at Westchester the following month. Earthstopper was later acquired by Anne Smith Wenden's Rivenrock Kennels in California.

Ch. Rivenrock Teak, an outstanding bitch of the c. 1950 era, whose pedigree traced back to Earthstopper. Teak was owned by Mrs. Donia Cline's daughter, Nancy Ann Oberg.

Ch. Celloyd Daniel, multi-BIS winner of the 1950s, owned and handled by the late Lloyd Case.

Am. & Braz. Ch. Damon v Benmarden, multi-BIS winner of the 1950s, owned by Mr. and Mrs. George Hendrickson and handled by Larry Downey.

Ch. Ezra v Benmarden, multi-BIS winner of the 1950s. Bred, owned and handled by Mrs. Marjorie Dennard.

73

Ch. Steve v Marienlust.

Ch. Herthwood's Saffron, bred and owned by Dorothy S. Prickett. Saffron typified the Marienlust line. —*Tauskey*

ample of the typical Marienlust look. Breeding at Herthwood is done in the classical manner of the old German kennels, with strict attention to soundness, movement and temperament. Type has long since been established through the Marienlust line. It was here that the Mehrers' last champion, Steve v Marienlust and his remaining kennelmates lived out their lives after Maria Mehrer's death.

The Picketts seem particularly fitted for this kind of a breeding program. Except for Dorothy's painting and embroidery, most of their activities are animal oriented — 4-H Clubs meet at their place in Huntington, Conn., young riders are encouraged to take care of their horses, there is a collection of bird houses and feeding stations to attract wild birds and their Dachshunds enjoy a smaller version of Peggy Westphal's open exercise areas. Indoors the dogs divide their time between their own quarters in the "dog room" and the Picketts' comfortable living room. Many of Dorothy's weekends are spent on judging assignments. She has been doing it well for a long time.

She tells this story of how they came to own Dachshunds. When they first bought their home and built the adjacent veterinary hospital, Dorothy wanted a dog. George pointed out that a dog in a veterinary establishment was like bringing coals to Newcastle. Besides, it might bite the paying customers. George had previously owned an Airedale who took his duties as guardian of the home seriously. But Dorothy persisted and after a few half-hearted objections, George agreed. Next came the problem of what kind of a dog. George based his choice of a Dachshund on the fact that those that came into his office were good natured and friendly, even to the vet. Dorothy just liked them; she didn't need a reason.

They approached their friends, the Bertrands, but they had no Dachshunds for sale at that time and suggested the Mehrers' kennels on Long Island. At the Mehrers they found Ava v Marienlust irresistible. The price was $200. Dorothy didn't hesitate. She had saved $200 for a new bathtub. It went for Ava instead.

It was the beginning of a lifelong friendship between the two families. Josef approved of Ava as a brood bitch as well as a show specimen and often went over his breeding ideas with Dorothy, with an occasional assist from George. The Picketts, so well educated in animal husbandry, marvelled at the skill of this self-taught man with no more education than most German children at that time had received. They are still convinced that he had a very special talent.

Josef Mehrer had great plans for the use of one of his dogs, Calvert von Marienlust, at stud. Calvert's untimely death from distemper robbed him of the chance to use the dog before he had done much breeding. Today, through the great progress made by veterinary medicine, we take for granted the freedom our dogs enjoy from this dread disease but until after World War II it was a constant threat to every kennel and many dogs succumbed to it.

Heartbroken at the loss of what he considered his top stud, Josef set out to

Ch. Velvet's Vance of Rose Farm, the Farm's first homebred champion.

Ch. Venture of Hardway winning a Group at the Bermuda Kennel Club under judge Percy Roberts. Handled by Dorothy Hardy. —*Shafer*

find a male puppy among the few litters that Calvert had sired and that had been sold. He traveled all over the United States looking at every litter and finally narrowed his choice down to two, a red male (one of a pair he had sold the Picketts) and another male that had been sold to a California breeder. Before making up his mind, Josef made another trip to Caifornia and then back to the Picketts in Connecticut. He finally chose the red male at the Picketts. The dog was Steve v Marienlust, and became Josef's last champion. Dorothy Pickett kept the sister.

Both Calvert and Ava appear in the pedigree of Herthwood's Saffron who is so typical of the Mehrer strain.

Nancy (Mrs. Pierce) Onthank was brought up with all the advantages that the children of the very rich enjoy. She was a world traveler during her school days and her talent for art was encouraged by lessons from the best teachers in painting and sculpture that were available. In such surroundings her appreciation of what she saw and the ability to analyze it in terms of form and beauty, came naturally to her. In her travels through England and the continent of Europe she came to know many Dachshund breeders and to appreciate the quality of their dogs. No visit, foreign or domestic, was complete for Nancy unless she returned home with some souvenir of her visit. Dachshunds proved to be the very best of all souvenirs.

She named her kennels "Rose Farm". Its first champion was Debutante of Fredelsa. The first homebred dog to make its championship was Ch. Velvet's Vance of Rose Farm.

Nancy was fortunate to have, near her Connecticut home, two good kennels, the Picketts Herthwood Kennels and Mrs. Cross' Hardway Kennels. Her wide acquaintance abroad, especially in England, gained her the confidence of British Dachshund breeders who, knowing her sincerity, were willing to part with their good stock, knowing the dogs would be shown and well treated.

Her family were amused at her absorption with Dachshunds and in this, as in other things they were indulgent. On learning that Nancy had been invited to judge a big Dachshund specialty in England during the '60s, her elder sister called her designer in Paris and had him make up a complete outfit for Nancy to wear in the ring. It was a brown silk dress with a pattern of tiny dachshunds woven in the fabric and a dark brown fur coat and hat to go with it. Like Ramona Van Court's Westminster outfit, it was perfect for the occasion.

Quality and disposition have always been Nancy's criteria for Dachshunds. Her knowledge of anatomy, through sculpture, has made her aware of the structure under the sleek Dachshund hide. Ch. Venture of Hardway and Ch. Herthwoods Mark of Rose Farm are perhaps the best indication of this ability, though of course there have been other fine dogs. She has never hesitated to buy a good one when she felt it was better than her own stock or could improve the quality of her own dogs. Her latest acquisition which marks her first step into breeding standard longhairs has been the purchase of a bitch from Mrs. Mary Howell's Bayard Kennels. I saw the litter in December of 1974 just after they had been whelped and I'm sure Mary would have been delighted with their quality.

The Rose Farm standard smooths and wirehaired Dachshunds and miniatures, mostly English imports, have been important contributions, especially to miniature breeders where the struggle to produce really good ones has been so difficult.

Ch. Venture of Hardway was "the most famous show dog I've ever owned" says Mrs. Onthank. He was the top Dachshund winner for 1956 and 1957. Another homebred, Ch. Herthwoods Mark of Rose Farm was Best in Show in three countries, Canada, United States and Bermuda. Through his dam, Herthwoods Maid Marion, he traces his pedigree back to Ava and Calvert von Marienlust.

Mrs. Onthank considers her six top dogs to have been Ch. Red Velvet of Fredelsa, who produced nine champions, Ch. Pondwick's Hobgoblin (a standard wirehaired bought in England in 1964), Ch. Venture of Hardway, Ch. Herthwoods Mark of Rose Farm, Ch. Mighty Fine von Walder (a longhaired miniature bought in England in 1961) and Ch. Debutante of Fredelsa.

She saw Mighty Fine during a judging assignment in England and was so taken with him that her husband, who had planned to make her a present of a mink coat, bought her the dog instead. Mighty Fine stayed in England until he had completed his English title and then came in to the United States. She spotted Hobgoblin at another English show, not in the ring but hiding under the chair of his disappointed owner who had just received third in a class of three with him. He was eight months old.

In the United States, handled by Frank Hardy, Hobgoblin was Best of Variety an astounding 98 of the first 100 times he was shown. As of the end of 1975, he has sired 64 champions. From his breeder, Mrs. Medley, Nancy also bought Pondwick's Queen of the Knight. Queen is the dam of Ch. Rose Farms Moon Rockette (Best of Opposite Sex in wirehaired Dachshunds at Westminster 1975) who is owned by Nancy's daughter, Dee Hutchinson.

More recent Rose Farm imports have come from England's Minutist Kennels, including a black and tan longhaired miniature, Minutist Goliath. Bred to Mighty Fine's sons, they are producing fine quality miniatures.

Most of the Rose Farm stud dogs, including Hobgoblin, are now with her daughter, Dee, who is following in her mother's footsteps as a breeder, and has recently received her judging license for the breed.

Although Nancy sometimes showed her own dogs, most of the Rose Farm dogs were shown by Frank and Dorothy Hardy. The Hardys were not only

Ch. Venture of Hardway. —*Tauskey*

Am. Can. & Berm. Ch. Herthwood's Mark of Rose Farm, Venture's son, a BIS winner.

among the top professional handlers but were Dachshund breeders too. Their Hubertus Kennels was as successful as those of the good amateur breeders whose dogs they handled.

Other professional handlers who also bred Dachshunds include Woodie Dorward (Red Locket Kennels); Jerry Rigden whose smooth-longhair cross, Ch. Guyman's Long Deal, contributed so much to Dachshund structure; Lloyd Case (Celloyd Kennels); Ben Klimkeiwicz (Bencelia Kennels); and just recently, Howard Atlee, amateur-turned-professional whose prefix is "Penthouse". But the Hardys were something special. Before a dog's campaign was over, their clients had become personal friends.

The election of Frank as president of the Professional Handlers Association lent dignity and cohesion to this hard-working, widely scattered group. It must have been a new experience at the American Kennel Club when a scion of German nobility went to bat for the PHA on matters affecting the organization. Frank set a standard for progressive ideas and constructive criticism to improve the quality of shows and the conditions under which professionals are required to work, a standard that more recent presidents of the PHA — William Trainor and Ray Holloway — are carrying on.

Frank's knowledge of dogs came from his family's kennels in Germany where showing and hunting with dogs, including Dachshunds, was a sport, not a profession. The outbreak of World War II found him stranded and penniless in the United States while his family, in Germany, had their fortune and their possessions swept away by the Hitler regime. Dogs were what he knew best and dogs were his start at wage earning in America.

Dorothy had been a successful professional handler prior to the war. Sporting dogs were what she was noted for, but she was skillful with both large and small breeds and a good judge of both. For her, the war had been an escape from a long and difficult divorce and her tour of duty in the K-9 Corps at Fort Riley was a welcome change. Once out of service she returned to her mother's home and resumed her handling career.

She and Frank met at dog shows and Frank admired a Dachshund that Dorothy owned and was showing at that time. He tried to buy it. Dorothy refused to sell, but Frank persisted and became a daily caller at Dorothy's home. At first it was to buy the Dachshund, which Dorothy still refused to sell; then it became a courtship which led to marriage. Dorothy's mother remained suspicious to the end. "He's marrying you for your Dachshund," she warned.

Harland and I got to know them well when they moved to a nearby town in Long Island shortly after the marriage. Once married, Frank decided that Dorothy's musical education had been neglected and he tried to interest her in the music of the great composers. I remember going over to their house one afternoon on an errand and was greeted, halfway down the block, by the swirling, crashing sounds of the storm scene from Wagner's "The Flying Dutchman." Entering the house I found Dorothy calmly grooming a Basset Hound. Above the sounds of drums, cymbals and woodwinds played at full tilt, Dorothy explained, "Frank thinks I'll understand it better if it's played loud."

Both of these prominent Dachshund figures are now licensed to judge all breeds. Ramona Van Court (now Mrs. John Marshall Jones) is pictured winning with Ch. White Gables Ristocrat under judge Herman G. Cox. —*Ludwig*

Mrs. Jeannette W. Cross, herself one of the most respected of Dachshund judges, showing Dixie Dachs Kruschina ("Gina") to win toward her Bermudian championship under judge James W. Trullinger. Mr. Trullinger is another Dachshund fancier who has become a judge of all breeds.

While they disagreed on music, their combined skills in establishing their Hubertus strain, particularly in wirehaired Dachshunds, was a great addition to the quality of dogs that came later. Frank's sudden death, shortly after one of the Queensboro Kennel Club shows, saddened us all. Dorothy still carries on their handling business from the lovely home in Pennsylvania.

The August Schuhmanns arrived in New Jersey about the same time the Mehrers came to Long Island. The two families were friends. The Schuhmanns were as expert in selecting and breeding Dachshunds as the Mehrers and their von Hoellental Kennels produced some fine dogs. One of the best known was Ch. Gauner v Hoellental. August Schuhmann used his knowledge of breeding principles to establish a very profitable mink farm. While it did not stop them from breeding Dachshunds it did put an end to showing them. The Schuhmanns were afraid of bringing back distemper or another equally deadly virus from dog shows.

Their dogs and their breeding program attracted breeders in both New Jersey and Pennsylvania, among them Mrs. Sara Peterman of Philadelphia. Mrs. Peterman bred Dachshunds, Beagles and Pointers over a period of more than twenty years. She now makes her home in an apartment in Philadelphia but her interest in the breed is still keen. It has been a great loss that due to advancing age, she is no longer able to judge. Some of her Dachshund champions include Ch. Peterman's Georgina, Peterman's Hugh III, Peterman's Candidate and Peterman's Gay Lothario. Candidate was Best of Breed at the Dachshund Club of California specialty and Best Hound at both Morris and Essex and the Eastern (Boston) Dog Show in 1952. Earlier, during 1948, her Ch. Georgina, on her way to her title, came from the Open class to take Best of Breed in Dachshunds and Best Hound at the Devon Dog Show.

Sara did not confine her activities to just showing and judging. She helped organize the Quaker City Dog Club, now the Penn Treaty Kennel Club. She was show chairman, secretary-treasurer and later president of the Bryn Mawr Kennel Club. She served for a while as vice-president of the Dachshund Club of America. Much of her breeding stock came from the Schuhmanns. She admired their dogs and their skill as breeders. "I used to sit at their feet" she said in speaking of her admiration of their kennels. I have a mental picture of this elegant Philadelphia lady sitting at the feet of a couple of mink farmers to increase her knowledge.

Mrs. Peterman also provided me with some information on the once important but now non-existent Waldbach Kennels of Mr. and Mrs. John Chaffe, who also lived in the Philadelphia area. The Chaffes bought Bavarian Lump from the Mehrers' friend, Louis Flecher, and Hans Sacher showed him to his championship. Another of their champions was Gale Wind of Blue Key, and they bought a dapple Dachshund from Mrs. Cellarius.

Mrs. Sara Peterman.

Ch. Peterman's Hugh III, by Message v Marienlust ex Peterman's Juliana. Bred by Mrs. Peterman and owned by Raymond S. Hill of Arizona.

Ch. Christi Dachs Challenge, multi-BIS winner of the late '50s. Owned by Miss Mary E. Cornet of Washington, D.C., and handled by George Rood.

John Hutchinson Cook is a name to conjure with in the Dachshund world. He possesses a fabulous memory about dogs and the people who own them and a library full of books on dogs, including Dachshunds, some now out of print and many of them collectors items.

John tells that he got off to a bad start in beginning his Kleetal Kennels at his family's beautiful, century-old Cloverdale Farm at Columbus, N.J. Peggy Westphal recounts the same experience in getting her kennels started. Breeders just would not sell them good dogs. These breeders felt that the enthusiasm of these new arrivals would be short-lived and good dogs, sold to them would be lost as breeding stock when the fun of showing wore off. When they were convinced this was not so, they sold good dogs to both Peggy and John. Some of the first of his good ones came from the Schuhmanns' von Hoellental Kennels.

John's eye for a good Dachshund improved on acquaintance with the good stock from the New York, Long Island, New Jersey and Pennsylvania area and his tour of duty in the armed services during World War II, placed him in California where he had a chance to see some of the Dachshund greats.

Following the war he resumed his breeding and enlarged his Kleetal Kennels. His work included some experimental breeding of dapples, although they were a rarity in the East. His kennels were extensive. They were capable of housing 100 dogs, which were shown often and with great success.

Unfortunately the kennels and the estate required more help in maintenance than could be found, a problem that estate owners throughout the country had already discovered. Upon the tragic early death of his wife, John and his children moved to a smaller home in Bordentown. Kleetal still continues but on a much smaller scale and many dogs bearing the Kleetal prefix are with other owners and breeders on breeder's terms. In the winter of 1975 I saw a litter of black and tan smooth Dachshunds, owned jointly by Mrs. Charles Merz of Merzdale Kennels on Long Island and Mrs. Elisabeth McNeill of Manhattan, which trace their pedigree to the Kleetal line. The pups had the best of two worlds, Mrs. Merz' country home and Mrs. McNeill's duplex apartment in Greenwich Village.

The Willard K. Dentons brought their considerable knowledge of breeding and showing fine animals, horses and dogs, to Dachshunds with the establishment of their Ardencaple Kennels at Mt. Kisco, N.Y. Willard Denton was at that time president of the Manhattan Savings Bank and while he accompanied his wife to weekend dog shows where their standard and miniature smooth Dachshunds were being shown successfully, he began to wonder if this public interest in dogs might somehow work out to the advantage of the bank in its public relations program. At that time television audiences were being assured that "You have a friend at Chase Manhattan". Without benefit of television, dogs found their friend in Willard Denton at the Manhattan Savings Bank.

Ch. Kleetal's Morgain, a 1950s bitch of John H. Cook's Kleetal Kennels.

Ch. Kleetal's Rondo, owned by Mr. Cook.

Two puppies from a litter carrying the Kleetal line, owned by Mrs. Marion Merz and Mrs. Elizabeth W. McNeil.

Mr. and Mrs. Willard K. Denton with their standard smooth, Ch. Jolly Dachs Falcon's Flame.

Mrs. Denton exhibiting her chocolate dapple, Mar-Bett's Girl O' My Dreams, at the annual exhibition held by the Manhattan Savings Bank in New York City.

He consulted with Thelma Boalbey, publicist for the Westminster Kennel Club. They decided that the bank's large rotunda just inside the entrance would be an ideal place to have an exhibition of dogs. The result has become the most elegant facsimile of a dog show ever seen anywhere in this country.

Dogs, not just any dogs but top winners including the Westminster Best in Show, were invited to come into the bank for a five-day exhibition that lasted from about 10:30 a.m. until 2:00 p.m. each day. With Mrs. Evelyn Monte, a noted field trial judge, as master of ceremonies, the dogs were brought into the ring within the rotunda one by one while Mrs. Monte described the breed and the particular dog and his winnings to a rapt audience of noontime New Yorkers. The Foley Dog Show Organization furnished the benching, but all resemblance to the Foley equipment vanished once it was set up inside the bank. The benches were covered with pastel antique velvet, and cushions to match were provided for the dogs. The edges of the benches that faced the spectators were framed in made-to-order picture frames, antiqued like those of fine paintings, and the dogs, curled up comfortably on their elegant cushions, were displayed like works of art. Red velvet ropes attached to polished brass stanchions created an aisle between the dogs and the spectators, who were encouraged to walk around the benching area and ask questions of the dogs' owners. The entrance to the show ring was also marked with velvet ropes, and the crowning touch was a sterling silver 14-inch Paul Revere bowl, full of chunks of chopped liver, and held invitingly by one of the Foley employees at this entrance so that exhibitors could give their dogs a treat during the performance.

It has become an annual educational fixture to which New Yorkers look forward, and which has done much to educate the general public in the infinite variety and types of purebred dogs. I have been showing dogs for many years but the first Bearded Collie I had ever seen was exhibited at the Manhattan Savings Bank. Willard Denton is now retired but the present officers and board of directors, with Thelma Boalbey still at the helm, continue to hold the show every Spring.

Until Mrs. Charles Stalter's death in 1975, her Barberry Knowe Kennels was one of the few of today maintained in the manner of those owned by George Semler and the Bertrands. Long before Mrs. Stalter became interested in Dachshunds she and her husband, Charles, were internationally known for their Scottish Terriers. A trophy room with all four walls lined with trophies was testimony of their success. Like Semler and Bertrand, they bought the best in Dachshunds to start their breeding program. This time there was no need to go out of the country for breeding stock. The United States had acquired the greatest number of good Dachshunds anywhere and the Stalters were able to reap the benefits of long past imports plus the more recently established lines created by American breeders after the second World War.

Their Ch. Crosswynd's Cracker Jack, bred by Mrs. Barbara Lovering, was the top winning Dachshund for 1968. He was retired the following year. Their Ch. Dunkeldorf's Jagerlust, another great winner, brought them the von Marienlust line. Mrs. Stalter's acquisition of Miss Delano's Knocknagree Kennels of longhaired Dachshunds brought her the best of the three founding lines of longhairs in America: the Howard Eric's Ch. Kobold v Fuchsenstein, a German import; Mrs. Thassilo Krug Von Nidda's English import Ch. Primrosepatch Rose Brocade; and Mrs. William Burr Hill Jr.'s Ch. William de Sangpur, whelped in the United States, a grandson of the famous "Welt and Derbysieger" (World Champion) Winnetou von Zinnowitz.

Coming into the '70s we find Miles K. McElrath of Columbus, Ohio with his Wagatomo Kennels reviving the dappled Dachshund in a big way. He began in 1960 with a smooth red puppy from Dr. Leo Manol, a Viennese living in Hawaii. Dr. McElrath went to his house on another matter, saw a litter of Dachshunds and bought the little red puppy on the spot. She turned out to have both Marienlust and White Gables breeding in her background and at first Dr. McElrath decided, as many novices have before him, that he wanted to breed Dachshunds as near the standard of perfection as possible.

Not one to jump into things hastily, Dr. McElrath researched the possibilities of his new-found hobby and decided, after a few attempts, that following an already established formula for breeding good ones, plus the fact that hundreds of other Dachshund breeders were trying to do the same thing, was not very interesting.

During the course of his reading on Dachshunds, he came across a rather uncomplimentary reference to dappled Dachshunds in Milo Denlinger's *The Complete Dachshund*. Here at last was a challenge for a serious breeder; creative, experimental breeding. He read everything he could find on color inheritance and dug up the names of Mrs. Justine Cellarius, whose Ch. Uhlan v Cellarius was the country's first dappled champion Dachshund, and others who had experimented with these odd colored dogs such as Mrs. Mary Fitzpatrick Dean, Mrs. Sarah Hoyt, Grayce Greenburg, Barbara M. Murphy and John Hutchinson Cook.

He named his kennels Wagatomo. It is an old Japanese word meaning "my companion." His first champion was a longhaired dapple, Ch. Wagatomo Tessella, the first dapple champion since Mrs. Cellarius' Uhlan. Others have followed Dr. McElrath's lead and dapples are appearing more and more at shows and winning too. But Wagatomo seems to have a head start. As of 1973, two littermates, Wagatomo Harlequin Tomtom and his sister, Wagatomo Harlequin Holly are both champions. Both are longhairs, although Mr. McElrath is more concerned with color than coat. Dr. C. William Nixon, the geneticist who has contributed importantly to this book, believes that if ever a white Dachshund is bred, it will be Miles McElrath who will do it.

Ch. Christi Dachs Camille, BIS winner and dam of champions.
Owned by Barberry Knowe Kennels.

Ch. Dunkeldorf's Falcon Forester who, as a young dog, won
Best of Breed at the Dachshund Club of America Specialty
from the classes. Owned by Barberry Knowe Kennels.

Ch. Crosswynd's Crackerjack and his son, Ch. Elfendorf's
Little Bit O' Jack. Owned by Barberry Knowe Kennels.

Ch. Willo-Mar's Lucky Star, 1960 BIS winner, owned by Mrs. Aileen P. C. DeBrun, and handled by Jerry Rigden.

Jerry Rigden has been identified as a top Dachshund breeder in his own right as well as one of the foremost handlers of the breed over many years. He is pictured here with Ch. Squier's Black Knight, a 1960s winner owned by Mrs. Frances G. Scaife.

No handler is more closely—or more brightly—identified with Dachshunds than Lorraine Heichel. She is pictured here with an outstanding trio from the Knolland Farm Kennels of Edward B. Jenner of Richmond, Illinois: Ch. Kemper Dach's Marcel, longhair, winner of many Groups and a Best in Show from the classes; Ch. Selkert's Randy, wirehair, consistent Specialty Best of Variety winner; and Ch. Moffet's Harvest, smooth, top winner for his variety in 1975.

Among the kennels that have risen to prominence in recent years are the Penthouse Kennels of Howard Atlee. Howard began breeding miniature and standard smooths in his Manhattan penthouse. The proliferation of Dachshunds soon reached the point where Howard was forced out of town to Stone Ridge, N.Y., where there was room enough to house his growing kennel. Fascinated with the sport, Howard turned from amateur to professional handler and was active in the early days of the Knickerbocker Dachshund Club. He still works on its show committee. Among his most recent winners are Ch. Midachs Penthouse Joker, the first dapple miniature to make its championship in this country. Two of Joker's progeny, Penthouse Tesselation and her litter brother, Penthouse Mosaic, were Best Brace in Show at the 1974 Knickerbocker Dachshund Club's specialty.

The Gordon Carvills of East Greenbush, N.Y., had their Villanol Kennels of standard and miniature smooths. The Carvills have long been active in the Albany Kennel Clubs all breed club and Gordon served as its president at one time.

Mrs. Eric Holmberg's Holmdachs Kennels — one of the major winning kennels in all three varieties in the early 1960s — came and went with Mrs. Holmberg's decision to sell her stock. However, some of it was given to her daughter Jane Paul, who still shows her own and the Holmberg breeding.

On the West Coast, Barbara Nichol's Nikobar and Joyce King's Joydachs Kennels are among the current winners. Mrs. Anna Boardman's Harmo Kennels, with William Trainor as its handler and manager, still continues most successfully at Amherst, N.H., and David and Raymond Thomas have their Ben Y Lan Kennels in the Midwest.

A look at the smooth entry at the 1975 Westminster show reveals a cross section of the old and new. Howard Atlee's miniature dapple Penthouse Mosaic was Winners Dog. He defeated, among others, an English miniature, Wendlitt Joseph (a son of Ch. Prince Albert of Wendlitt, pictured among the English dogs in this book) owned by Dr. Peggy Clark. The reserve winner was Joydachs Showcase of Nikobar, a joint enterprise of Joyce King and Barbara Nichols. Best of Variety was Mrs. Dorothy Muse's Sandwood Musette and Best of Opposite Sex was Dunkeldorf Gunther, bred by the Dunks and owned by the Lemuel Strausses.

Mrs. Muse's win was a triumph of research and breeding that would have done credit to the Mehrers or the Horswells. Here is the story in her own words:

"Jim, my late husband, and I were always interested in dogs but since we were apartment dwellers in Washington, D.C. (while working in the U.S. Senate and Air Force) and then in New York City and Cincinnati (while he was in the uniformed Air Force) it was not until he was retired from the Air Force and discharged from the V.A. Hospitals in 1949, that we felt we were

Another of the handlers long identified with excellence in Dachshunds is Woodrow Dorward of Chatsworth, Calif. Mr. Dorward's Red Locket Kennels contributed many champions to the breed. He is pictured here with Ch. Barbadox Ironside, a current winner owned by Barbara Haisch.

Ch. Tywell's Pegeen, standard smooth, scoring Best in Show under Mrs. Jeannette W. Cross. Pegeen was top bitch winner of 1974. Owned by Robert A. Hauslohner's Trebor Kennels in Rosemont, Pa., and handled by Howard Atlee. Mr. Atlee is another in the tradition of Dachshund breeders that have become successful professional handlers.

in a position to have dogs. At that time we moved to Mountain City, Tennessee, where I now live.

"During all those years we attended dog shows wherever we were living and we both always liked Dachshunds, particularly since they were shown naturally, without any apparent trimming. We acquired our first two Dachshunds early in 1951."

The Muses had gained a practiced eye for a good Dachshund through their years of attending dog shows. At their first show they showed their Dachshunds themselves, complete novices at showing, and their dogs took Winners Dog and Reserve Winners Bitch.

"We bred nice Dachshunds but not good enough to be big winners," she states, "so I quit and waited six years until I could own a bitch of the breeding I always liked — the Gera lines. I acquired Timbar's Honeymoon Limited and completed her title in the U.S. and Canada. I bred her to Ch. Nixon's Double Concerto and from that litter four finished their titles and the other two were pointed. The four were Am. & Can. Ch. Museland's Alysia; Am & Can. Ch. Museland's Atlantean; Ch. Museland's Athena and Can. Ch. Museland's Allegra. Jim died in 1970 before Aylsia and Atlantean had started on their show careers. Atlantean was his favorite — he was the only male in the litter. Every evening when Jim would come home he would pick up the little fellow and hold him on his lap while he read.

"I bred Alysia to Ch. Nixon's Fleeting Encounter and three of their get have already finished their championships. They are Ch. Museland's Cygnet, Ch. Muselands Cymric and Ch. Muselands Cybele. A fourth, Museland's Cyril, is well on the way to his title. At the Alabama Dachshund Club Specialty in November, 1975, seven month old puppies sired by Atlantean out of my Ch. Dunkeldorf's Drachen, did extremely well. The bitch puppy, Dagmar, owned by Paige Bolus, daughter of my handler David Bolus, was best smooth puppy in Sweepstakes and her littermate, Darius, was second in Sweeps. In the regular classes, Darius was first in Puppy, Dogs, Winners Dog and Best of Winners for a major. He repeated the next day at the all-breed show. Not bad for puppies at their very first show.

"I never campaigned Atlantean after finishing his championship because frankly, I couldn't afford to keep two dogs out at the same time, but in the short time he was shown he won a Hound Group First.

"Alysia won 64 BOVs, 37 BOS, and 14 Group placements including a First. She was Best of Breed at the Metropolitan Washington Specialty, Alabama, Knickerbocker and Louisville Dachshund Club Specialties. She was Best Opposite to the Best of Breed at seven Specialties, and was selected Best Smooth Dachshund in 12 Specialties, twice at the Knickerbocker Dachshund Club, twice at Metropolitan Washington, twice at Pennsylvania Dachshund Club, twice at Alabama and once at the Greater Syracuse Dachshund Club, Metropolitan Atlanta Dachshund Club, Reserve Dachshund Club and Louisville Dachshund Club."

Dorothy Muse with Am. & Can. Ch. Museland's Atlantean.

Am. & Can. Ch. Museland's Alysia.

Ch. Lucene's Tanner, red standard Smooth, Best of Breed winner at the Dachshund Club of California 1975 Specialty, is banner-carrier for Mrs. Jeanine A. Sudinski's Lucene Kennels in California. Whelped in 1968, by Ch. Lucene's Lanson ex Ballenger's Ballerina, Tanner is the product of concentrated breeding from progeny of Int. Ch. Aristo von Marienlust and Ch. Favorite von Marienlust. With this foundation, the breeding at Lucene's (established in 1955) is now a blending of Ch. Falcon of Heying-Teckel, Ch. Hainheim's Lance and Ch. Blauruckenberg Firebrand. Tanner and his sire have each produced five champions, and two of Tanner's sons have produced three champions to date. Tanner's two sisters have each produced a champion also, and one of the get has already produced a champion in its first breeding.

Mr. and Mrs. Lemuel Strauss (Stradachs Kennels) of Somerset, New Jersey, have owned Dachshunds for the past 25 years, and have shown them — most successfully — over the last fifteen. Their famous Best in Show winner, Ch. Dixie-Dachs Pong, has passed on, but his place has been well taken. Ch. Dunkeldorf Gunther, a handsome red heavy with Marienlust in his background has won four Specialties and 20 Hound Groups, and was Number One Smooth for 1974. He is equally impressive as a sire and has a number of champion get. His most recent champion son, Farmeadow Light Up The Sky, finished undefeated in four shows, with 18 points.

Ch. Dunkeldorf Gunther, red Standard, top winning smooth of 1974 and sire of champions. Owned by Lemuel Strauss and handled by Bobby Barlow. Gunther is pictured winning Best of Breed at the Reserve Dachshund Specialty under judge F. L. McCartha, Jr., with show chairman Dave Thomas holding the trophy. —*Klein*

Ch. Lucene's Tanner, handled by his breeder-owner Mrs. Jeanine A. Sudinski, winning Best of Breed at Dachshund Club of California Specialty in 1975 under judge Larry Krebs.

Ch. Kobold v Fuchsenstein, red, bred by August Kessler, Germany, and imported in the '30s by Mr. and Mrs. Howard Eric of Stamford, Conn.

Ch. Bartonbury Vex, red, bred by Mrs. Violet Rycroft and owned by Pam Johnson Patterson. Mrs. Patterson was one of the early importers and breeders of longhaired Dachshunds.

THE LONGHAIRS

Longhaired Dachshunds did not appear in the United States until 1930. A few occurred, recessives, like those in Mr. Alt's litter, and some were brought in from Germany as pets, but the dog show fancy and the American public were not familiar with them. It was not until 1931 that the first longhaired Dachshund was registered with the American Kennel Club; her name was Beauty.

Two longhaired Dachshunds were entered that same year at the Dachshund Club of America's Specialty show. By 1936 the Specialty had an entry of 24 longhairs. Entries increased gradually but in the '40s there was a sharp drop, followed by a rapid increase through the '50s and '60s. Today, entries of 60 to 100 longhairs at the specialty shows are not uncommon.

About 1931 or '32, Howard Eric of New York asked Mrs. Anna Gargett, a breeder of smooths and a well-known judge of Dachshunds, to get him a good longhaired Dachshund the next time she went to Germany. She did. She bought for him a young dog, Kobold v Fuchsenstein, who became the first longhaired champion.

About that time Best of Variety title was approved for longhairs, who were required to compete in a division of the Open class; by 1939, longhaired Dachshunds were competing for Best of Breed as is done in Specialty shows today. It was not until 1943 that longhaired and wirehaired Dachshunds were shown in the Hound Group along with the smooth winner.

The year 1939 was a significant one for longhairs. It marked the establishment of three bloodlines which appear in practically all winning longhaired Dachshund pedigrees today.

In that year, the Thasillo Krug von Niddas, who had left Germany to make their home in Boston, went to England on a visit. Mrs. Von Nidda was a Scotswoman and liked to visit relatives and friends in Britain. She was charmed with longhaired Dachshunds and bought Primrose Patch Rose Brocade from Mrs. Smith-Rewse. Breeders now had two good bloodlines from which to start a program. The third dog which came at about that time was William de Sangpur. He was bred in Germany and whelped in the United States. Mrs. William B. Hill, Jr. (Grace) bought him as a puppy from Bertrand d'Alexandre. It was the start of her De Sangpur (French for pure blood) Kennels which, although much curtailed at this writing, is the oldest longhaired kennels in the United States.

Ch. Kobold was bred to two different bitches, one from Mr. Eric's Riverbank Kennels and one from Maude Daniels Smith's Dachshafen Kennels near Philadelphia. Both bitches were German. The Erics got Tommy Tucker of Riverbank from their mating and Mrs. Smith got Koboldina v Dachshafen. Tommy Tucker was sold to Mrs. Max Zabel who was beginning her Gypsy

Ch. William de Sangpur, Best Longhair at Westminster 1948; at Morris & Essex 1946, 1947 and 1948; and at the Dachshund Club of America Specialty 1946 and 1948. Owner, Mrs. Wm. B. Hill, Jr.

Ch. Crespi's Happy New Year, 1950s longhaired winner, owned by Mrs. Donia Cline.

Barn Kennels near Chicago. Koboldina remained in the East and was bred to Rose Brocade. Two direct descendants of that breeding were Ch. Roderick v d Nidda and Ch. Pegremos Paragon.

Tommy Tucker won his championship easily and gave Mrs. Zabel the start she wanted in the longhaired field. Her three best known champions were: Zarky of Gypsy Barn, born in 1943; Antonio of Gypsy Barn, born in 1944; and Tytucker of Gypsy Barn, born in 1946. Antonio was sold to Mrs. Charlotte Sibley of San Francisco of the Forever Kennels. He was the first longhaired Dachshund to win Best in Show. One of his daughters, bred to Mrs. Virgilio Cheda's Golden Ransom v Teckelhof, produced Ch. Forever Golden Antonio, who was sold to Miss Margaret Taylorson, also of the San Francisco area. Golden Antonio won seven Best in Show and 21 Group First awards and came East to take Best of Variety at Westminster two years in a row, 1953 and 1954.

Longhairs, at least in California, were holding their own against smooth competition. For three years, at the Golden Gate Specialty, the show's Best of Breed went to longhairs — Ch. Golden Lightning of Marin in 1957, Forever Golden Antonio in 1958, and Ch. Graf Spee von Richtofen in 1959.

Until the time of her death in the early '60s, Mrs. Cheda's Marin Kennels was among the tops in longhairs. Her Golden Lightning of Marin, sired by Forever Golden Antonio out of Ch. Golden Christine of Marin, came East to take Best of Variety at Westminster in 1957.

Mrs. Hill's William de Sangpur was equally productive. He provided the founding sire of Mrs. Charles (Donia) Cline's longhaired Dachshund additions to Crespi. Beginning in 1949 with the purchase of Ch. Saqui de Sangpur, a William son and Ch. Carla v d Nidda, Mrs. Cline bred Ch. Crespi's Zilly, a lovely bitch. Bred to Ch. Antonio of Gypsy Barn, she then had Ch. Crespi's Happy New Year. Happy won Best of Variety at the DCA Specialty in 1958.

His granddaughter, Jessell's Sea Witch, was also a granddaughter of Roderick v d Nidda by his son, Bayard le Marin. She was bred back to Roderick in December of 1962 and sent to England to Barton Emanuel and Mrs. Muriel Rhodes. It was the first litter of really top flight American longhaired Dachshunds to be whelped in England. Through both their sire and dam they carried the bloodlines of the three dogs that started longhairs on their way — Kobold, Rose Brocade and William de Sangpur.

Mrs. Von Nidda imported three more dogs from Primrosepatch, Ch. Gay Lancer and two bitches. Her Ch. Vicki v d Nidda, a daughter of Rose Brocade and Ch. Koboldina v Dachsafen, was the mother of Ch. Hussar v d Nidda, Best of Variety at the Dachshund Club of America's Specialties in 1949 and 1952. Another descendant of Ch. Antonio of Gypsy Barn was Ch. Bergmanor Rumplestilskin, owned by Mr. and Mrs. Edward F. Hirschman of Los Angeles. He did well on the West Coast during the '60s.

Two years before her death, Mrs. Von Nidda's final litter was born. From it came Roderick v d Nidda. His dam was Ch. Liebling, a Vicki daughter and the sire was Ch. Hihope Ladies Man, owned by Mrs. Zelie Ely of New Jersey.

Roderick almost missed the show career that was to make him famous. Mrs. Von Nidda sold him and his litter sister to a friend as pets. The friend had some illness in the family and asked Mrs. Von Nidda if she would keep the pair at her kennels for the weekend. Mrs. Jeannette Cross was staying with Mrs. Von Nidda and when they took one look at Roderick, now a year old, their eyes popped. Fortunately his owners were willing to sell him back. They had discovered that he had bred his sister and puppies were on the way.

Roderick had an outstanding show career. Born in 1955, he died in December of 1965. During his lifetime he won 11 Bests in Show, 77 Hound Group firsts, 10 Best of Breed awards, and a record-setting 296 Bests of Variety. Mrs. Von Nidda lived long enough to see his greatest victory: he won Best of Breed at the Dachshund Association of Long Island Specialty in June of 1958 over an entry of 314 Dachshunds. That night he was flown with his handler Jerry Rigden, to Los Angeles and the next day won Best American-bred in Show at the Harbor Cities show. There were 2,400 dogs entered at Harbor Cities. When Mrs. Von Nidda died, she left Roderick to her friend, Mrs. Osborne Howes, who continued to show him. His show career ended soon after he won Best of Variety at Westminster in 1963.

Ch. William de Sangpur was a top winner in longhairs during the 1940s and as the owner of one of his sons, Ch. De Sangpur Traveling Man, C.D., I am embarrassed to say that I cannot recall his record. His major victories were Best of Variety at the Dachshund Club of America Specialty twice, in 1946 and 1948, and winner of the same honor three times at Morris and Essex. He took another Best of Variety at Westminster in 1948. I believe he held the record at one time for siring longhaired Dachshund champions (38). He was then eleven years old and still going strong, so there may have been more. My own Ch. De Sangpur Traveling Man had an excellent record in breed and did well at field trials although he was never in the top class of Mrs. Goodspeed's dogs. In Obedience he just squeaked by. He obeyed sullenly with an "Oh, lets get it over with" attitude, although he was very obedient in the house. His son, Ch. Frederick v.d. Isar — out of Camelia v d Isar, owned by Mrs. Frances Anthofer — had the same disposition. He too, had a good record and won several Best of Variety and Hound Group placings.

Another William son I owned was Ch. De Sangpur Traveler's Trix, out of one of Mrs. Hill's bitches. Trix had the best record of my three, including a Best of Breed at the St. Louis Dachshund Specialty and several Hound Groups, one of them at the Westbury Kennel Club all-breed show under the English judge Leo Wilson.

Present day kennels carrying some of the de Sangpur bloodlines are the

Ch. Hussar v.d. Nidda, DCA Specialty winner in 1949 and 1952. Owned by Mrs. Thassilo Krug von Nidda. —*Tauskey*

Ch. Hihope Ladies Man, 1950s Specialty winner, sire of Ch. Roderick v.d. Nidda. Bred, owned and handled by Mrs. Hiram B. Ely.

Ch. Forever Golden Antonio, a 1952 champion longhair, winner of 7 Bests in Show and one of the great sires. Owned by Margaret F. Taylorson of California.

Ch. Roderick v.d. Nidda. —*Tauskey*

Ch. Jo-Del's Nicholas. —*Shafer*

Stonybrook Kennels of Mrs. Robin Gianapolous and the v Hohenhorst Kennels of Dr. and Mrs. Helmut Adler. Through Frederick v.d. Isar, C.D., the Thorn Pines Kennels have passed on the William De Sangpur strain. Mrs. Thorn was quite taken with "Freddie" and bred several bitches to him. Mrs. Anthofer also used both Frederick, which I bought from her, and Ch. De Sangpur Traveler's Trix. Her German-based v.d. Isar Kennels (no longer active) carried the De Sangpur line. Mr. and Mrs. William Blair and their Moorehope Kennels have the v.d. Isar bloodlines and those of Mrs. Thorn through their Ch. Raubatz v.d. Isar and Ch. Tithonius of Thorn Pines. Mrs. Charles Merz has a Trix son that goes back to v.d. Isar breeding, Ch. Merzdale Long John.

Grace Hill's interest in Dachshunds, from her acquisition of William De Sangpur, is, in a large measure, responsible for the continued popularity of the breed and the strength which the Dachshund Club of America exerts over its regional clubs. She has been its secretary for more than twenty years and through her efforts, along with those of Horswell and other presidents, major splits have been prevented and arguments settled — if not to everyone's complete satisfaction, at least to a point of peaceful co-existence. Her parallel job as an officer of the National Miniature Dachshund Club has had a like influence and has helped to smooth the differences between it and the American Miniature Dachshund Association.

It was her efforts as president of the Dachshund Association of Long Island and her running of its annual Specialty Show that earned her the reputation of "the Pearl Mesta of the Dachshund world." No effort was spared in the year-long work on the show to make it the biggest, the best, and so pleasant that even the losers looked forward to returning the following year.

When the available show grounds were not to her liking, Gracie ripped up her rose garden and turned it into a lawn big enough for two rings. The roses were replanted around the border, attractive striped tents — the kind used on the large estates for outdoor parties (Gracie felt those drab brown ones from the Foley Dog Show Organization were inappropriate) — were set up, and the menu (prepared by the club's best cooks, including Gracie with gourmet John Cook supervising) was alone worth the trip through Long Island traffic to the show site. In such a setting even the most mediocre Dachshund looked beautiful and the losers *did* come back year after year. Half the fun of showing Dachshunds went out of the game when Gracie closed down her Hicksville home and moved to Jacksonville, Florida.

The Knocknagree Kennels of Miss Laura Delano at Rhinebeck, N.Y., were known for their Irish Setters long before Miss Delano decided to breed long-haired Dachshunds. Advancing age, her own and that of her kennel manager and handler, Fred Kunze, was the reason for the switch. The big red dogs were just too much for either of them in the ring. She admired the Dachshund

A 1958 picture of three of the great ladies of the breed—Dorothy Hardy handling Ch. Roderick v.d. Nidda, Nancy Onthank judging, and Roderick's breeder-owner, Mrs. Thassilo von Nidda. —*Shafer*

Miss Laura Delano, dressed for her judging assignment complete with jewelry, is pictured awarding Best Brace in Show at Adirondack KC to Vera Jackson's miniature duo, Geam's Wee Teddy and Geam's Wee Lady, handled by Frank Hardy. —*Shafer*

spirit and the longhaired variety looked a good deal like a smaller version of her Setters, so she chose them.

Miss Delano and I were members of a now-defunct club called the Amateur Dog Judges of America. It was the brainchild of the late Madeline Baiter, Miss Adele Colgate and Mrs. L. W. Bonney. I don't think men were barred from membership, but I don't remember one who ever dared attend this meeting of strong-willed dowagers. Meetings were held at the Women's Republican Club in Manhattan. Miss Delano took her judging assignments seriously and as a compliment to the show committee she was always beautifully dressed. As accessories, she wore fabulous bracelets, at least three or four to each arm, and equally dazzling rings. With such a collection she should have chosen Doberman Pinchers for protection.

Some Dachshund exhibitors objected to this display. It was not that they didn't admire the jewelry, but masses of clanking bracelets descending over their heads as Miss Delano examined them caused some Dachshunds to duck and jerk away as she approached them. Quite a few owners asked me if it was possible to have the Amateur Judges Club call this to Miss Delano's attention in some tactful way so that she would leave off her shining accessories during Dachshund judging. I passed the word on.

At the next meeting Mrs. Bonney was chairman. Tact was not one of Mrs. Bonney's virtues. She spoke her mind plainly. So when the matter of judges dress was brought up she voiced the complaint about judges wearing too much jewelry. As a concession to Miss Delano, she did not mention any names. It didn't work. Miss Delano sprang to her feet and declared, "I feel that criticism is aimed at me. As a breeder of hunting dogs, I believe that any Dachshund who is afraid of a lady's bracelet has no place in the show ring." The discussion ended then and there.

Miss Delano's founding stock came from Gypsy Barn. She bought Tytucker and My Fair Lady of Gypsy Barn from Mrs. Zabel in 1940. She bred first class longhairs and the sight of Fred Kunze waiting outside the Dachshund ring with four or five of Miss Delano's dogs on leash was enough to send all of us scurrying for our brushes to put the final touch on our own entries in the face of such competition. I remember particularly her Ch. Flori of Knocknagree who won Best of Variety at the Dachshund Club of America Specialty in 1959, and again in 1961. On Miss Delano's death, the Knocknagree stock went to Mrs. Charles Stalter's Barberry Knowe Kennels where both Scottish Terriers and Dachshunds help to fill the enormous trophy room with their wins. Mrs. Stalter managed to even improve the Knocknagree strain. Heads are more elegant and their size, which tended to be large, has been somewhat reduced.

Mrs. Hiram B. Ely (Zelie) started her Hihope Kennels in the late 1940s with two puppies, Saqui and Roddy de Sangpur. Saqui was sold to Mrs. Cline in 1949 soon after he won Best of Variety at Westminster. Roddy, a grandson of Rose Brocade, brought fame to the kennels and sired Mrs. Ely's best dog, Ch. Hihope Ladies Man, who took the Best of Variety at Westminster twice, 1955 and 1958. Among his progeny was Ch. Roderick v d Nidda. Mrs. Ely's sudden death right after a morning session of the Westminster show, shocked us all.

Mrs. Harry Howell, (Mary) of Virginia began breeding longhairs in 1951. She took the kennel name of Bayard and her kennels are still among today's winners. Her founding sire was a dog from German stock, Ch. Karl Hans v Ritter Bayard. She bred to both the Von Nidda and De Sangpur lines and her Ch. Split Rock's Electra, which she bought from Howard Rumpf on Long Island, was the dam of my own Ch. De Sangpur Traveling Man, C.D. and ten other champions. Mrs. Howell has always been active, in the Metropolitan Washington Dachshund Club and worked hard to make their specialty shows successful. Her talent as a hostess made the shows a delight and the parties that followed were remembered long after the winners' names were forgotten.

Peter Monks began his breeding in 1950. He lived in Massachusetts at that time and bought Mrs. Von Nidda's English bitch, Primrose Patch Black Satin, whom he bred to Ch. Hussar von der Nidda. He soon found out that his place was not large enough for his new-found hobby and moved to Virginia. His Pegremos Kennels produced Ch. Pegremos Paragon and many other champions. While he now devotes most of his time to judging, Mr. Monks still breeds some longhairs.

The outstanding longhair in the 1960s was Ch. Jo-Del's Nicholas. Dr. William Koss of Indianapolis was the registered owner but his sister, Dr. Betty Koss and her associate, Miss Dolores Farley, sponsored his show career. His sire, described in more detail in the Obedience chapter of this book, was Ch. Gustav v Steinwald, whom Dr. Betty bought in Germany. Nicholas' wins included 25 Best in Show awards, 261 Bests of Variety, and 109 Firsts in the Hound Group. He was retired in September of 1967. His last two shows were a crowning touch for his career. He took Best of Breed at the St. Louis Dachshund Specialty and finished with a Best in Show at the Lima all-breed show. Dr. Betty Koss said "Miss Farley and I feel that to retire him at the height of his career is the least we can do for this great Dachshund and great friend."

Another longhair, Ch. Covara's Tabasco, owned by Mrs. Vera Gunn was whelped in January of 1959. He died in 1972, and at this writing stands as the No. 2 longhaired sire (all-time) with 34 champions to his credit. There may be more. One of his grandsons, Ch. No Ka Oi's Omar Wagatomo, bred by Dr. Miles McElrath, won his championship in 1973. Omar is owned by Mr. and Mrs. Bruce Boone of Boone's Farm Kennels.

Tabasco was sired by Ch. Red Locket Stevedore and was handled by Woodie Dorward, who like the Hardys, bred good dogs of his own at his Red Locket Kennels. Tabasco was a very dark red. Some of the most successful

Mrs. Harry Howell handling her standard longhair, Ch. Bayard Le Souvenir to Best of Breed at the 1966 Dachshund Association of Long Island Specialty. The judge was Frank Hardy, and Mrs. Wm. Burr Hill, club president, presented the trophy. —*Klein*

Ch. Bayard le Fenelon (Ch. Robdachs Familiar Stranger ex Berthe de Bayard), bred by Mrs. Harry Howell and owned by Beverly and John Kelly of Hillsborough, California, is pictured being handled by Mrs. Kelly to win under judge Robin Hernandez. This young dog was Best of Variety at the Dachshund Club of America Specialty, and has a Hound Group and several California Specialty Best of Breed awards to his credit. —*Langdon*

109

breedings to him were bitches from the De Sangpur line. I remember William De Sangpur (No. 1 longhaired sire of all-time) was also a dark red.

The Gordon Carvills added longhaired stock to their Villanol Kennels with great success and the Edward Hirschmans' Bergmanor Jack Horner is in many longhaired pedigrees.

Mr. and Mrs. Peter Van Brunt bought the British Primrosepatch Kennels and brought the kennel name and its remaining stock to their home in Lake Placid, N.Y. They continued to breed but it was almost entirely miniature longhairs. During the early '70s the Van Brunts returned to England and their kennel name there is "Riverlawn."

Among the Californians still active in breeding are Maria Hayes, whose Maxsohn Kennels date back to 1946, and Mr. and Mrs. Sanford Roberts, who got their start in the 1960s. The Roberts' Ch. Robdachs Espirit sired four champions in one litter. Among Esprit's grandchildren are Ch. L and C's Gay Personality, UD., described in the Obedience chapter; Ch. Enido's Taggert (whose pedigree also includes Ch. Guyman's Long Deal), owned by Enid Officer and Carol J. Douglas and Ch. B's Javelin de Bayard, the third top ranking Dachshund for 1972.

Two Canadian breeders have recently imported longhairs. Mrs. Linda Konkol of Scarborough, Ontario, bought American and Canadian Ch. Pegremos Pinnacle, a combination of Pegremos and Bayard lines, and Canadian Ch. Bayard l'Ottoman from Mrs. Howell's kennels in Virginia. Her Von Ayres Kennels should benefit from this. The other is Barbara J. Maxedon of Quebec who bought Ch. Bizet von Kotthaus from Karl and Iona Kotthaus of Phoenix, Arizona. Bizet has both Ch. Maxsohn Victor and Ch. Covara's Tabasco in his background.

Ch. Hubertus Shooting Star, owned by Dr. and Mrs. Lyle Cain, is another arrival among the champions of the '70s. His sire is Ch. Lucifer of Knocknagree and he carries both Bayard and Pegremos blood.

American, Canadian and Mexican Ch. Karlew's Triton, bred and owned by Carl and Marjorie Lewis's Karlew's Kennels in California, is a Best in Show and multi-specialty winner with dozens of Group placements. He carries in his pedigree the prefixes of Dachs Ridge, Robdachs, Holmdachs, Bergmanor and Covara's Tabasco.

The glossiest record by a longhair in the 1970s has been achieved by Am. & Can. Ch. Von Dyck's Mr. Bojangles, co-owned by his breeder Dr. Helen G. Tiahrt and Mrs. George S. Hendrickson, and handled by Mrs. Hannelore A. Heller. Bojangles, whelped in 1972, followed upon his win of Best of Variety at the Dachshund Club of America and Houston Dachshund Club Specialties in 1973 with win of the Ken-L Ration Hound Group Award for 1974 (an award given each year to the Hound winning the most Groups during the year.) He scored 27 Group Firsts, in complement to his 7 all-breed Bests in

Ch. Robdachs Familiar Stranger winning Best of Breed at the Knickerbocker Dachshund Club's first Specialty show in February 1971. Judge, Mrs. Robert V. Lindsay; handler, James Swyler; presenting trophies: Bill Blair and Howard Atlee. Stranger, winner of Best of Variety at both the DCA Specialty and Westminster in 1970, has a Hound Group and win of Best of Breed at 10 Specialties from coast to coast to his credit. He was the top producing longhaired male in 1972 and 1974. Bred and owned by Sanford and Patricia Roberts of El Cajon, California. —*Gilbert*

Ch. Robdachs Party Princess, longhair bitch, winning Best of Breed at Golden Gate Dachshund Club's 38th Specialty under breeder-judge Ernestine Carlson. Owned by Burt and Evelyn Newmark of Burlingame, Calif., and handled by Mrs. Newmark. —*Francis*

111

Show, in that year, and then closed out his show career in spectacular style with win of the variety and Second in the Group at the 1975 Westminster Kennel Club show. Bojangles is sired by Ch. Han-Jo's Flaming Flare, and on his sire's side is pure Bayard breeding. His dam is Ch. Dachs Ridge Midnight Blues, and her background is mainly Dachs Ridge with an outcross to Robdachs.

Am. & Can. Ch. Von Dyck's Mr. Bojangles, standard longhair, winning Best in Show at Northeastern Indiana KC 1974 show under judge Peter B. Thomson. Bojangles' win of 27 Groups (along with 7 BIS) in 1974 not only made him the top winning Dachshund of the year, but also earned him the Ken-L Ration Award over all hound dogs in America. Co-owned by Dr. Helen G. Tiahrt (breeder) and Mrs. George S. Hendrickson, and handled by Hannelore A. Heller. —*Booth*

THE WIREHAIRS

Past history of wirehaired Dachshunds in America shows that the generally accepted practice, here as in England and on the continent of Europe, has been to occasionally breed to a smooth Dachshund to improve conformation. When this has been done by knowledgeable breeders, it has worked out with a fair amount of success; but novices in the wirehaired variety, and those who wanted to breed wirehairs in a hurry to meet public demand for the increasingly popular dogs, have abused the practice.

In 1955, Herman Cox, writing in *Popular Dogs*, sounded this warning: "The crossing of smooths with wirehaired Dachshunds has been practiced for years by breeders of experience but, to my knowledge, the privilege has not, until recently, been abused. In the past several years the popularity of the wirehair has been steadily increasing. Breeders, in their efforts to secure wirehairs have perniciously interbred smooths and wires without knowledge of the damage they have been doing."

"Those of us familiar with the wirehaired variety know that it is not a purebred, that it was developed by crossing the smooth and the Dandie Dinmont or sometimes the Griffon or the German Pinscher. Over the years it has been necessary to cross wires with smooths to instill body conformation and short length of leg. These crosses have proved two points: first that the wire coat is dominant over the smooth and secondly, that the body conformation of the smooth is dominant over the wire."

Mr. Cox goes on to give this advice: "Do not consider cross breeding unless it is for the purpose of improving the conformation of the wirehaired offspring; never breed a smooth with a silky-textured coat to a wirehair and never breed a smooth to a wirehair whose pedigree shows a smooth-coated animal within four generations."

The reader will note Mr. Cox's statement that the wirehaired variety is not a purebred but a crossing of Terriers with smooth Dachshunds. In earlier chapters of this book I have presented the beliefs of some eighteenth and nineteenth century writers, that the smooths, the longhairs and the wirehairs all began about the same time. However, the wirehairs were kept by hunters and as a result of hard usage and indiscriminate breedings to produce a keen hunting dog, no matter what its looks or its breeding, the original wirehaired almost disappeared. They were later reconstructed from the original pure specimens through the Terrier crossings. Captain G.A. Graham did much the same thing in England with Irish Wolfhounds. Taking the few remaining specimens he crossed them with a variety of the larger breeds until he achieved the reproduction of the original that bred true to type. Early German breeders of wirehairs tried to do much the same thing, according to these past century writers, and it is their belief that wires did not *originate* from these crossings but were *reestablished* through the process.

Whichever belief is correct, it is safe to assume, as did Mr. Cox, that the American wirehaired Dachshund came from these reconstructed crosses, and as a result they have had the same problems with soft coats and other Terrier inheritances as breeders in other countries, which have made it necessary to continue to cross wires with smooths.

Done with caution and skill it has obviously produced good results. Of the five top producing sires of Dachshunds for the past thirty-five years (as of 1973), three were smooths — Ch. Favorite of Marienlust, Ch. Falcon of Heying-Teckel, and Ch. Dunkeldorf's Falcon's Favorite, and two were wires, Ch. Pondwicks Hobgoblin and Ch. Draht Timothy.

Only one wirehaired breeder appears to have disagreed with this crossing of varieties — Mrs. Thirza Hibner. Her belief has been that good wires came from good wire backgrounds and that it is possible to put good hard German wirehaired coats on wires with American conformation. Captain Zuchschwert, prior to 1914, had almost succeeded in achieving good wires without cross breeding, but the war interfered and both the Ditmarsia stock on which he depended and his own dogs were dispersed. American breeders had a better choice, although admittedly not pure wire background, in the Sports kennel in Sweden and the German kennels of Paulinenberg, Grossenhagen, Konigshuffen and Holzgarten.

Wirehaired breeders had probably their best friend and severest critic in Dr. Herbert Sanborn, who expressed himself on them during the 1940s and early 1950s. Without question Dr. Sanborn knew more about Dachshunds than anyone in the United States and more than many foreign breeders. His blunt, often harsh opinions were all the harder to accept because he was so frequently right. Here is his criticism of wirehaired Dachshunds in 1949: "Unfortunately the breeding of the wirehaired dog in this country has suffered even more from ignorance of history and ideals of breeding than is the case with the other varieties, and especially from the lack of correct information. . . . Some of the very best dogs of this variety from Germany and Sweden have disappeared here, lost to the breed. Only recently in Chicago there was the descent in the second generation from the famous Wicht St Georg — not merely the greatest wire of all time, but perhaps one of the greatest Dachshunds of all varieties; yet this inheritance was allowed to disappear through ignorance of its value and the means of its conservation. There have been untold similar instances where mere collectors have been a menace to the development of this variety and others."

How much influence Dr. Sanborn's criticism had on the wirehaired breeders is hard to say but from the 1950s on, wirehairs, both American-bred and imported did not disappear but were shown to their championships and better, and bred more to bring an outcross into an already established strain than to improve it.

Wicht von St. George, bred and owned by Edmund Wagner.

Ch. Thomanel's Lola, standard wirehair, winner of the Hound Group at Westminster 1952. Owner, Stan Todd.

Eng. & Am. Ch. Wylde Surmise, standard wirehair, Best of Variety at Westminster 1953. Surmise had 5 CCs in England before his exportation to America. Owner, Stanley F. Todd.

Ch. Brentwald Joshua, whose record as the top winning wirehaired Dachshund still stands today, contained many generations of pure wire on his sires side and a strong infusion of wire blood on his dam's side with a smooth outcross. He was whelped in October of 1946 at the Brentwald Kennels of Mr. and Mrs. Harold Patrick. Both his sire and dam came from the Frank Hardys. His sire, Ch. Lumpacious Hubertus, was sired by Ch. Vagabond v Paulinenberg, a German dog by World Champion Wicht v Paulinenberg ex Liesel v Paulinenberg. Hubertus' dam was Mermaid v Dachshafen, owned by Maude Daniels Smith and sired in turn by the Swedish wirehair, Ch. Sports Buster, brought to the United States by Mrs. Richard Pell for her Hildesheim Kennels. Mermaid's dam was Nixe v Grossenhagen, another German wirehair, pure wire breeding for at least three generations.

Joshua's dam, and the only dog to defeat him in his show career, was Ch. Jerry Hubertus, sired by the smooth champion Leutnant v Marienlust. Jerry's dam was Ruthie Hubertus, sired by Lumpacious Hubertus ex Valentine Hubertus, both wirehairs.

During his show career Joshua was handled by William Ake, a professional who bought him from the Patricks in 1947. The Akes called him "Buzz." Beginning in 1948 he was taken on a whirlwind campaign of 15 shows in 11 states during a five-month period. By the time he was 14 months old, he was a champion. Before the year's end he had taken Best in Show at Louisville, Ky. The following year he was sold to Herman Cox, breeder-exhibitor-judge and owner of Dychland Kennels. Cox continued to show him and he won Best in Show at Daytona Beach, Best of Variety at Westminster in 1949 and 1950 and the same honors at the Dachshund Club of America's specialty in 1948 and 1949. Shown at Morris and Essex in 1949, he took Best of Variety there too. When Joshua's show career ended he was purchased by Mr. and Mrs. Neville Stephens for their Tubac Kennels in Arizona, where he became the kennel's top stud dog.

It was no coincidence that there were enough good wire bitches to breed to Joshua. Eastern breeders in the '40s and early '50s had imported a number of good English and some German dogs. Louise Magary, now a Dachshund judge, talked to me about her experiences at that time.

She was an apprentice handler in 1943 to Mrs. C.V. Blagden at her Ruffy Kennels, under whose charge the wirehaired Dachshunds of Miss Emilie S. Bromley's Edgemere Kennels were conditioned and handled. The Edgemere wires were almost unbeatable. Ch. Impudence of Edgemere won Best of Variety at Westminster in 1944, Ch. Gremlin of Edgemere won it in 1945, Ch. Impudence won it again in 1946 and 1947 and in 1948, Charlotte Sibley's Ch. Prejudice of Edgemere was the Westminster BOV. Joshua ended this winning streak by taking Best of Variety at Westminster in 1949, 1950 and 1951.

During this time, Miss Magary, who was working with Mrs. Blagden, bought an Impudence puppy for a friend, Mrs. Ethel A. Thomas, who lived near her in Greenwich Village. Mrs. Thomas registered her kennel name as

Frank Hardy, whose Hubertus Kennels produced both the sire and dam of Ch. Brentwald's Joshua, pictured with Joshua.

Ch. Brentwald's Joshua, the top winning wirehair of all time, with William Ake, who handled him throughout his show career. Joshua, whelped in 1946, was purchased from his breeders Mr. and Mrs. Howard Patrick by Mr. Ake in 1947, and sold to Herman G. Cox (Dychland Kennels) in 1949.

117

"Thomanel". Louise handled the dogs at shows and planned the matings. The pups and grown stock were farmed out with the theatre people in the neighborhood, who enjoyed having them as house pets and sometimes even used them in their vaudeville acts. "They were born showmen" Louise told me, "the people and the dogs." Thomanel's Lola was one of these. Early in life she developed the winning personality that brought her fame as the first wirehaired Dachshund to win the Hound group at Westminster, in 1952. Here is Louise's description of the scene: "Unawed by the huge gallery at Madison Square Garden, she stood at the end of her lead and invited their applause. Stanley Todd, who had bought her reluctantly, suddenly found himself in the final circle of six contenders for the Best in Show. It was his finest hour."

While Stanley Todd never did much breeding, he liked to show his dogs and he bought English wirehairs. His Ch. Wylde Surmise took Best of Variety at Westminster in 1953 and was shown successfully at Eastern shows but never came as close to Best in Show as Lola. He bought Prejudice of Edgemere from Mrs. Sibley and imported Grunwald Melody, sired by Eagle of Dunkurque, bred by Mrs. Littmoden.

Miss Bromley had been the breeder of Prejudice and she was equally successful with her homebreds and her imports. Ch. Duplicate of Edgemere and Ch. Second Edition of Edgemere were among her own dogs, and she imported Ch. Ajax of Ouborough of Edgemere (English) and Greygates Prelude of Edgemere (Irish). Maude Daniels Smith's wirehaired bitch, Dearest v Dachshafen, was sired by Prejudice in 1951.

Mrs. David B. Doggett of Dachscroft Kennels in Wisconsin imported six English wirehairs, four bitches and two dogs from the Hollyhill Kennels. They were noted for their pack of hunting Dachshunds, as well as their show stock. They included Hollyhill Sivershell, already in whelp to a well-known English champion Hollyhill Petrouka. She produced a litter of five puppies a month later. Others were Hollyhill Piper-Piper and Hollyhill Gisella. Dachscroft Hapence, one of the results of these English bloodlines bred at Dachscroft, was sold to the Neville Stephens.

The J.A.R. Irvings imported from Major T. Ellis Hughes' Wytchend Kennels, Ch. Georg of Wytchend and a young bitch. Thomas Ladd of New York bought Gretchen of Wytchend, sired by Eng. Ch. Mercury of Seaton.

The Neville Stephens' Tubac Kennels in Arizona, where Brentwald's Joshua spent his final years, began as a hobby and grew into a business. They had Dachshunds of all three varieties and miniatures too. Their interest in wirehairs began when Mrs. Raymond Hill bought Ch. Brentwald Toni. Raymihill was noted for its smooth Dachshunds but in 1951 Mrs. Hill decided to add wires. Neville Stephens bought a half interest in Toni. In June of that same year Mrs. Hill bought The Witch's Brat from his handler and breeder, Jerry Rigden. Neville Stephens bought the litter sister at the same time. She was named Black Magic Zipper. Both were sired by Joshua out of Zipper of Badger Hill.

Ch. The Witch's Brat, a Joshua son, bred by Jerry Rigden and owned by Mrs. Raymond Hill and Anne E. Applegate.

Ch. Hush Hush v.d. Stephens, standard wirehair, by Ch. The Witch's Brat ex Brentwald Toni. Owned by Stanley Orne.

Ch. Pinocchio of Raymihill, littermate of Hush Hush, owned by Anne E. Applegate.

The Witch's Brat won the puppy class in 1951 at Westminster. It launched him on a winning streak that brought him his championship at Morris and Essex in 1952. He was a Hound Group winner and was an outstanding showman. One of his accomplishments was to sire a litter which produced three champions. They were Pinocchio of Raymihill, owned by Anne E. Applegate; Ch. Hush Yo' Mouf Liza, owned by the Neville Stephens; and Ch. Hush Hush v.d. Stephens owned by Mr. and Mrs. Stanley Orne.

Joshua was used so much as a stud that practically all American wirehairs at that time had him in their pedigree. There was a need for a good true wirehaired stud to provide for an outcross to this line. It was provided by the Fay-Dachs kennel of Mr. and Mrs. Gene Nesbitt in California. They imported Strolch vom Holzgarten from Germany. He was the product of true wire breeding. The Nesbitts bred him to a smooth bitch. Ch. Minton of Heying-Teckel, and the result was Ch. Fay-Dachs Mindora, who was sold to Mrs. Hill and completed her championship in 1954.

About this time, Martin Shallenberger of Kentucky imported a German dog, Klausner von Mentor Line. Its name would indicate Ditmarsia in its background, the strain that Captain Zuchschwert used so successfully in eliminating smooth coated dogs from his breeding program. However, there seems to be no record as to what it sired or whether or not it was shown.

The Heyings, already famous for their Favorite v Marienlust, got their start in wires by breeding Favorite to a wire bitch, Cerka v Drasky, an import owned by Katherine Knapp. The offspring was Ch. Barb Wire of Heying-Teckel, whelped in 1950. She was their foundation dam. They bred her to a Joshua son, Ch. Brentwald's Copyright, and got another champion, Live Wire of Heying-Teckel. They were off to a good start in producing wirehaired champions.

The Stanley Ornes have played a dual role in the world of American Dachshunds. First, as breeders they imported two Irish dogs, Greygate Prima Donna and Greygate Intermezzo. They also purchased Hush Hush v d Stephens. They bred Prima Donna to Joshua and the result was their first homebred champion, Fir Trees Coco, CD. There were other champions but it was their work as editors of The American Dachshund that won them not only the admiration of Dachshund owners but an award from the Dog Writers Association of America for "The Best Breed Magazine." Sanford Roberts, the magazine's present editor, whose Robdachs Kennels is contributing much toward longhair improvement, carries on in the same tradition.

One of the reasons for the improvement in wirehairs in a relatively short space of time has been the addition of the variety to the kennels of so many good smooth breeders. They already knew the skills involved in breeding Dachshund champions; the challenge of the wire coat and the engaging dispositions of these whiskery little dogs made it interesting to add them to their breeding programs.

Ch. Fay-Dachs Mindora, standard smooth, by Strolch vom Holzgarten ex Ch. Minton of Heying-Teckel. Owned by Raymond S. Hill.

Dachscroft's Tweed Jacket, by Hollyhill Petrouka (Eng.) ex Ch. Hollyhill Silvershell. Owned by Margaret C. Smith.

Ch. Happy Go Lucky of Willow Creek, standard wirehair, winner of 75 Bests of Variety in the year 1961 alone. Owned by Elizabeth Holmberg's Holmdachs Kennels.

Ch. Live Wire of Heying-Teckel, owned by Mr. and Mrs. Fred W. Heying. —*Ludwig*

Ch. Fir Trees Coco, CD, mid-50s standard wirehair conformation and Obedience winner. Owned by the Stanley Ornes. —*Shafer*

Unretouched photo of Ch. Westphal's Wandering Wind, Group-winning wirehaired Dachshund of the mid-60's. A son of Ch. Pondwick's Hobgoblin, bred by Peggy Westphal and owned by Dorothy S. Pickett.—*Shafer*

Dr. and Mrs. George Pickett were among these. Their wire Ch. Herthwood's Holiday was Best of Variety at Westminster in 1955. Ch. Fir Trees Coco. CD. won it in 1956.

The Charles O'Hara's imported Moat Arab, another English wirehair.

Presently two dogs, one American-bred and the other an English import, are exerting the greatest influence on the wirehaired variety. These are Peggy Westphal's Ch. Vantebe's Draht Timothy and Dee Hutchinson's Ch. Pondwick's Hobgoblin.

Timothy's breeder, Mrs. Betty W. Schlender is to be congratulated on her skill in combining the pedigrees of dogs from four countries to produce this famous champion and outstanding sire. Timothy was sired by Ch. Abner W, a son of Joshua. His dam was Westphal's Nettle, a Wylde Cantata daughter. His American background contains Brentwald, Heying-Teckel, Hubertus, Tubac, Dachshafen, Marienlust and Crespi. His English inheritance comes from Wylde, Seton and Dunkerque and through the Seton line, Swedens Sports Kennel and through the von Marienlust, German breeding. Joseph Mehrer himself couldn't have done it better.

His owner, Peggy Westphal, also deserves great credit. Perhaps she took Herbert Sanborn's words seriously, for she certainly campaigned the dog vigorously and with her breeding program, there is no chance that his inheritance will be allowed to disappear.

Ch. Pondwick's Hobgoblin has been described earlier in this chapter, in our coverage of the Rose Farm Kennels. He came at the right time as a good outcross from Timothy's progeny. Mrs. Onthank believed this to be so when she bought him as an eight-months-old puppy, and her judgment has been proven right. On his sire's (Moat Hall-Mark) side, he is all English breeding; on his dam's (Pondwick's Christina) side, he is all Swedish. English kennels represented in his pedigree are: Pondwick's, Moat, Clouds, Solo, Tumlow, Simondswood, Rytona, Craigmere and Wylde. Swedish kennels are Sports, Backstugans, Garpabackens and Tivedens.

As of the end of 1975, "Gobbie" stood as the sire of 64 champions, and "Timmie" with 58. Since both were still very much alive at that point, these totals seem certain to grow.

A typical German Dwarf Dachshund, Kerlchen-Perkeo, a black and tan, bred by Ernst Hass and owned by Frau Schuchardt.

Peterchen v.d. Jeetzel, kaninchenteckel, bred and owned by Wilhelm von Daacke, Jr. The Von Daake strain in miniatures was brought to America by the Fritz Kroeffs' vom Osterholz Kennels.

Henrietta von der Festigkeit, kaninchenteckel, bred by Jane Johnson and owned by Laurence Horswell.

THE MINIATURES

Just as there are dwarfs among humans, perfectly formed small replicas of normal-sized people, so there are dwarfs in the dog world — including Dachshunds. Dachshund breeders in past centuries did not have the modern knowledge of genetics and hereditary characteristics, so these dwarfs were considered freaks or curiosities. Some were kept as pets and others were destroyed.

These people could not have realized that in many cases these tiny dogs were probably mutants and could have been bred to each other, thereby accomplishing the goal that it has taken our modern breeders so long to achieve, a miniature Dachshund.

A demand for the miniature Dachshund was created long before the first eleven were registered in Germany in 1902. Two widely different groups sparked this demand; city dwellers and hunters.

The growth of dog shows with its attendant prestige of owning and showing a winner appealed to city dwellers. It was much cheaper than owning a race horse, a sport which only the rich could afford; and the dog, if it was small enough, could even be kept at home in the apartment. Since it was just as easy to win with a small dog as with a large one the demand for smaller dogs increased. Standard Dachshunds had no special appeal over dogs of similar size but small Dachshunds called *Kaninchenteckel* were beginning to appear in the show rings. They seemed just right to apartment owners and there was a great demand for them as pets.

At the same time a group of German breeders, horrified at the ever-increasing size of the standard Dachshunds and the emphasis on beauty which won them prizes at dog shows, regardless of their ability to hunt, began breeding smaller, lighter Dachshunds that could cope with a variety of underground conditions, including the sandy soil of north Germany where many of the standards became trapped in burrows by cave-ins. Along with this came the impulse to breed a Dachshund small enough to pursue rabbits and other small game underground. So they began to breed these very small Dachshunds (kaninchenteckel).

Foresters, who wanted good small hunting dogs in a hurry, were impatient with the slow careful process of selective breeding to produce the kaninchenteckel. They took a short cut, bred the smallest standards they could find to any one of the toy breeds. The result looked something like a Dachshund; it was small, and it had many of the toy dog characteristics including a desire to sit in its owners lap rather than hunt rabbits. These toy-Dachshund crosses were called *Kaninchenhund.*

Then there were the true dwarfs (*Zwerg*) Dachshunds which were being brought out by their owners at dog shows, once a class was established for small Dachshunds.

At first all three were shown in one classification which was called Kaninchenteckel.

Foresters found a ready market for their kaninchenhunds in the apartment dwellers. Useless as hunters, they made fine pets and they were something to show at dog shows. Commercial breeders produced even more of these crossbreds.

Kaninchenteckel breeders were reluctant to part with any of their dogs since their breeding programs were still in the experimental stage and, too, their dogs were slightly larger and a great deal more fiery in disposition than the kaninchenhund. The owners of the dwarf Dachshunds were few in number and most of them had no desire to part with their pets.

This left the market open to the kaninchenhund. As a result, a great deal of harm was done by the widespread breeding of the kaninchenhund and the public's confusing it with the other two small Dachshund varieties, since they were all shown in the same class.

But by 1913 the contrast among these three was so great that a division of the class was made. There was the zwerg Dachshund, about 8 to 9 pounds, which was now beginning to be purposefully bred to produce a small replica of the standard; the kaninchenhund, equally small but with terrier-like heads, bat ears, light bones and flat chests; and the slightly larger kaninchenteckel, bred slightly higher in the leg for hunting ability.

Eventually competition at dog shows and in the hunting field eliminated the kaninchenhund. Show dog owners who had purchased them found they could not win against the beautiful miniatures produced from the dwarfs; hunters finding their breeding program unsatisfactory gave it up in favor of the kaninchenteckel. However, the harm had been done and for a long time breeders would be suddenly confronted with apple-headed, goggle-eyed pups in their litters, throw-backs to the Toy crosses. By 1935, the kaninchenhund influence had almost disappeared and owners of miniature Dachshunds today can be assured of pure miniature stock from which to breed.

Miniatures were not introduced into the British Isles until after World War I. And of those introduced in the period between the two wars, few traces — other than their show records — remain. Even with their growing popularity, the belief that they could not be bred without either causing the death of the tiny mother or, if she survived, the development of the puppies into standard sized dogs, held back breeding efforts, and many fine dogs went unused. Mrs. Smith-Rewse, the owner of Primrosepatch Kennels, England's largest in longhaired standards, decided to put this belief to the test. She bred some of the very small standards that appeared from time to time in her litters to the smallest miniature stock she could find. She found the small standards whelped without trouble and the puppies when full grown remained small. The progeny of this cross were mated to pure miniatures, who also whelped

126

Ch. Primrosepatch Diamond, first longhaired miniature Dachshund to win AKC championship (1948). Diamond, an English import, was owned by Miss Avis Earle, Tinyteckel Kennels, N. Hollywood, Calif.

Miss Avis Earle and her five English imports: Gracechurch Fairy Dream, Primrosepatch Zinnia, Smokyhole Rolfi, Smokyhole Mimi, and Ch. Primrosepatch Diamond.

Ch. Smokyhole Rolfi, miniature longhair imported from England and finished to American championship in 1951 by Miss Earle.

Early miniatures of the three varieties, all owned by Mrs. Wm. Burr Hill's De Sangpur Kennels: wirehaired, Fant von Osterholz, CD; longhaired, De Sangpur Bon Bon; and smooth, Chota's Achilles.

Ch. DeSangpur Wee Allene, a 1954 miniature longhaired champion, bred and owned by Mrs. Wm. Burr Hill.

without difficulty and whose litters remained small when grown. The results of these experiments were so superior over pure miniatures that other breeders began to follow her lead.

Like the crossings of smooth with wires to produce good conformation in wires, the crossing of standards with miniatures to improve quality was also abused by the ignorant and the greedy who wanted to breed miniatures in a hurry to meet a growing market. (I can remember Grace Hill worriedly screening purchasers of her miniatures to make sure that the new owners knew what they were doing in the way of future breeding plans.) The standard-miniature crossing has long since stopped and miniatures are now bred to miniatures to produce championship quality in the little dogs.

To Miss Avis Mary Earle, who brought longhaired miniature Dachshunds from England and Hollywood talent scouts to the door of her Tinyteckel Kennels in Beverly Hills, California, goes much of the credit for bringing the miniature to public attention in the United States. In 1948 Miss Earle left England for California bringing with her the best longhaired miniature stock she could buy as foundation stock for Tinyteckel. These were Primrose Patch Zinnia, Gracechurch Fairy Dream, Smokeyhole Mimi, Smokeyhole Rolfi and Ch. Primrose Patch Diamond. Diamond made his championship at California shows in competition with standard longhairs. He was the first longhaired miniature champion in the United States.

Before he left England, Diamond had sired a litter of longhaired miniatures, among them a dog called Jeffrey of Paddenswick. Jeffrey went Best in Show at the London City and Suburban Show in May 1948 and Diamond became the first miniature to sire a Best in Show winner. There was more to come. His son, Tinyteckel Ever Ready, earned a CD title in Obedience. Thus Diamond was also the first miniature to sire an Obedience winner.

Ever Ready's obedience title, plus his style and showmanship inherited from his famous father, earned him the job, over twenty-two well-trained motion picture dogs, as the canine lead in "Fancy Pants," which featured Bob Hope. Ever Ready's successful debut into show business brought more calls from producers for Tinyteckel Dachshunds. Tinyteckel Buttercup was the four-footed star of the Dennis Day show on TV. Buttercup, who weighed four pounds had a wardrobe of hats, lace dresses, sweaters, raincoats and even a "mink coat" made up for her by the studio's wardrobe department. Tinyteckel Cuddles joined the Ray Bolger TV show. Ethel Thomas's wirehairs never achieved such fame in spite of their theatrical upbringing.

Before they left England Diamond and Zinnia had been mated, and four days after Miss Earle's arrival in Beverly Hills, Zinnia whelped a litter of eight. It was a record at that time, the largest litter of miniature Dachshunds. All of the Tinyteckel miniatures did well in the show ring and in the early '50s, Miss Earle returned to England in search of an outcross for her kennel. She returned with a smooth red miniature, Tinyteckel Magical of Seale bred by Mrs. M. Howard. Through his sire, Minivale Magical, he carried the Minivale bloodlines which combined successfully with Miss Earle's established stock.

Two American breeders bought offspring of Smokeyhole Rolfi. Tinyteckel Millicent went to Mrs. Cordelia Skapinsky's Belleau Kennels, and another daughter, De Sangpur Juliette, went to Mrs. Hill's De Sangpur Kennels.

The first wirehaired miniatures were brought over by Dr. Lyman R. Fisher of Ithaca, N.Y. They were Alex Friedwaldau and Adda v Swartenbrook, from Germany. His Limelight Kennels produced the first miniature wire champions, Ch. Limelight Breslauerlicht and Ch. Limelight Berlinerlicht. Mrs. Charles Cline showed Berlinerlicht to her championship in California for Dr. Fisher. This lady, so well known for her smooth and longhaired standards, was amazed to find she had made Dachshund history by winning the first wirehaired championship in the United States.

The Fritz Kroeffs of New York City brought over two smooth German miniatures in 1948 — Kasco v.d. Jeetzel and his litter sister Kaeti v.d. Jeetzel, bred by Wilhelm von Daacke.

Mrs. Hill's beautiful black and tan De Sangpur Wee Allene, sired by Tinyteckel Black Silk ex Shantee Linda De Sangpur, became the first American-bred longhaired miniature champion.

The twin problems of breeding good miniatures and winning with them against the really superb standards that were being bred and shown in America is illustrated by the scarcity of miniature champions during the first twenty years from 1941 (when Dr. Fisher's wirehairs achieved their goal) up to 1961 when miniatures took a giant step forward into the winners circle. In these two decades, 44 miniatures gained their championships. Of these, 22 were wirehairs, 15 were longhaired and 7 were smooths. Here is the list of these early champions:

Wirehairs

1941
Limelight Berlinerlicht
Limelight Breslauerlicht

1946
Mikosz v Teckeldorf

1947
Misery v Teckeldorf

1953
Ursel v Osterholz

1955
Shandor Fantasia
Ulla v Osterholz

1956
Stardust v Teckeldorf
Tubac's Wee Johann

1957
Erdman v Osterholz
Gracie of Teckelheim
Sketch v Teckeldorf
Tubac's Wee Miss Piffle

1958
Garners Cutie Pie

1959
Garners Wee Jingle Bell
Garners Wee Josh
Garners Wee Noel
Tubac's Sweet William
Tubac's Wee Schmaltzie

1960
Garners Miss Special
Garner's Something Special
Tubac's Wee Lightning Bug

130

Ch. Limelight Breslauerlicht, one of the first wirehaired miniature champions in America (1941), bred by Dr. Lyman R. Fisher.

Ch. Mikosz v Teckeldorf, third miniature wirehair to win AKC championship (1946). Owned by Mrs. Katharina Lehfeldt.

Am. Can. & Mex. Ch. Tubac's Wee Johann, a top winning miniature wirehair of the 1958–60 era. Owned by Neville Stephens.

Judge Ramona (Van Court) Jones awarding Best Brace in Show at San Francisco to Neville Stephens' miniature wires—Ch. Tubac's Wee Lightning Bug and Tubac's Wee Firefly. Handled by Mr. Stephens. —*Ludwig*

Best in Show team of wirehaired miniature Dachshunds owned by Neville Stephens' Tubac Kennels. —*Ludwig*

Ch. Edmonston's Teddy Boy, 8½ lbs., second male miniature longhaired Dachshund to win championship (1959). Owned by Neville Stephens.

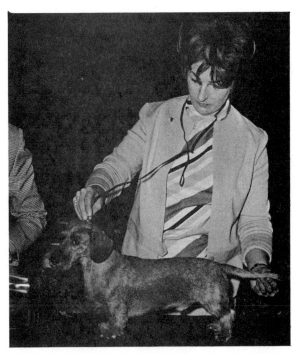

Ch. Elenbusch Jiminy Cricket, miniature wire, multi-BIS winner of the 1960s, owned by Beverly and Sherry Snyder, and handled by Evonne Chashoudian.

Longhairs	1959	Smooths
1954	Edmonstons Teddy Boy	1956
De Sangpur Wee Allene	Geam's Penny of Midge	Aldwin's Jewell
	Geam's Pretty Penny	Dach's Den Eric M
1956	Mausie v Bilstein	De Sangpur Wee Memmy
Edmonston's Livin' Doll	Sherwood Petra	
	Von Kralc Wee Goldie	1958
1958		De Sangpur Wee Lancelot
Bayard Chantilly	1960	
	Edmonstons Yazzy Begay	1960
	Goldie's Little Alex	Garners Wee Hans
	Mindox Tiny Tim	Geam's Wee Trudina
	Tubac's Sweet Marie	Johannes Strauss

Reading these statistics, one can only admire the courage and persistence of these breeders who seemed to accomplish so little during a twenty year period. Teckeldorf with only four champions Tubac with six, Mrs. Dwight Garner with seven, Dr. Fisher with two, Osterholz with three, Geam with three, De Sangpur with three, Edmonston with three, Bayard with one, Hardy with one and Dachs Den with one. What a debt we owe them for their continued efforts in the face of such slow and discouraging progress.

Their efforts paid off. There is no lack of miniature champions now and many breeders have entered this field. In 1972 there were 74 miniature championships made in one year.

Wirehaired miniatures seem to have held the head start they earned. The first miniature to win Best in Show (in 1966) was the wirehair Ch. Elenbusch Jiminy Cricket, owned by Beverly and Sherry Snyder of Torrance, California, and handled by Evonne Chashoudian. During his lifetime he won 4 Bests in Show and 20 Hound Groups, 3 Best of Variety at Specialty shows and one Best of Variety at Westminster.

Ch. Tubac's Wee Johann, a wirehair owned by Neville Stephens, was American, Canadian and Mexican champion and the top winning miniature, all coats for 1958, 1959, 1960.

Mrs. Charles Mays was another wirehaired breeder of about the same period. Her Garners Wee Josh was the sire of twelve champions. Mrs. Mays' Ch. Mays Tyna-Mite, owned by Mary Germany, was the first miniature to win the variety at the Dachshund Club of America's specialty show. She finished her championship at eleven months. Her show career started in 1961 and ended in 1967. During that time she was a Hound Group winner. Dorothea Metzger was her handler during her show career and became her owner after she was retired.

134

Ch. DeSangpur Wee Lancelot, red smooth miniature (8 lbs.), 1958 champion bred and owned by Mrs. William Burr Hill.

Ch. Johannes Strauss, 1960 smooth miniature champion, owned by Frank and Dorothy Hardy. —*Tauskey*

Eng. & Am. Ch. Mighty Fine von Walder, longhaired miniature, wh. 1960, made each of his championships in just four shows. Imported to America by Rose Farm Kennels. —*Tauskey*

135

The fame of Mrs. William B. Hill as a Dachshund breeder gained more prestige when her De Sangpur Wee Ad Lib won its championship in 1964. No other person had bred miniature champions as well as standard Dachshunds in all three coats. Mrs. Garner was the first to breed miniatures in all three coats and make them champions, but both she and Mrs. Mays, who also had champions in all three of the miniature varieties, bred miniatures only.

Miniature wires and those of other coats found a firm friend and supporter in Dr. C. William Nixon. As a geneticist, the problems of breeding miniatures intrigued him and he set about trying to improve both breeding practices and the quality of the dogs. He bought his first dog in 1951. Following Mrs. Smith-Rewse's method, which so improved the English miniatures, he began with a small standard black and tan bitch and bred down for size. From the smooths he went to the miniature wires. He chose a son of Ch. Garner's Wee Josh, Ch. Rayes Little Maynard, bred by Mrs. Mays and owned by Mrs. E. Olson. He was shipped from California to Dr. Nixon at Randolph, Massachusetts. He sired 13 champions and proved Dr. Nixon to be on the right track with his breeding program. Dr. Nixon is also working on the breeding of dapple Dachshunds. Elsewhere in this book is a reference to his latest acquisition, piebald Dachshunds.

The Wilheen Kennels also used Wee Josh in their breeding program. Their Ch. Wilheen's Winnie of Way-Hi was Best in Show in 1970 at the Greater Miami Dog Club show with an entry of 1,123 dogs. She was owned by Dorothy Turco and handled by Dick Vaughn. Ch. Garner's Miss Special was owned by the White Gables Kennels and Ramona Van Court enjoyed showing this tiny wire with such an outstanding personality.

In 1969 Wyndel Kennels, a newly begun effort, had its first champion. From this start, the kennel has produced eight wirehaired miniature champions with more surely on the way. Ch. Wyndel's Kiss Me Kate, was a sensation at the Dachshund Club of America's Specialty in 1972. The National Dog System of top fifty Dachshunds for 1972 placed Pat Wynne's Ch. Wyndel's Kiss Me Kate seventh on the list.

American, Canadian and Mexican Ch. Little John v Maradon was the top winning wirehaired miniature for 1970 and 1971. At a Mexican show he went Best in Show over an entry of 1,400 dogs. He is owned by Marjorie Pepper. Ch. Sir Lawton v Maradon is another miniature Best in Show winner, scoring February 4, 1973 at St. Joseph, Missouri, with 1,285 dogs entered. He is owned by Florence Pointdexter, and handled by Jack Brenneis.

Among the best known wirehaired miniature imports were dapples from the Cumtru kennels of Mrs. Shelagh Willoughby, who bred all three coats. Ch. Calpreta Print of Cumtru CD and Ch. Witching Hour of Cumtru were imported by the Stanley Ornes. Calpreta Print won her CD in three shows taking Best of Variety and two Bests of Opposite Sex in the breed classes at the same three shows.

136

Ch. Ardencaple's Wee Bronze Penny, shown by her breeder-owner Mrs. Willard K. Denton, is pictured scoring Winners Bitch at the 1974 Dachshund Club of America Specialty under judge Jeannette W. Cross. —*Klein*

An outstanding representative of Westphalen miniatures, Ch. Patchwork Hill Calliope, longhair sire of 13 champions. Calliope was bred by Patricia Beresford.—*Tauskey*

Mrs. Blanche Schoning more than doubled Miss Earle's record for importing miniatures. She came to the United States in 1963 with twelve wirehaired miniatures. They represented three leading British kennels: Sillwood, Coobeg and Orkneyinga. Mrs. Schoning's kennel prefix, Scoshire, starts with the first three letters representing each of these kennels. To these bloodlines was added a fourth, Blufelt Kennels and in 1964, Orkneyinga Angus of Scoshire was added to the kennel. He was a chocolate 7½ pound dog. Mrs. Schoning's most recent champion is Ch. Scoshire Black Narcissus, an eight pound black and tan wire. He is all German breeding on the side of his sire, Illo vom Jagdhaus Bewingen. His dam, Scoshire Lysee Little, is homebred Scoshire with the original English dogs in her pedigree.

In longhaired miniatures, Mrs. Hill's Wee Allene had 27 Bests of Variety, a Hound Group first and 6 Group placings when she was retired in 1958. Her sire, Tinyteckel Black Silk also sired the third longhaired miniature champion, Bayard Chantilly. Chantilly had both standard longhair and miniature smooth in her background. Her granddam was Ch. De Sangpur Penelope, a standard. Bred to a smooth miniature, she produced Bayard Astarte. Astarte, bred to Tinyteckel Black Silk produced Chantilly. She began her march to championship in 1956 by going from the puppy class to Reserve winners bitch. She finished in 1958 with three majors including a five pointer.

During the sixties while Tubac, Garner and De Sangpur continued to breed and show, others joined in, among them Paul Tolliver and Patricia Beresford. Tolliver was a fairly new arrival in breeding standard smooth and wirehaired Dachshunds but he was intrigued by the longhaired miniatures and bought Wee Keli Jean of Wayne, bred by Ruby Arnot. It was his first champion. Keli Jean was sent to Rhodesia in 1964 where she was shown, whelped a litter and was returned to Mr. Tolliver. Tolliver's best known champion was Ch. Taunuswald Wee Sakura, sired by Ch. Goldie's Little Alex, one of the four 1960 champion miniature longhairs. She finished her championship at the age of nine months. In her show career, from January 1965 through November 1970, she was shown 133 times, with 93 wins from that total. She retired in a blaze of glory at the age of seven, taking Best of Breed at the Cascade Dachshund Club Specialty. At that time her coat was the best it had ever been.

Patricia Beresford chose Mrs. Onthank's great winner, Ch. Mighty Fine von Walder as the foundation sire for her Patchwork Hill Kennels. Bred to De Sangpur Wee Rouge, the litter contained Patchwork Hill's first champion Ch. Westphal's Merry Mite. The second litter from a repeat mating gave her five champions, quite a start for a beginner in the miniature field. She now has five generations of Patchwork bloodlines, all show quality, proven in ring competition, among them Ardencaple's Melody d'Amour owned by Kenneth Fields.

Another English import, Sunara Firecracker, brought over by the Charles

Mays, was not shown much but proved a fine stud dog. He sired eleven American champions and three Canadian ones.

During the late sixties Ch. Patchwork Hill Calliope, owned by Peggy Westphal was probably the top winner. Her full brother Ch. Patchwork Hill Johnny Come Lately was among the top twenty longhaired winners in 1971. Mr. and Mrs. Paul Nakamura's Ch. Nakamura's Wee Willie was seventh in the same list and the number one bitch was Paul Tolliver's Ch. Taunuswald Nefertiti.

The seventies were marked by the appearance of Ch. Ace-Hi Little Tootsie, owned by the Donald Taylors of Council Bluffs Iowa. Tootsie won her American, Canadian and Mexican championships, and her kennelmate Ch. Sugar Creek's Wee Robin Hood also won his championship in the same three countries and received an award from *Dogs in Canada* magazine for second place in Miniature competition in that country.

Sylvan Dante, an Irish import bred by Mrs. O.M. Rutledge, has been brought to this country by Barbara J. Nichols for her Nikobar Kennels in California. A clear red, the dog is sired by the English champion Delphik Dario who carried Dephik and Reedscottage bloodlines. His dam is Sylvan Holiday, with mainly Kinlough breeding in her background including the Irish Ch. Kinlough Oscar. He should be an important contribution to longhaired miniatures, not only at Nikobar, but elsewhere in the country.

The smooth miniatures were the last to arrive in the winners circle. It was not until 1956 that the first three champions achieved their titles. I remember Aldwins Jewell, an exquisite little black and tan, who was never bred by her owners, the Richard Farnhams, for fear of losing her at whelping. De Sangpur Wee Memmy a red bitch went to Mrs. James Ball. Dachs Den Eric, the first male smooth miniature champion was one I never saw. Mrs. Newhauser, whose miniatures were so successful during the sixties, tells of seeing him when he was quite old. Even then, she described him as "... very correct. His front was lovely." His owner, Mrs. Lynda Beard was a pioneer in smooth miniatures in a very real way. She lived in Lincoln, Nebraska where dog shows were few and far between and since she couldn't drive, she had to take the train to dog shows. This sometimes meant three or four days of travel, often with an unsuccessful day at the show. It has been the determination and self confidence of breeders like Mrs. Beard that modern miniature breeders can thank for their present success.

The second male champion in smooth miniatures, Mrs. Hill's Ch. De Sangpur Wee Lancelot, faced a different problem in achieving his title. It was competition, a lot of it, all very good and plenty of dog shows. It was not good enough, however, to beat this eight pound red dog. In less than two months he had two Best of Variety wins and fourth place in the Hound group in five consecutive shows. He never placed below Best of Winners.

Ch. Garner's Wee Hans-M was sold to Mr. and Mrs. James Ruffell of Bellvue, Washington, in 1960 and did much for miniatures in the Northwest.

That same year Mrs. Carolyn Strauss gave a four month old miniature smooth puppy to Frank and Dorothy Hardy as a Christmas present. He became Ch. Johannes Strauss and made his championships in United States, Canada and Bermuda. The sixth dog to finish his championship was a red, Groff-Nix Little Shotgun and the seventh was Ch. Groff-Nix Tiny Tim.

Tiny Tim was bought by the Herman Newhausers in 1961. They have a remarkable record as miniature breeders. Ch. Tiny Tim was Lo-Dachs breeding. His dam was Lo-Dachs Wee Cover Girl and his sire, Lo-Dachs Mr. Lucky. As a mate, the Newhausers bought Lo-Dachs Miss Fabulous and promptly bred the pair. It was the start of their success. Hoping to combine Eastern and Western miniature blood they bred Muriel's Timalee (who had Lo-Dachs bloodlines) and the Hardy's Ch. Johannes Strauss (who brought Eastern blood to the mating). The result was Ch. Muriel's Semper Fidelis, born in January of 1964.

An indication of the time and effort which went into the planning and selection of the Newhauser dogs for breeding and showing can be seen in the results at dog shows. At the Cleveland Dachshund Club specialty in 1967, the Newhauser dogs placed first, second, third and fourth in the Open bitch miniature class. First was Muriel's Miss Bam, second was Muriel's Fabulous Timette, third was Muriel's Esprit de Corps and fourth was Candy of the Loughs, a daughter of Semper Fidelis. Mrs. Newhauser handled Miss Bam, Mrs. W. Dorward handled Timette, Herman Newhauser showed Esprit de Corps and Peggy Westphal handled Candy.

It was in the sixties that we first had occasions where all three Dachshunds representing their breed in the Hound Group were miniatures. It occurred twice. In 1965 at the Rio Grande Kennel Club show the Dachshunds in the Hound group were: the wire miniature, Ch. May's Tallyrand, who placed second in the Group; the smooth, Ch. May's Pallette, placed fourth; and the longhair Ch. Taunuswald Wee Sakura, unplaced. Again, in 1968 at the Kennel Club of Pasadena, the Dachshunds in the group were: the smooth, Ch. Muriel's Miss Bam; the longhair, Ch. Taunuswald Wee Sakura, who placed fourth this time; and the wire, Kula of Running D Ranch.

Semper Fidelis, bred to Ch. Hubertus Teddina, sired Vernon's Vici, owned by Mr. and Mrs. Thomas Curit's Dachs Haven Kennels. He began his career in 1968 and before the year was finished he was the top smooth miniature male according to the Thomas System.

The sixties also saw the beginning of the Ardencaple Kennels of Mr. and Mrs. Willard K. Denton in the miniature Dachshund field. Their De Sangpur Wee Ebony Doll became the fifth smooth miniature bitch to win its championship, making her title in 18 shows, an accomplishment for any Dachshund. Their Geam's Miss Ting Tang, a daughter of Mrs. Hill's De Sangpur Wee Lancelot, made her championship in 1961.

Mrs. Raymond L. McCord has accomplished what every breeder hopes for: a Best in Show team, all of them children or grandchildren of her Kordach's

Ch. Tori Jarice's Wee Nicodemus MS, handled by owner Miss Jeanne A. Rice, pictured winning Best Miniature from the Open Class at the Knickerbocker Dachshund Club Specialty in February, 1975, under judge Sterling Brown. On June 27, 1975, Nicodemus became the first Smooth Miniature to win a Specialty Best of Breed—scoring over 252 Dachshunds at the Reserve Dachshund Club Specialty at Cleveland.—*Gilbert*

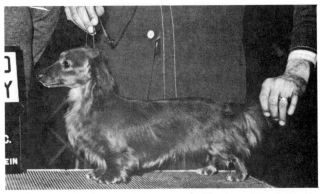

Ch. Delfisk L'Enfant D'Amour, miniature longhaired Dachshund, is establishing new marks for a longhaired bitch with wins that include 6 Group Firsts and more than 50 Bests of Variety. Owned by Robert A. Hauslohner and handled by Howard Atlee. —*Klein*

Wee Red Pepper. Mrs. McCord scored her first team Best in Show win at The Hoosier Kennel Club show in 1966 with a team of reds, her second win in 1968 with a black and tan team and a third win in 1970 with another team of reds. All were bred, owned and handled by Mrs. McCord. Some champions from her Kordachs Kennels were Ch. Kordachs Wee Copper Candi in 1969 and Ch. Kordachs Wee Pinochio in 1970.

Neville Stephens accomplished a similar win with his team of wirehaired miniatures.

Hawaii, where there are only three shows a year, had its first miniature champion in the smooth miniature Little Guy of Aiealani, bred by Elisabeth Ling and owned by the B.H. Beams. Little Guy earned his first points when he was nine months old and finished his championship when he was five years old.

The seventies have seen the Tallavast Kennels of Dr. Walter and Mrs. Ida Thomas come to the fore with three generations of champions, plus others, from their Florida home. They began with Tallavast Frank (a son of Ch. Johannes Strauss), followed with Frank's son, Ch. Tallavast Eddie, and then Eddie's son, Ch. Tallavast Shiloah.

Mr. and Mrs. Thomas Knox' Knox Knoll Kennels are the breeders of American and Canadian champion Gottlieb of Knox Knoll, owned by Lucille Deying. The Albert Ross' miniatures carry Taunuswald and De Sangpur bloodlines and there is the breakthrough of Mrs. Jean Rice's Ch. Tori Jarice's Wee Nicodemus, a black and tan smooth, the 28th miniature smooth to win its championship and the first smooth miniature to win Best of Breed — scored in June of 1975 at the Reserve Dachshund Club specialty at Cleveland. The Rice's kennels were begun in the sixties and Mrs. Rice is the current president of the National Miniature Dachshund Club. An interesting footnote to this win is that Nicodemus' litter sister is being shown by none other than Mrs. William B. Hill, Jr., whose De Sangpur kennels were the first to show both standard and miniature Dachshunds in all three coats.

One of the most dramatic illustrations of the impact of the past on the present in Dachshund breeding is the startling success of Mrs. Patricia Beresford's Patchwork Kennels. Started ten years ago as "Patchwork Hill," a change of location eliminated the original hilltop site and it is now simply "Patchwork."

In ten years from 1965 to 1975, Mrs. Beresford has succeeded in producing a third generation homebred good enough to take Best In Show at the Cape Cod all breed event in 1975—the longhaired Miniature, Ch. Patchwork Peter Piper. Peter Piper is one of the two longhaired miniatures to top an all-breed event; the other is Ch. May's Rhapsody, owned by Frances Keaton and handled by Mrs. Judy Murray.

Mrs. Nancy Onthank's daughter, Dee Hutchinson, is enthusiastically carrying on the Rose Farm tradition. She is pictured here with the Farm's impressive English import miniature longhair, Ch. Minutist Goliath. —Shafer

Ch. May's Hap-Pea Torpedo MW, miniature wire, Best in Show winner. Torpedo was the top winning wire of 1974. Owned by Elsie Riddick of Newark, California, and handled by Ray McGinnis. —Henry

Mrs. Beresford's foundation stock was De Sangpur Wee Rouge, a miniature bitch bought as a pet from Mrs. William B. Hill's kennels at Hicksville, L.I.

Tracing Peter Piper's pedigree, one comes upon such familiar names as Smokyhole Rolfi and Gracechurch Fairy Dream, discriminatingly imported in 1948 by Avis Earle for her Tinyteckel Kennels. Mrs. Hill's acumen in breeding to Mrs. Earle's dogs is apparent in Wee Rouge's pedigree. Rouge's sire and dam (De Sangpur Wee David ex De Sangpur Wee Alissa) both go back to Tinyteckel Black Silk.

Other familiar names appear. Ch. Mighty Fine von Walder, Mrs. Nancy Onthank's valuable contribution to the miniature Dachshund variety, and Mrs. Mary Howell's breeding is represented in Ch. Bayard le Pierrot. More recent English imports such as Sunara Firecracker and Printshop Danjor Little Pipit are others that show the careful selection by both the older and more recent breeders from which Mrs. Beresford has benefitted so richly.

It was not entirely a matter of beginner's luck with Mrs. Beresford. While she was new to the Dachshund breed she was by no means ignorant of sound breeding principles. A flock of sheep — a joint project of Patricia Beresford and her young son — are producing meat, wool and skins in testimony of her knowledge of breeding larger animals.

While she had the benefit of well-known English dogs to use in her breeding program, it was sheer chance that introduced a German strain into it. During the showing of her Ch. Patchwork Love Bug at an all-breed show she was approached by a German couple, Gizella and Joseph Rich, who admired the little dog and asked Mrs. Beresford if she would breed him to their bitch. They really didn't want any puppies, they explained, Mrs. Beresford would be welcome to the whole litter, but they did want their pet to experience motherhood. Intrigued by this unusual offer, she went to see the bitch and look at the pedigree. She found her gay and attractive with two German lines, von Fraunenbruennen and vom Gosenbach in her pedigree. So the mating took place and, in due time the litter arrived.

Three of the pups became champions: Ch. Patchwork Pandora, Ch. Patchwork Marigold and Ch. Patchwork Peter Piper. Besides his Best in Show wins Peter Piper has three Group firsts and nearly a dozen other Group placings. In 1974 he was Best of Breed at the Dachshund Specialty at Palm Beach and in 1975 he was Best in Show in Canada at the Canadian Miniature Dachshund Show. He holds a Canadian championship, too.

Love Bug is, in Mrs. Beresford's opinion, her present best sire. His two most important breedings were the one to the German bitch, Nired von Fraunenbruennen and the other to Ardencaple's Melody d'Amour, sired by Patchwork Hill Calliope ex a recessive longhair, Ardencaple's Wee Surprise. Melody d'Amour is owned jointly by Ken Fields and Mrs. Beresford. Love Bug has an outstanding show record; top miniature longhair in 1972 under the Thomas system and among the top ten longhaired Dachshunds and top twenty

144

Three generations of Patchwork miniature longhaired Dachshunds. In the center is the start of it all, De Sangpur Wee Rouge; on the right, Ch. Patchwork Johnny Come Lately; and at left, a puppy, Patchwork Antigone. All bred and owned by Mrs. Patricia Beresford of Winchester Center, Conn. —*Gilbert*

Ch. Patchwork Peter Piper, miniature longhair, being shown (by his owner, Robert Crews) to Best in Show all-breeds at the 1975 Cape Cod show under judge Harry Thomas. —*Gilbert*

Dachshunds, all varieties in 1972–73. To date he has sired six champions. From Melody d'Amour's litter came Ch. Delfisk Roi d'Amour and Ch. Delfisk l'Enfant d'Amour, owned by Robert Hauslohner and Howard Atlee. According to Mrs. Beresford, Delfisk l'Enfant d'Amour is the top winning longhaired miniature bitch of all time and the top longhaired bitch of both sizes.

Looking back at Mrs. Beresford's early attempts, in 1965 it was a combination of Ch. Mighty Fine von Walder and De Sangpur Wee Rouge that got the kennel off to a flying start. They were bred twice. The first mating produced six puppies one of whom Ch. Westphal's Merry Mite was among the top longhaired bitches in 1967 and represents Peggy Westphal's brief excursion into Miniatures. The second mating in 1966, also six puppies, gave the kennels five champions: Ch. Patchwork Hill Calliope, now a sire of 12 champions, owned by Peggy Westphal; Ch. Patchwork Johnny Come Lately, who finished his championship in a burst of glory taking Winners Dog at the Dachshund Club of America's Specialty the day before Westminster and Best of Winners the next day at the Garden Show. Johnny now has six champions to his credit; Ch. Patchwork Hill Calypso, owned by Peggy Westphal; Ch. Paul's Julie of Patchwork Hill, owned by Paul Nakamura of California; and Ch. Patchwork Hill Cassandra.

Cassandra was bred to Ch. Bayard le Pierrot and produced Ch. Patchwork Punchinello. Punchinello, bred to Ch. Paul's Julie of Patchwork Hill produced a champion for Mr. Nakamura — Ch. Nakamura's Wee Willie, a Group winner. Punchinello, bred to Patchwork Firefly, the only puppy from a mating of Printshop Danjor Little Pipit (mainly Coobeg bloodlines) to Sunara Firecracker, produced Love Bug. Love Bug, outcrossed to Nired von Fraunenbruennen, produced Peter Piper.

Ardencaples Wee Surprise (the granddam of Delfisk l'Enfant d'Amour), bred and owned by Mrs. Willard K. Denton, is the top producing longhaired dam in the American Dachshund's list of top producers in 1975. She has nine champions to her credit.

As we go to print, Ch. Spartan's Sloe Gin Fizz MW is rewriting much of the record book—not only for miniatures, but for all wires. Whelped March 24, 1974 out of a smooth-wire mating (Tori-Jarice's Wee Angus MS ex Spartan's Mynni Wyre MW), at just past two years of age "Gin Fizz" has already won 14 all-breed Bests in Show and 30 Group Firsts. Included in his winning was Best of Variety at the 1976 Westminster Kennel Club show under judge Dr. Lyman R. Fisher, who produced the first miniature wirehaired Dachshund champions back in 1941. "Gin Fizz" is owned by Mrs. C. Gordon-Creed, Oldland Kennels, Camden, South Carolina, and handled by Jerry Rigden.

Ch. Pondwick's Hobgoblin, sire of 64 champions. —*Tauskey*

Ch. Vantebe's Draht Timothy, sire of 58 champions.—*Tauskey*

The Top Producers

WITH THE SERIOUS Dachshund breeder, first emphasis has been on the dog's potential as a sire or dam, rather than on its winning. Here, compiled for us by Sanford Roberts of *The American Dachshund* are the dogs in each variety that have been sires or dams of the most champions (as recorded through December 1975):

Top Producing Smooth (Standard) Males	*Sire of:*
Am. & Can. Ch. Favorite von Marienlust	95 champions
(Owned by Fred and Rose Heying)	
Ch. Dunkeldorf Falcon's Favorite	90 champions
(Owned by Mr. and Mrs. Thomas Dunk, Jr.)	
Ch. Falcon of Heying-Teckel	82 champions
(Owned by Fred and Rose Heying)	
Top Producing Smooth (Standard) Bitches	*Dam of:*
Ch. Moffett's Rosanne	15 champions
(Owned by Mr. and Mrs. Russell Moffett)	
Ch. Albion's Own Penelope	13 champions
(Owned by Mr. and Mrs. Harry Sharpe)	
Dunkeldorf's Gimlet	10 champions
(Owned by Mr. and Mrs. Thomas Dunk, Jr.)	
Top Producing Wirehaired (Standard) Males	*Sire of:*
Ch. Pondwicks Hobgoblin	64 champions
(Owned by Dorothy O. Hutchinson)	
Ch. Vantebe's Draht Timothy	58 champions
(Owned by Peggy Westphal)	
Ch. Westphal's Shillalah	41 champions
(Owned by Peggy Westphal)	

Top Producing Wirehaired (Standard) Bitches

	Dam of:
Westphal's Berry	9 champions
(Owned by Frank and Mary Castoral)	
Ch. None Such Bumble Bee	8 champions
(owned by Terry Childs)	

Top Producing Longhaired (Standard) Males

	Sire of:
Ch. William de Sangpur	38 champions
(Owned by Mrs. Wm. Burr Hill)	
Ch. Covara's Tabasco	34 champions
(Owned by Alva and Vera Gunn)	

Top Producing Longhaired (Standard) Bitches

	Dam of:
Ch. Split Rock's Electra	12 champions
(Owned by Mary Howell and Grace Hill)	
Sweethaven Suzi Chenile L	8 champions
(Owned by Barbara J. Nichols)	
Ch. Robdachs Gypsy Rose	8 champions
(Owned by Sanford Roberts and	
Beatrice A. T. Medes)	
Ch. Fantasy v Kotthaus	8 champions
(Owned by Robert and Alice Dildine)	
Ch. Haleajo's Periwinkle	8 champions
(Owned by Martha Prendergast)	

Top Producing Longhaired (Miniature) Bitch

	Dam of:
Ardencaple's Wee Surprise	8 champions
(Owned by Mrs. Willard Denton)	

Ch. Vantebe's Draht Kahlua, standard black and tan wirehaired bitch, at age of 6 years winning Best of Breed at the 1975 Bay Colony Specialty under judge Peter Monks, with Howard Nygood handling. Kahlua's remarkable winning through 1974–75 included 17 BOVs, BOV at the Knickerbocker Specialty, Best Bitch in Show at DALI, and a weekend sweep in which she was BOV—on to Best Bitch in Show—at the 1975 Dachshund Club of NJ, BOV and on to Group second at Bucks County, and BOV at Trenton. She is owned by Dr. and Mrs. George G. Pickett's Herthwood Farms.

Cutting the cake at the Golden Jubilee banquet of the Dachshund Club of America in 1945 was part of a two day endurance contest for Laurence Horswell. He was chief speaker at the banquet, held November 25 at the Pennsylvania Hotel in New York City, and then next day judged 250 Dachshunds. Below, looking a bit weary, Mr. Horswell is seen at conclusion of the show. The dog at left is Ch. Arnett von Dachshafen, Best of Opposite Sex, owned by Maude Daniels Smith. At right is Ch. Gunther v Marienlust, Best of Breed, owned by Jeannette W. Cross. The 14-inch bronze plaque was cast from the original sculpture by Katherine Ward Lane, and is the only one of that size ever awarded. The only other 14-inch DCA plaque hangs in the picture gallery of the American Kennel Club in New York.

Laurence Alden Horswell

LAURENCE ALDEN HORSWELL is one of the best known and most controversial figures in the dog world. He joined the Dachshund Club of America in 1932 and Dachshunds were his primary concern from that time on. He later became a judge of all hound breeds and a writer, lecturer and authority in the field of dogs. To all these endeavors he brought his own innovative ideas. He made as many enemies as he did friends but everyone respected his opinions and his judgment.

Those who have known him for the past four decades will agree with a statement by Mrs. Jeannette W. Cross, a fellow Dachshund judge and one of his longtime acquaintances. In a letter which she read to me, before mailing to *The American Dachshund* for publication in its January 1975 issue, Mrs. Cross said, in part, ''In my opinion, one of Laurence Horswell's greatest achievements was carrying the breed through World War II without a single objectionable cartoon appearing about Dachshunds — no derogatory news stories, no unpleasant incidents; in fact, the breed emerged more popular than ever in this country when the war was over.

''People who are old enough to remember World War I will tell you things were very different then. It took real courage to keep Dachshunds during the war hysteria of that period.

''People who owned them kept them hidden and only took them out after dark. Dachshunds were stoned in public places and their owners threatened. By a shrewd and energetic public relations program, Mr. Horswell averted such cruelty and stupidity. We all owe him a great deal.''

Laurence Horswell's vigilance and determination to protect the breed from adverse publicity continued after the war years. Shortly after the war ended he received a letter from Gustav Alisch, a famous German Dachshund breeder and judge with whom Laurence had become friendly prior to the war. Alisch described the results of a large German field trial and an elaborate hunt dinner which followed it. He also gave the results of an all-breed show held in Berlin about the same time. The letter worried Laurence. He felt it might adversely affect the breed if the American public, still mourning its dead and caring for its wounded, was made aware of the fact that their recent enemies were pursuing "business as usual" in their way of life, including such luxuries as field trials and dog shows. He cut the information down to the bare facts and published it only in magazines and newsletters devoted exclusively to Dachshunds.

Horswell did not become interested in Dachshunds until just before his marriage to Dorothy Allison White of Ocean Grove, N.J. When the young couple moved to New York City they decided they wanted a dog. Remembering a chocolate-colored Dachshund they had seen in Chicago they decided to get one like it. The odd color was hard to find.

They went to the Westminster Kennel Club show every year from 1926 to 1930. Finally they found one. In talking to an exhibitor whose black and tan Dachshund had just won Best of Variety at the show, they learned that a litter sired by the dog had been born that very day and that there was a chocolate Dachshund in the litter.

They named her Martha v Solligen. When she outgrew her puppy awkwardness, she won the "Dachshunds any other color class" at Westminster. The Horswells never bred her. Laurence's investigation of the then known facts on chocolate breeding convinced him that it would not be practical. Martha remained their house dog for seventeen years.

Mr. Horswell was not involved with the Dachshund Club of America until 1932 when he became a member. Within a year he was named secretary and information chairman. He remained as its secretary until 1937. In 1946 he became president and his term of office ran through 1950. He was a director again in 1952 to 1965 but his job as information chairman was his chief pleasure and he never relinquished it until illness put an end to most of his activities.

I have my own recollection of him at this work. In 1970 at the Dachshund Club of America's 75th anniversary show held at the Hotel Manhattan in New York City, he spent the day at the ringside marking press catalogues, providing feature material and seeing to it that reporters covering the event got all possible information. The show dragged on late into the night. Walter Fletcher, the reporter for the *New York Times*, sat beside him nervously watching the clock and wondering if the show would be over in time for him to meet his paper's deadline.

Finally the three Best of Variety dogs had been named but before the Best of Breed could be chosen from among these three there were a number of special classes and one or two ceremonial events that would cause more delay. Walter's nervousness increased as the deadline got closer and closer.

Laurence was equally aware of the difficulty. Both men were remembering an occasion in the recent past where a Working breed specialty had run well beyond the deadline of all the morning papers. As a result the press refused to cover the show the following year. Suddenly, with characteristic abruptness,

Laurence turned to Walter and thrust a sheet of paper into his hands. It contained the complete show record of each of the three finalists and background material on all three dogs, their owners and handlers. "Go back to the office" he said. "I'll phone you when they pick the winner." Walter rushed back to the *Times* offices at 43rd street.

His story on the show with its class winners and summaries had long since been completed. All he needed now was an opening paragraph on the show winner to finish it. Sitting down at his typewriter he wrote three separate paragraphs one on the longhaired, one on the wirehaired and one on the smooth Dachshund. In each he proclaimed it the winner and filled it with the wealth of detailed information such as only Laurence, with his vast knowledge of Dachshunds, could provide. Then he sat back to wait for the call. Five minutes before the deadline, with the sports editor irritably demanding the story, the phone rang. "It's the smooth" said Laurence. Walter attached his paragraph on the smooth Dachshund to the body of his story and handed it to the editor.

Horswell's family background explains a good deal about the controversial effect he had on people he knew and with whom he worked. The family came of pioneer stock. His grandparents had migrated from Plymouth, England, to Canada. Their large family and a lack of enough money to support them all sent their children, including Laurence's father, Charles, out to seek employment at an early age.

Charles Horswell homesteaded in Wisconsin until he had earned enough money to pay his tuition at Northwestern University. While there he met and married a young schoolteacher and a graduate of the University, Nellie Miranda Redfield. The couple moved east while Charles completed his Ph.D. at Yale, and then back again to Northwestern where Charles had gained a teaching job at Garett Biblical Institute, a graduate school associated with Northwestern. Here he taught Greek, Hebrew and Biblical research. Nellie studied Arabic so that she could help him in the translation of some of the old manuscripts.

Nellie came of pioneer stock, too. The Redfields were transplanted Yankees who traced their ancestry back to John Alden and his Priscilla.

Young Charles was often at odds with the school board and his students. He was demanding and uncompromising in his insistence on detail and accuracy. He was impatient with his students at what he thought was a frivolous approach to their studies. Finally he resigned.

After several more teaching positions he finally accepted the ministry of a small parish, the Kennilworth Union Church, near Evanston, Illinois. It was here in Kennilworth that Laurence was born on the fourth of July, 1893. He was the first of three children. A sister, Carol and a brother, Richard were to follow.

Shortly before Carol's birth, little Laurence contracted polio. It left him with a withered and useless leg and since then he has worn a cumbersome built-up shoe and metal leg brace. It has never slowed him down. He has treated it as an annoying inconvenience rather than a crippling defect. He drove his car, piloted a weather observation plane and when working in New York he frequently ignored the escalators at Penn Station on his way to the office. He skipped up the long flights of stairs with the agility of a mountain goat while fellow commuters stared. He felt his sedentary job at the office called for some exercise before the start of a day's work and this was his way of getting it.

Even as a small boy Laurence had a practical approach to his problems. During the long and painful recovery from polio he was told that the angels had brought him a baby sister.

"Well," said Laurence, "I hope the angels will take care of her because I need mamma to take care of me."

In High School his ingenuity in publicizing the senior play caught the attention of a local businessman. With his encouragement Laurence eventually entered the advertising field and got a job with a Chicago firm.

Like his father, Laurence was accurate and uncompromising in his assessment of the products he publicized. There was no glossing over any of the features, good or bad. This sometimes embarrassed his employers and offended the manufacturers and after several changes in employment he was finally hired by a New York firm looking for someone to conduct a "Truth in Advertising" campaign that they were about to launch.

They found the right man in Laurence. As time went on, the original board of directors and members of the firm retired and were replaced by younger men with different ideas about advertising. They found Laurence's refusal to color fact with fancy a drawback to expanding business and so, at sixty, he was out of a job.

For the dog fancy and for Dachshunds this was a tremendous gain. He turned to writing as a livelihood. His spare time activities with Dachshunds and the Dachshund Club of America, his wide acceptance as a judge at dog shows and his general knowledge of the sport plus a real talent for research proved to be saleable material. His published critiques, lectures and writings have provided dog fanciers with a rich heritage that will continue on long after Laurence Horswell, 82 at this writing, has passed on.

He liked to illustrate his writings with graphs, charts and statistics. His diagram of a Dachshund in show pose has been widely distributed among individuals and regional Dachshund clubs. Many of these diagrams were wall-sized and are still in use. In a lighter vein he once designed a catalogue cover for the Dachshund Association of Long Island for one of its specialty shows held at Hicksville. It showed a map of the Island with Dachshunds romping over it toward Hicksville. The Association still uses it for the covers of its premium list and its catalogue. Only the date and show site have been changed.

156

The polo helmet was one of Mr. Horswell's identifying labels. He wore it all summer long to help him keep his cool. He is pictured here at the 1956 Specialty of the Dachshund Club of America (held with the Westchester Kennel Club show) at which he awarded Best of Breed to Ch. Steve v Marienlust, the last champion to be shown by the Marienlust Kennels. Peter Knoop, now an all-breed judge, was the handler.

A year later, Mr. Horswell again was a judge at the DCA Specialty held on the sun-baked fields of the Westchester show—and awarded Best of Variety in wires to Am. Can. & Mex. Ch. Tubac's Abner, owned and handled by Neville R. Stephens. Abner was the top winning wirehaired Dachshund in the United States for 1956 and 1957.

Horswell on Judging

When he began judging in 1934, Mr. Horswell kept notes on the dogs he judged and later transposed them onto cards for a permanent record. He soon tired of this time-consuming method and came up with his own original idea on the subject — judging cards. He marked them in the ring while looking at the dogs without delaying the judging and when his assignments were finished, he put them in his card files. One of the many uses of these judging cards was to trace the progress of the breed.

In an article in April 1940 issue of *Popular Dogs*, Mr. Horswell explained his use of the cards in judging Dachshunds at Westminster that year:

> For a long time I have wanted to make systematic notes on a number of Dachshunde sufficiently large for a subsequent analysis of the data to be representative of the present status of the breed. The notes of the German judges in 1937 and 1938 did not serve the purpose, as their notes for each dog usually contain only one essential: the "limiting fault" by which the dog is rated "*Ungenugend*", insufficient; "*Gut*", good; "*Sehr Gut*", very good; or, without which it could be rated "*Vorzuglich*", excellent.

> For my purpose it was necessary to be sure that notes were recorded of every significant deviation from a fair passing agreement with the standard, whether differentiated by superiority or by faultiness, and not just a selection of the most important fault and one or two compensating notes of praise.

> Working from notebooks used during previous judging engagements, I arranged on cards of convenient size, the names of the parts of the dog in an order easy to follow, primarily to save time otherwise required to write these words again and again, and secondarily as a check list to assist in systematic inspection of the dog.

> The four references to "running gear": Front, Back, Hindquarters, and Rear, have room for two notes each, (standing) and (moving).

> The armband numbers and initials to identify the class are filled in on the first line before the class is judged, and the exhibitor is asked to state the age of the entry. Each dog is placed on a firm table for close-up noting of teeth, eyes, ears, pigment, head, neck, feet, nails, coat, skin, proportion of shoulder blade to upper arm, extension of breast bone behind foreleg, quality of muscular development — all the details which must be inspected at close range or by touch.

Posture Judged on Floor

On the other hand, no notes are made involving posture of the dog while on the table, as many dogs are at a disadvantage at this unnatural height and will not pose with the confidence necessary to display their quality to advantage. Newspaper flashlights of winning dogs, hastily placed on a none-too-secure table, distracted by competitive photographers under pressure to meet deadlines, all too often record and promulgate likenesses unfair to the dog, the owner and the judge, but in the long run, most unfair to the breed.

The dog is then lowered to the floor where the grass matting gives him a firm footing, to stand unposed on slack leash for views from front, side and rear; and gaited fore, aft, and side for verification. Throughout this operation the exhibitor is given every opportunity to maneuver his dog into favorable position, encouraging him to advance by easy steps, and halt in show position; but if the exhibitor stoops to manipulate the dog by hand, any such posing is disregarded, and the dog advanced to a self-assumed pose before being noted. Similarly, if the first attempt to gait the dog is unsuccessful, a second and even third opportunity is given in order that the record may credit the dog with the best stance and gait of which he is capable.

After each dog has been noted, each class is gaited in a circle until first place can be assigned on over-all appearance, type, balance, performance and soundness, the cards being used only as supplementary references with respect to details of soundness not visible at that distance. After the best dog is assigned the first place, and its card so noted, the circle continues per dog. Considering that the level above which notes would be made for superiority was set at a fair passing agreement with the standard of perfection of the breed, it is encouraging to record that the average number of notes of superiority above that level averaged 1.5 per dog. The number of negative notes per dog averaged for smooths 3.8, longhairs 4, wirehairs 4.5 and miniatures 4.9. Without adjustment for "serious" or "minor" classification of the respective items, the number of such notations could be interpreted as indicating fair agreement with the standard, to the extent of an average of 86% of the items.

Statistical Analysis of Faults

Since the show, I have had an opportunity to tabulate the frequency of plus and minus notations item by item, and where some of the items are related to tabulate some of them in permutations and combinations.

The fault most frequently noted was upper arm shorter than shoulder blade, 45%; of which 33% were within the ratio of 4/3, and 12% had ratios up to 3/2 and 2/1. Faulty stance viewed from the front 37%, of which turned out feet represent 19%. Faulty gait from the front 42%.

However, further analysis of the data shows that of the 42% noted for faulty front gait, 11% were free from fault in front stance, another 10% free from fault in shoulder proportion, and in addition, 6% free from either; leaving only 15% of the total which combined faulty shoulder, faulty front stance and faulty front gait. Within this last 15%, however, appear nearly all of the dogs whose shoulder ratio was disproportionate to the extent of 3/2 or more. Amazing as it may seem, the number of Dachshunde which had creditable front gaits, and nevertheless a fault either in shoulder ratio or front stance, was 25% of the total, and no less than half a dozen individuals had structural faults in both and still were able to walk as straight as a chalk line.

From close observation of a number of Dachshunde of varying but unmistakable degrees of inclination to knuckle over, a conviction is growing that there is another factor which cannot be overlooked in this relationship. The forearm, extending almost vertically from elbow down to wrist, appears to have displacements which can best be described as "tortional" in the relation of the axis of the elbow joint to the axis of the joint composed of the combined small bones of the wrist. Considering these axes as if they were the pins of hinges attached to the upper and lower ends of the forearm, the properly constructed Dachshunde

159

No. _70_   Class _S&O red_

Age. _2 yr_   Color _red_

Teeth _✓_   Pigment _✓_

Eyes _⊂⊃_   Neck _X_

Ears _✓_   Skin _✓_

Head _X_   Coat _✓_

Feet _⊥⊥_   Shoulder _<_

Nails _✓_   Elbow _✓_

Fore _–_   Chest   After

        (standing)   (moving)

Front | | | | ·•

Backline _▬▬▬▬_   _▬▬_

Hindqtrs X   ∧   ∧

Rear | | | |

Loin _✓_   Bone _✓_

Tail _✓_   Type _X_

Cond'n _✓_   Temp'nt _X_

General

                                           _BV_

Rating _EX_   Placing _1 WD BW_

Show   Date

Judging cards, like this one, were part of Horswell's creative ideas on judging. The class is standard, Open dogs, red. Dog number 70 has its good qualities indicated by check marks, its excellent qualities by crosses. The oval in the "Eyes" notation indicates that the dog had the correct almond-shaped eye. A fault, flat feet, is also indicated by drawing. The marks opposite Placing indicate that the dog was Winners Dog, then Best of Winners, and on to Best of Variety.

160

has these hinge pins in parallel alignment, whereas individuals too frequently can be observed in which these axes are so rotated with respect to each other that when either is placed at right angles to the lengthwise axis of the body, the other is automatically forced out of alignment. Such a tortional displacement of the axes of these joints has been observed without interruption through series of four to six generations. That this fault frequently has been inherited simultaneously with a short upper arm should not distract from its significance or its importance.

Before leaving the forequarters, it should be noted that there were 26% flat front feet, many of these combined with turned out feet and spread toes; and that the number of elbows with too much play was 13%.

The faults in backline represented 31%; chests too short 12%, shallow 8%, too deep 2%; narrow or weedy, 14%, but of these such a share were in the large puppy classes where adult development would be abnormal, that this last figure must not be given undue significance.

Faulty rear gait was noted on 38% about evenly divided between gait too narrow, or walking with a "dancing" motion like tandem-coupled windshield wipers. The rear stance fault of cowhocks was noted on only 14%, greatly reduced in recent years; other structural hindquarter faults, steep, over-muscled, bowed legs, etc., 11%. Light eyes were noted 10% in smooths and wirehairs, 72% in longhairs; eyes improperly set in head, 9%, of which more than half were too prominent. Poor coat was noted to the extent of 16%, poor type 10%, skin with wrinkles 8%. Only 3% could be criticized for fit of teeth, and an equal number for all other teeth faults, including distemper, puppy teeth retained in adult dogs, teeth worn or broken, or tartar.

The number of heads with the notation of superior quality was 16%, compared with a total of 13% for combined faults of short, coarse, fine, domed, etc. Faults of ear or tail, including carriage, were below 5%.

So much for analysis of the notes. If another such opportunity is presented in years to come, it will be interesting to compare the percentages to see what trends may be disclosed.

Mr. Horswell did get to compare percentages. He judged the parent DCA Specialty in 1945 and again in 1956. Matching the cards from both assignments, he found that half the dogs he judged in 1945 had faults in angulation, shoulders and hindquarters, whereas in 1956 only one third of the entry had the same faults.

At the 1940 Westminster, Mr. Horswell had surprised by placing Ch. Helmar Flottenberg to Best of Variety over the immortal Ch. Herman Rinkton. His account of the judging is a very interesting exposition of what — in his mind — a judge should be looking for in the ring:

> There has been enough discussion of the decision for best smooth Dachshunde to suggest that readers may be interested in reasons for that placing.
> During 1938 I placed Herman Rinkton best Dachshunde at two shows, but at the Garden it did not appear that he approximated previous condition or perfor-

mance. Several of the dogs which came into the ring for best smooth Dachshunde had decisive advantages over him in structure, or condition, or gait, or combinations of these three factors. As the contest narrowed down, the problem was to select which of these, while under the scrutiny of judgment, gave the most consistent exhibition of winning quality. Factors of structure and condition do not change during the time that a dog is under judgment, nor are they subject to the dog's mood or the skill of the exhibitor. In matters of posture and gait I believe a dog should be judged, not on instantaneous or accidental faulty position unless repetition confirms it as habitual, but rather upon its best consistent performance. Knowing that whatever the outcome, it would be impossible that there should be unanimous approval, I kept Herman in the ring until the end, in order that competent and unprejudiced observers, free from the psychology of hero worship or other emotional reactions, might have adequate opportunity to record their impressions of the significant differences which outweighed Herman's always popular showmanship.

For instance, when Hanko Flottenberg first stood down from the table, he presented a picture anyone would find hard to fault in any particular — later, he carried his back high, standing and walking; Heidi Flottenberg in spite of the handicap of an underline showing the effects of recent maternal duties, presented a preponderance of agreement with the standard, but at critical moments, stood with her hind feet too far forward under her body for her backline to remain level.

Faults of posture, such as these, come and go from moment to moment, and the dog which improves as the final decision is made, becomes the winner. Helmar Flottenberg excels in bone and substance. Compared with his final competitor his stance in front and rear is equal. His type and balance were distinctly the better. His rather heavy coat for a smooth Dachshunde somewhat obscured his muscular development which is hard as iron without being muscle-bound or over-muscled. When he was gaited his hindquarters did not at first hit their stride. But in the final and decisive comparison, when the field was narrowed down to only two contestants, in three parallel trips the length of the ring and back, Herman's gait never straightened out in front or behind, and Helmar's gait never broke or wavered for a single step.

While he and Dorothy never bred their chocolate Dachshund, Martha, they did decide to breed a bitch that they had shown to championship. It was a highly successful mating. Three of the litter made their championships and their mother went on to place in the ribbons at Dachshund field trials for the first twelve years during which the trials were held.

Raising a litter of pups in a New York City apartment is not a good idea. Like many enthusiastic dog owners before them, Laurence and Dorothy decided that once was enough and thereafter they contented themselves with treating their Dachshunds as house dogs. This did not stop them from vigorously pursuing their interest in the breed. Together they wrote *The Pet Dachshund* which sold 65,000 copies. It is now out of print.

Recognition of his abilities came early in Laurence's career. In 1945, The Gaines Dog Research Center inaugurated its "Fido" awards to be given to

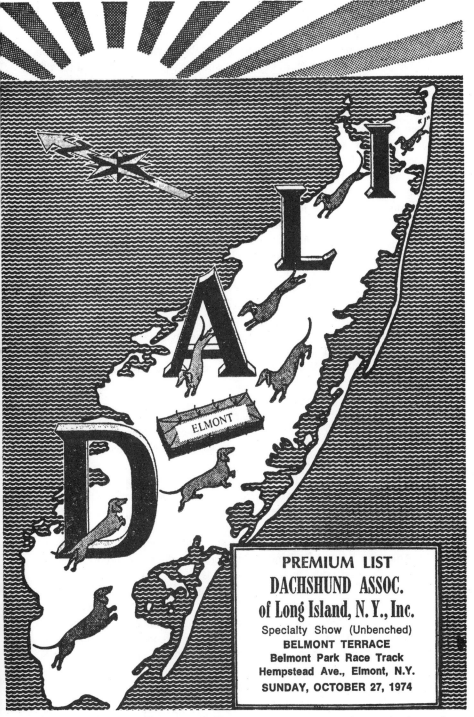

PREMIUM LIST
DACHSHUND ASSOC.
of Long Island, N.Y., Inc.
Specialty Show (Unbenched)
BELMONT TERRACE
Belmont Park Race Track
Hempstead Ave., Elmont, N.Y.
SUNDAY, OCTOBER 27, 1974

Cover for the premium list and catalog of the Dachshund Association of Long Island annual specialty, designed by Laurence Horswell in the 1960s, and still being used—only the date and location have had to be changed.

prominent contributors to the dog world. These awards were made by balloting a wide section of breeders, veterinarians, breed clubs, dog show officials and the press. Laurence won it that year and became the first to hold the title "Dogdom's Man of the Year." In 1963 he won the "Dog Writer of the Year" award from the Dog Writers Association of America.

The Dachshund Club of America made him an honorary life member and fifteen regional Dachshund clubs gave him the same title. The latest was the Connecticut Yankee Dachshund Club in 1975. I visited him at the nursing home in New Jersey shortly after the letter telling him of the Connecticut club's award reached him. He was very pleased. The letter was propped up on his nightstand where he was able to reread it often.

During the late 1960s Rachel Page Elliott began a book on motion in dogs. Horswell had done considerable research on the subject and Mrs. Elliott consulted him on some of the material. While the book was still in the making, the Professional Handlers Association learned about it. They asked Mrs. Elliott and Laurence if they would present it in lecture form at their 1967 Educational Conference at Gaithersburg, Maryland.

They did, complete with Laurence's cherished slides, plus more slides and movies done by Mrs. Elliott. Later they gave the same lecture at one of the Dog Fanciers' Luncheon Club meetings at the Overseas Press Club in New York. Mrs. Elliott titled the completed book "Dogsteps." It was published in 1963 and won the Dog Writers Association of America's award for that year.

One of the high points of Laurence's judging was that of the Dachshund Club of America's Golden Jubilee Specialty Show in 1945 at the Hotel Pennsylvania in New York. He needed all the strength he inherited from his pioneer forebears for the task.

It began the day before the show where Laurence was the guest speaker at the Club's banquet. Naturally his speech was accompanied by color slides and the whole affair lasted well after midnight. The next day he judged an entry of 250 dogs, a record entry for any Dachshund specialty at that time.

This included all three coats and both standard and miniature Dachshunds. The American Kennel Club now considers 175 dogs per day the absolute maximum that one judge can handle.

Dorothy Horswell shared Laurence's enthusiasm for Dachshunds and dog shows. A Wellesley Graduate, an avid reader (about 100 books a year according to her close friends) and a witty conversationalist, her presence at the ringside during his judging assignments brought her in contact with most of the Dachshund exhibitors in the country. Many of them became her close friends. Like many spectators, she indulged in ringside judging and frequently discussed her opinions with Laurence when his judging was finished. As a result of these discussions Laurence encouraged her to apply for a judging license. She did and in 1950 she had her first assignment. It was the Westbury Kennel

Club all breed show at Old Westbury, Long Island. The Dachshund entry was 119 dogs, one of the largest single breed entries at the show. Laurence recollects that she judged 30 shows from 1950 through 1966, passing judgment on 2,000 dogs. Failing health put an end to her show-going activities and she died in 1968.

During the time both were judging, the Horswells went to great lengths to avoid influencing each other's decisions.

Mrs. Lester Fox of Le-Dor Miniature Dachshund Kennels at Baldwin, Long Island, shares with me the memory of two shows in Cleveland where Laurence judged a Saturday specialty at the Central Armory and Dorothy judged the Dachshund classes at the all-breeds show the next day. The shows were the Reserve Dachshund specialty on March 31, 1962 and the Western Reserve all-breeds show (which that year was unable to use its regular show site, the Public Auditorium, and was moved to the Arena, a group of public buildings built for spectator sports). The temporary location at this show left much to be desired as a site for dog shows. Here, in Laurence's own words, is what happened:

> When Dorothy and I accepted the invitations to judge these two large overlapping entries of Dachshunds on successive days, we decided to test, objectively, how closely or widely our interpretations of the standard would be.
>
> She did not get into Cleveland from our home in Flushing, Long Island, until Saturday night. The Western Reserve Club had reserved a room for her at a motel near the Arena and she spent the evening at the Club's buffet dinner.
>
> Sunday morning I judged several other breeds at the opposite end of the Arena and not until she was more than half way through the judging did I get to the Dachshund ring. There Dave and Ray Thomas, working at the trophy table away from the ring, told me that my wife's choice for Best of Variety and Best of Opposite Sex in longhaired Dachshunds, had coincided with mine.

Laurence, who had spent the night at the Auditorium Hotel and had been guest speaker at the after-show dinner there, settled back in his ringside seat to watch the rest of his wife's judging. Mrs. Horswell repeated five of the six top awards that her husband had made the previous day. Laurence concluded that their long association with Dachshunds and ringside discussions at dog shows for more than 30 years had brought their interpretations of the standard into substantial agreement.

At right, Maria Mehrer. Below, Josef Mehrer showing Ch. Success v Marienlust, who was finished to championship in 1953 with four majors. Success was the last of the Marienlust dogs personally handled to championship by Josef.

The Josef Mehrers

T HE JOSEF MEHRERS were probably the most dedicated and skillful Dachshund breeders to appear in America within recent years. Breeders of the greatest producing sire of any Dachshund variety, knowledgable in their analysis of the results of their breeding program and with what amounted to almost genius for selecting the most productive sires and dams, their "Marienlust" suffix is in the pedigree of many of today's best Dachshunds.

Coupled with all this talent was a set of circumstances beyond their control which put them in the right place at the right time. Bear with me while I look back at the extraordinary events that helped to boost them to fame.

World War I had ended. Tired and discouraged young men from the defeated German Army, discontent with the unemployment and general confusion that plagued the Fatherland, were packing up their possessions and coming, with their families, to America. Josef Mehrer, weakened by food poisoning from his wartime service and his wife, Maria, were among them. It was 1923. The language barrier and the fact that many of them had known very little employment outside of their army training, put them into the low pay, unskilled labor force. They tried to supplement their wages by extra work.

In this group were some of the men and officers from the famous German War Dog patrols and training centers. Some brought with them their beautifully trained German Shepherd Dogs and Doberman Pinschers that had served with them in the Army.

Some of the lucky ones found employment in American kennels, well below their abilities as trainers, but financially profitable until they could afford their own training and boarding kennels. Others snatched at the first job available and kept their dogs as house dogs. American veterans seeing their dogs in their neighborhoods and remembering the performance of these German dogs in wartime, sometimes asked their owners to display some of the things the dogs had been taught. In no time exhibitions of attack work, for a small fee, became a way of bringing in a little extra money. It proved to be a two-edged sword. People were at once attracted and repelled by these exhibitions of what seemed to them savagery. The American public knew dogs only as pets, show

167

dogs or hunters. Obedience training was unknown and these audiences were unable to grasp the skill and control with which the dogs were handled. They saw only the swift, frightening violence of the attack and the raw animal power of the dogs.

I witnessed one such performance as a small child. The memory of it is as clear and disturbing today as it was many years ago when my grandfather took me to a small park in Hoboken, New Jersey, one noontime. My grandfather who shared and understood my passion for dogs and horses, explained that we were about to see a beautiful dog trained better than anything I had ever seen in a circus. I sat down beside him on the park bench in happy anticipation. The noon whistle blew and workers from a nearby factory, clutching their lunch pails, came over to the park to eat and relax. Among them were two thin young men with a German Shepherd Dog on leash walking between them. I had never seen a German Shepherd and like my grandfather, I thrilled at the sight of this powerful graceful dog gliding through the crowd of shuffling workmen. Now and then the dog would turn, tail wagging, and look at its master with such obvious pleasure and devotion that we were all charmed. Several of the men touched it as it passed them and I asked my grandfather if I too, could pat the dog. At my grandfather's request, the young man willingly permitted it. The dog's head was level with mine and as I approached it, its eyes looked past me at its master. I put my hand on its neck and felt the rock-hard muscles under the soft fur. It was like touching a furry stone.

The man's companion asked us to form a large circle and to please be quiet. He stepped back and dog and master had the ring to themselves. First came a demonstration, off leash, of jumping over park benches, crawling under them, sitting, staying, coming on command, refusing food from the crowd, all done with the master standing well away from the dog and sometimes only giving hand signals rather than a spoken word. We were all spellbound. It seemed like magic. The performance ended with a bow from dog and master but it seemed there was more to come.

The second man reappeared in the ring. This time his one arm was covered with a straw filled burlap bag and the hand that protruded from it held a pistol! I was suddenly afraid for the beautiful dog. Were they going to hurt him? I turned to look at him as he sat quietly at his master's side.

Something seemed to be happening to him. He was tense, quivering; his front paws shifted nervously and his eyes no longer looked at his master but stared at the approaching man with the pistol. Suddenly the man raised the burlap covered arm as if to aim the gun at dog and master. The dog exploded into action.

Hurling himself at the man with jaws wide open, he grabbed the upraised arm with such force that the man was knocked to the ground and the pistol fell from his hand. Growling fiercely, the dog continued to hang onto the arm with such violence that the man's whole body was tossed about like a rag doll on the grass.

168

His master uttered a word and instantly the dog let go and stood quietly over the man's prone body. The master picked up the gun, helped his companion to his feet and motioned him to walk forward in front of him. The man did as he was told. All at once he began to run as if to escape. Instantly the dog was on him again but as soon as the man stopped, the dog released him and stood watchfully beside him.

The master came up and put on the dog's leash. His companion removed the burlap bag from his arm and both of them laughed and petted the dog, who reverted to almost puppylike glee at this praise. All three bowed and the young men passed their hats for whatever money the crowd wanted to donate for the performance. Then they went back to the factory entrance, sat down on the steps and ate their lunches which they shared with the dog. As the workers walked past them into the building they gave the dog a wide berth. Nobody tried to touch him. I felt that I had seen an evil beauty, one to be more feared than admired.

Performances like these were common all over the country and did immeasurable harm to the German Shepherd Dog and Doberman Pinscher breeds in America. In spite of overwhelming evidence to the contrary, a large segment of the public still believes that these beautiful, versatile dogs are savage killers, not to be trusted.

The Mehrers were shocked at this turn of events. They loved German Shepherds. Josef had given Maria a Shepherd puppy during their courting days. "He wouldn't marry me until he was sure that I loved dogs as much as he did," she once told me laughingly. They had talked about raising a litter of Shepherds when their finances would permit it. They had found a place to live on Long Island. Josef had a job of sorts and Maria opened a boarding kennel to supplement his income. Josef spent most of his spare time working in the kennel.

The immaculate kennel so near New York City, run by the young couple who loved dogs and were so expert in their care, attracted the attention of wealthy New York and Long Island dog owners and soon Josef was able to give up his job and devote full time to the boarding kennel.

Thrifty, shrewd and practical, Josef and Maria saw no future in breeding German Shepherds. The undeserved reputation for viciousness and the exploitation of the breed as "guard dogs" presented a very limited market. On the other hand, another German breed, the Dachshund, was being widely accepted by the American public as house pets.

American soldiers brought them home from Germany by the hundreds. Most of them were not concerned with registrations or show quality; they were enchanted with these gay little dogs that fitted so happily into American family life. Comic strip artists added to this pleasant presentation of the Dachshund by showing the dogs as engaging, mischievous clowns that accompanied their comic strip characters. Now that the war was over, the persecution of American Dachshund owners and their dogs ceased and Dachshunds gained in popularity as pets.

Some of these Dachshund owners brought their dogs to the Mehrers for boarding. Josef was worried at the poor quality of a breed he knew so well. From childhood he had been familiar with the breed and while he may not have known personally many of the great German breeders, mostly wealthy sportsmen and aristocrats with large hunting preserves, he had haunted dog shows for years and had seen top specimens of the breed walking the city streets where wealthy Germans vied with each other in owning show winners. He had formed in his own mind a mental picture of a perfect Dachshund and knew, from memory, the pedigrees of many German winners.

Blunt and outspoken, he criticized his customers' dogs, but along with the criticism he made suggestions as to how and where better dogs could be found. Many of his customers followed his advice and soon he was importing and breeding good quality dogs with their pedigrees carefully handwritten by Maria. These handwritten pedigrees were a trademark of the Mehrers. Every one was the loving end result of the Mehrers' dedication to the breed. Maria could never bring herself to use a typewriter for this final seal of their guarantee of good quality.

While all this was going on, German artists, singers, musicians, stage and motion picture stars, directors and deposed nobility were coming to America. These people knew a good Dachshund when they saw one and they began to see them at the homes of their American friends. More often than not, they found these dogs came from the Mehrers' kennels, so, when they wanted a Dachshund for themselves they made the trip to Long Island to own, once more, a beloved Dachshund and to hear again in a strange land the language of the Fatherland.

At the same time American theatre stars were discovering Great Neck on the North Shore of Long Island as the "in" place to live. From Madame Alda to Eddie Cantor they bought and built handsome estates and beautiful residences right in between the greatest market for their talents, New York City, and the greatest monetary source of support for the arts, the millionaire families of Old Westbury. To own a Dachshund, like those of their internationally famous contemporaries became a status symbol which quickly developed into a genuine affection for the little dogs. Owning and showing a Dachshund was also another chance to appear in public, off stage with plenty of photographers around to see that they appeared sometimes twice in the same paper, on the same day, once in the theatre section and again on the sports page.

In 1936, the Mehrers decided to move from Flushing to a less crowded suburb of New York. They chose a corner plot in the unfashionable town of West Hempstead, Long Island. It was about 30 miles from New York and about 10 miles in either direction from both Great Neck and Old Westbury, right smack in the middle of their greatest market for boarding dogs and selling top quality Dachshunds. Their future seemed secure at last.

They now had the opportunity and the means to breed the ideal Dachshund. By the time the theatre set had deserted Great Neck and New York for Hollywood, and the millionaires of Old Westbury were selling their estates for real estate developments, the Mehrers were established as one of America's leading breeders of Dachshunds.

They still kept their boarding kennels. Josef made one restriction, no Irish Setters. The big red dogs seemed to have an uncanny ability to open kennel gates and climb eight foot fences. After chasing their charges desperately over the Hempstead plains, Josef and Maria admitted defeat.

All this does not alter the fact that Josef and Maria Mehrer worked hard to attain their success. The well-run kennel was no accident. Before they opened it they had gone to a school for dog grooming and kennel operation. This newly acquired schooling plus their own knowledge and affection for dogs made their Marienlust Kennel and its operation outstanding even in an area where the best gamekeepers and professional dog handlers from Great Britain and the continent of Europe were being imported by Long Island estate owners to care for their show stock.

At first the Mehrers thought of raising Terriers. Josef was fond of Welsh Terriers and even had a few of his own in the kennels but Maria wanted a Dachshund so Josef, looking for quality right at the start, went to Anton Kappelmier, whose Wittelbach Kennels in New York City were known for good domestic and German dogs. He bought a bitch puppy which they named Friede of Marienlust, the first Dachshund to bear the Marienlust name. (Marienlust translates as ''Maria's happiness.'')

Now came the task of what was to be a lifetime work — studying pedigrees and looking at Dachshunds to select the right pair for breeding. Josef had seen a good imported German male, Arri von Luitpoldsheim, which had been brought over, along with a female, for breeding and showing by Mr. and Mrs. William Z. Breed. The Breeds were Boxer exhibitors but on their trips to Germany they had become intrigued with Dachshunds and bought a pair for show and breeding purposes. Josef arranged a breeding of Friede to Arri. The result was Zep von Marienlust, who was to sire eleven champions during his lifetime and become one of the founders of the Marienlust line. Poor Arri did not fare so well. It was the first and last time he ever sired a litter outside the Breeds' kennel. In one of those unpredictable kennel accidents both Arri and his kennelmate were killed by the Boxers.

Pleased with Zep's quality, Josef and Maria looked about for a suitable mate.

About that time their good friend, Louis Flecher, decided to take a trip to Germany. Flecher was a chef at the Lido, a well known Long Island club with a fine restaurant. In the winter, Flecher was chef at an equally posh restaurant in Florida and when he went South, he boarded his Dachshunds with the

Certified Pedigree

of

Günther v. Marienlust

SELLER Mr. & Mrs. J. Mehrer	**BREED** Dachshund **COLOR** red		**SEX** male
ADDRESS OF SELLER West hempstead L.I.	**DATE WHELPED** Aug. 10/39 **REG. No. (If registered)** A 35848.		

PARENTS	GRANDPARENTS	GREAT GRANDPARENTS	GR. GR. GRANDPARENTS
		Arri v. Luitpoldsheim	ERWIN von Luitpoldsheim
	Champ. Zep von Marienlust		FREYA von Luitpoldsheim
		Friede of Marienlust	Ch. Felix v. Wittelbach
Champ. Leutnant v. Marienlust			JANE von Wittelbach
		Hansi v. Holzgarten	Cito von Adlerschroffen
	Champ. Senta v. Luitpoldsheim		Coely von Westhoff
		Herta v. Luitpoldsheim	Erwin von Luitpoldsheim
			FREYA von Luitpoldsheim
		Bavschle v. Adlerschroffen	Rotfink Schneid – Suchen Siege
	Champ. Cid v. Werderhavelstrand		FERNA von Luitpoldsheim
		Sascha v. Werderhavelstrand	Rotfink Schneid – Suchen Siege
			KATERL von Werderhavelstrand
Moya von Marienlust		Ch. Felix v. Wittelbach	Champ. Held v. Erlbachtal
	Friede of Marienlust		Wittelbach Dora
		JANE v. Wittelbach	FAUST von Falltor
			Gloria von Wittelbach

Pedigree of Ch. Gunther v Marienlust in Maria Mehrer's writing. The handwritten pedigrees were a trademark of the Mehrer Kennels.

172

Mehrers. The two families had become friends and Flecher shared Josef's knowledge and enthusiasm for good Dachshunds. Josef asked that Flecher, while he was in Germany, buy him the winner of the Senior Puppy Bitch class at the Reichssieger Show which was being held at Cologne. Louis brought him Ilka v Holzgarten. She had won deservedly. Josef was delighted with the beautiful elegant prize-winner. Flecher had bought himself the second place winner of the same class, Senta v Luitpoldshiem. She was heavier and more robust than Ilka but she carried the Holzgarten line through her sire, Hansi v Holzgarten and the Luitpoldshiem line through her dam, Hetta v Luitpoldshiem. Louis Flecher felt that he had the best of two well-known German kennels and he had kept his promise to Joe to bring him back the winner. He was well pleased with second best. Leaving the dogs with Joe, he departed on his annual trip to Florida.

Looking at the pedigrees of the two bitches, Josef chose Senta as a mate to Zep. He arranged to lease Senta from Flecher. The litter of four produced three champions. One, Leutnant v Marienlust, sired 36 champions in nine years and his name is still found in the pedigrees of many of today's winners.

Josef then bred Ilka to Leutnant and kept a bitch from the mating, Vera v Marienlust. He bred Vera back to the Holzgarten line through Theo v Holzgarten. This mating produced Bruce v Marienlust. Bruce was then bred to a granddaughter of Leutnant, Melinda v Marienlust. The pair produced Favorite v Marienlust, described by one man who saw him as a puppy "a veritable atom bomb of a Dachshund." Favorite became the sire of the greatest number of Dachshund champions in America.

This combination of the best of American and German lines became a trademark of Josef's skill as a breeder. He ignored the common practice of "breeding a good one to a good one" favored by some of the gamekeepers and kennel men in Old Westbury. Every pedigree was thoroughly researched. Every pair selected for breeding were personally inspected by Josef who insisted on seeing not only the dogs, but their get. He traveled all over the United States and made frequent trips to Germany to see for himself what the dogs looked like before he made his final decision about breeding. Maria recalls that even during his last illness he would wake her on nights when he couldn't sleep and together they would get out the records and pedigrees and Josef would make up a five generation pedigree on the dogs he was considering for breeding. Sometimes he felt it was right. More often than not he would decide against it. Even in the hospital in the months preceding his death he kept putting pedigrees together.

Mrs. George (Dorothy) Pickett, a Dachshund breeder who came to know the Mehrers well, believes that there was more to it than skill and personal observation. "Josef had a quality of almost genius for selecting the right animals for breeding," she said. "He would look at a litter of four or five month old puppies and after he had selected those he thought would make their championships, he would say, 'This is the one to use for breeding.' He was invariably right.''

When it came to ideas on the right way to breed and show Dachshunds, Josef was firm and uncompromising. He kept his breeding kennel small. There were never more than six bitches at one time and he and Maria never raised a great many dogs. He wanted bitches that produced small litters. If a bitch had seven or eight pups, he would wait a year and then breed her again. If she still produced a large litter he would sell her. He was against the practice of taking some pups away from the mother so that she would not be weakened by nursing so many puppies. He believed it was already too late — that the mother's strength had already been depleted by the development of the pups within her body.

He was utterly sincere in wanting to make good studs available to Dachshund breeders and never charged more than $50. for a stud fee. Even during the 1940s and '50s it was a very reasonable figure.

Neither he nor Maria ever tried to choose good puppies until they were four or five months old. Younger puppies, they decided, were apt to grow unevenly; the shapes of their mouths and their bites were not fully developed at six or eight weeks and disposition, always an important factor in a show dog, was more readily apparent at four to five months.

He was equally strict in his ideas about showing. He always showed his own dogs. It was his pleasure and he didn't want another person or a handler to deprive him of it. There was one exception. During his last illness, while he was in the hospital, Peter Knoop, a Long Islander and at that time a professional handler, took a red Dachshund, Steve v Marienlust, to the Dachshund Club of America's Specialty show held in conjunction with the Westchester Kennel Club's all breed event in September of 1956. Steve finished his championship that day and took Best of Breed. The judge was Laurence Horswell.

If Josef had been awarded major points at a show he never showed that dog under the particular judge again. He felt it was unfair to the judge. He never showed a dog in the Specials class after it had finished its championship and never showed in the Hound Group. Once the dog had completed its championship, he never showed it again. There were reasons for this. He was not interested in comparing his dogs with those of other Hound breeds and since he had sold a number of good Dachshunds to people who were aiming at Group and Best in Show honors, he did not want to compete with them.

He felt that twenty months was early enough to start a dog on its show career. Until then it was not likely to be fully mature and had not had time to build up resistance to contagion to which all dogs are exposed at crowded dog shows. In spite of these precautions his kennels were depleted twice by epidemics.

Josef Mehrer died in 1956. True to his code, Maria never showed Steve again. But she did not keep her promise to Josef that she would stop breeding Dachshunds after his death.

To continue the work they both loved was a comfort to her and so, with the help of Bill Thompson, their faithful kennel man, who had helped Maria nurse Josef until hospital treatment was the only help left, she continued to operate both Marienlust Dachshund kennels and the boarding kennels until her death, at 69, in October of 1965.

When the estate was finally settled, most of the Marienlust Dachshunds, including the now aging Steve, were taken over by their good friends, Dr. and Mrs. George Pickett.

Best of Breed at the first independent specialty held by the Dachshund Club of America on May 6, 1934, was the German import standard smooth, Ch. Held vom Erlbachtal, bred by F. M. Wiedemann and owned by Mrs. Gussie Held of Jersey City. The judge was veteran breeder Mrs. C. Davies Tainter, and there were 204 Dachshunds entered.

Drawing from the cover for the booklet on German show dog rules and regulations emphasizes the Dachshund in its field capacity.

The Dachshund Club
of America

THE DACHSHUND CLUB OF AMERICA was organized in 1895 and is the eighth oldest breed club to become a member of the American Kennel Club. There were, of course, Dachshunds in America before that date. Eleven were registered between 1879 and 1885 and the organization was formed because of Dachshund breeders' concern over the breed's growing popularity. They must have felt a need for some sort of regulatory group.

The Club's first president was Harry Peters, Sr., and the Club was incorporated in New York in 1932.

Its first independent Dachshund Specialty was held on May 6, 1934 at Greenwich, Conn. It drew an entry of 204 Dachshunds, a record for any single breed event at that time and the judge was Mrs. C. Davies Tainter, whose Voewood Kennels was among the country's best. The Best of Breed was Held v Erlbachtal, a smooth black and tan owned by Mrs. Gussie Held.

From 1936 through 1941, the Club's Specialty was held in conjunction with the Morris and Essex Kennel Club at Madison, N.J. German judges drew big entries at these events. Herr Marquand judged 276 Dachshunds and Herr Heinrich Stroh drew an entry of 311 dogs.

The earliest independent regional Specialty show was held in California in 1932. It was the first independent licensed Dachshund Specialty ever held in America. The Best of Breed was an English import, Int. Ch. Kensal's Call Boy, owned by Mrs. Grayce Greenburg. The judge was John Sinnott and the show-giving club was the West Coast Dachshund Club, which later became the Dachshund Club of California.

With the cancellation of the Morris and Essex show, the Club held annual independent Specialties in New York City on the day preceding the Westminster Kennel Club's all breed show.

In 1960, at the DCA annual meeting, which was usually held on the day of the Specialty (either during the lunch break or after the judging), members

177

Scene from the Walt Disney movie of "The Ugly Dachshund", G. B. Sterne's classic story of the Great Dane who believed himself to be a Dachshund. This photo gives hint of the sights possible when—as they were until 1929—Dachshunds were shown in the Working Group. Then, for a period of about two years, Dachshunds were shown in the Sporting Group, and since 1931 in the Hound Group. It was not until 1943, however, that Best of Variety was established for each coat and that the long-haired and wirehaired winners went into the Group finals along with the smooth.

voted to alternate the location of the Specialty between New York and other parts of the country. One of the largest of these was held in 1963 at Del Monte, California, when Mrs. Ramona (Van Court) Jones and John H. Cook divided a judging assignment of 314 Dachshunds between them.

The Club weathered many storms. Arguments and firm convictions on the part of highly individualized and dedicated breeders are a healthy sign in most dog clubs. The most serious and disruptive in the DCA have been the controversy over the conduct of the Dachshund field trials in the 1930s, which cost the club a temporary loss of some of its most substantial members and the argument over whether or not Miniature Dachshunds should become a separate variety, which occurred in 1951. Tempers flared as supporters of the plan openly accused the directors of the DCA of interference with their efforts. (These controversies are discussed in greater depth in the chapters on Field Trials and The Miniature Dachshund Clubs.)

An indication of the Club's current growth, solidarity and maturity is illustrated by its latest undertaking. It has appointed a committee and approved funds to research the disc problem in Dachshunds. While this problem is more prevalent in Dachshunds than in other breeds, it is by no means limited to them and the results of this effort should benefit all dogs from the show winner to the house pet.

Dorothy Hardy in 1953, handling Primrose Patch Tiny Teckel, miniature longhaired owned by Mrs. Peter van Brunt, to Best of Winners at the DALI Specialty. —*Shafer*

Dorothy Hardy in 1966, handling German import wirehaired miniature, Elfie von der Lonsheide, owned by Fred Doell, to Best Miniature in Show at the Metropolitan Washington Specialty under judge Norman Lough. —*Bushman*

The Miniature
Dachshund Clubs

THE ORIGIN of the American Miniature Dachshund Association tion is the story of an enthusiastic group of people who possessed a great knowledge of Dachshunds but saw only one narrow point of view and looked no further. More careful consideration of the problem as it related to the sport as a whole, and more careful study of the American Kennel Club's policies regarding breed changes, would have spared them the bitter disappointment and the divisive results among breeders that time has finally healed. Elsewhere in this book I've urged novice exhibitors to read the rules to familiarize themselves with the sport as a whole before entering the ring with their Dachshunds. The founders of the American Miniature Dachshund Association were no novices, but they were shortsighted and naive in their belief that the American Kennel Club would grant their request simply because a sizeable and organized group requested it.

The ebullient Grayce Greenburg, at that time editor of *The American Dachshund,* was one of the originators of the idea of having Miniature Dachshunds classified as a separate variety. Mrs. Greenburg had acquired some smooth Miniature Dachshunds in 1948. The following year, she and Mr. W.W. Giles and a number of other Miniature breeders formed the American Miniature Dachshund Association. It was incorporated in New York in July of 1950.

Its constitution stated that one of its main purposes was "to seek changes in the AKC-approved standard of the Dachshund so that the Miniature Dachshund will have a separate standard and classification of its own."

Mrs. Greenburg gave the separate variety movement full exposure in the magazine. Every issue contained letters from exhibitors, judges, breeders, pet owners and just breed enthusiasts who favored the idea. It was a high pressure campaign worthy of a politician running for office. Mr. Giles, Mrs. Greenburg and the others were convinced that all they had to do to win the American Kennel Club's approval was to organize Miniature Dachshund owners and present their plan.

In 1951, the Dachshund Club of America asked Mr. Giles, who was chairman of its Miniature Dachshund committee as well as a director of the American Miniature Dachshund Association, to make a survey and get opinions, pro and con. The survey indicated that Dachshund owners were in favor of a separate variety for Miniatures; that they wanted them to be judged in the Toy group; that they would set a weight limit of nine pounds and that they wanted a separate parent club. Dr. Lyman Fisher, then president of the DCA, forwarded the survey to the American Kennel Club. Backers of the separate variety movement believed that the AKC would routinely accede to their request.

It did not. The letter from John C. Neff, then executive Vice-President of the AKC, to Dr. Fisher rejecting the proposal was a masterpiece of diplomatic wording and sound reasoning. I have quoted most of it here:

> The expressed desire of a substantial number of Dachshund breeders and exhibitors for a separate show classification for dogs which, when mature would weigh 9 pounds or less is, in itself, I fear, not sufficient reason for taking such a step. As we all know, the modern quest for points would find many exhibitors interested in more and more separation by weight, by height or by color, which would make exhibiting more productive pointwise. Such interest cannot in itself be considered a tenable position from which to advocate a new separation as it clearly would contribute nothing to breed improvement — would, in fact, in most cases lead to breed impairment.
>
> Nor would the contention that the 'Miniature' is handicapped when shown against the 'Standard' be a convincing reason for a separate variety — unless it is also contended that the quality of the former approximates that of the latter but that a judicial prejudice exists which frequently produces unfair results.

Mr. Neff went on to say that the Dachshund already had three varieties, highest number for any breed, and that the creation of a special variety for Miniature Dachshunds would make a fourth and quite probably result in six varieties for the breed since Miniatures would be entitled to compete in all three coats just as the Standards. He continued:

> It is assured that the interest in a separate variety for Miniatures cannot be assigned to either of these two causes; some real practical difficulties still must be faced and overcome. Your organization's assistance in working toward a solution of these difficulties is solicited, as I have said. Following are some particular problems to which study might be given:
>
> Since a variety (in whose winners class points are awarded) may offer competition in all six of the regular official classes (puppy, novice, bred-by-exhibitor, American-bred, open and winners) what definition can be established for the Miniature Dachshund which will give assurance that nothing but Miniature Dachshunds will compete in these classes? Can it be said that a Miniature Dachshund is one that weighs no more than so many pounds, stands no more

than so many inches at six months, at nine months, at twelve months, at a later date? Or, as has been suggested, could it be said that mature dogs are not to go above a certain height and weight limit and that younger dogs will be considered to be Miniatures if their parents become 'recorded' as being Miniature when mature? No facilities exist for obtaining and maintaining such records. It is clear some major rule changes (which now apply uniformly to all the 111 breeds) would have to be prepared to meet the particular problems presented here. In those breeds where variety separation exists, interbreeding between varieties is allowable even when variety groups are involved. An example is the Poodle. Poodles are Poodles so far as the stud book is concerned; show requirements or limitations as to size are entirely unrelated to registration procedures. If we are to assume that this problem could in some way be met, we would then be confronted with problems such as these:

Is the Miniature Dachshund stabilized so that a reasonably good specimen (with the currently accepted weight limit of nine pounds) may be expected from breeding Miniatures without recourse to an occasional breeding to a Standard to regain quality which may be lost in the search for small size? If the Miniature is not thus established, the plan as suggested in the preceding paragraph (to recognize Miniatures on the basis of 'recorded' status of the parents) would lead straight to retrogression simply because the needed quality of the Standard would be unobtainable.

The present rules applying to determining heights and weights at a show would be quite inadequate. They allow for an official determination of a dog's height and weight upon application at the show, but before the judging. Doubtless it would be little practiced, but exhibitors would demand assurance that no loop-holes in the rules would permit an unscrupulous exhibitor to dehydrate or withhold food from a dog near the weight limit prior to an early morning weighing, followed promptly by corrective measures before the dog enters the ring. Dealing as we are with very small weights and heights, an actual weighing and measuring of all entries at the ring would be an indicated solution. While this is common practice in Europe, American exhibitors have shown a dislike for such procedures. If such a plan were adopted, it might be predicted that exhibitors themselves would in a short time completely nullify the plan. They would consider it unsporting to question the representation made by an exhibitor on his entry form and even if the procedures of weighing and measuring all entries at the ring were adopted, the practice might quickly become superficial.

We doubt whether those who advocate a separate variety for Miniatures have fully realized the problem involved. Unless you can provide a solution not yet apparent to us, it would seem that several really major rule changes prepared specifically for your breed would be necessary to establish safeguards.

As I have said to you, our minds are not closed on this subject. It does look formidable from a practical standpoint. I cannot close this letter without again raising the question as to what is best for the Miniature Dachshund itself. Will the dog improve under a plan for variety separation? May it not improve faster and more surely if it continues to compete in the winners class against Standards by means of a special open class for mature dogs of nine pounds and under?

When these dogs start defeating Standard dogs in the winner's class, when Miniatures bred to Miniatures quite regularly produce Miniatures which can do that, then the question of defining a Miniature will no longer be a problem such as it is today. The need for special legislation and safeguards will have disappeared. The dog will have defined itself.

Amazed and angry at this turn of events, Mr. Giles and other members of the AMDA accused Laurence Horswell and others in the Dachshund Club of America of everything from foot dragging to outright opposition to their movement. A number of East Coast breeders, among them Mrs. William Burr Hill, who was also secretary of the DCA, were disturbed by Mr. Giles' forceful writings and talks. They resigned from the AMDA and formed the National Miniature Dachshund Club. This new club avoided the issue and simply stated that it was dedicated to the improvement of the Miniature Dachshund.

Miniature breeding suffered a sudden drop but the really dedicated breeders continued their programs. By the end of the 1950s most of them had set aside their aim of a separate variety and had devoted their efforts to improving Miniatures. This time they were more successful. Gradually the Miniatures began to hold their own and, on occasion, even defeat a Standard entry, and this encouraged renewed interest among exhibitors.

Both the National Miniature Dachshund Club in the East and the American Miniature Dachshund Association, which had now moved its headquarters to the Pacific Northwest, held national round-ups in conjunction with established Specialty shows. By the late 1960s, these round-ups were attracting entries of 100. At the Dachshund Specialty in San Diego in 1968, there was an entry of 94 Miniatures and at the Dachshund Association of Long Island, held that same year, the Mini entry was 100. Since then the trend has increased. At present both clubs seem to be on a parallel course which is obviously benefiting not only Miniatures but the entire Dachshund fancy as well. Friendly rivalry exists in seeing which club can draw the most entries but they seem to be mainly in agreement as far as producing good dogs is concerned.

Jerry seeing Jerry win. President Ford's presence added considerable luster to the Best in Show scored by Ch. Spartan's Sloe Gin Fizz, MW, at Northeastern Indiana KC, May 2, 1976. Also pictured are handler Jerry Rigden, judge Edward Bracy (at left) and club president George Bruning. "Gin Fizz" is owned by Mrs. Christy Gordon-Creed of Camden, S.C. His fast march toward all-time records (see Page 147) may make him the dog to prove that Mr. Neff was right in speculating that when miniatures begin winning over standards with any consistency, the wish to see them shown as a separate variety might evaporate.

Ch. Jackdaw, whelped 1886, was undefeated through a long show career in England, and was—in his time—considered the ideal of the breed. The Jackdaw Trophy, honoring his name, is awarded annually to the top winning Dachshund—all coats, all varieties—in England.

Ch. Swansford Brigg of Truanbru, standard longhaired, winner of the Jackdaw Trophy for 1972, and of the St. Aubrey Award (for top winning dog of all breeds) for the same year. Brigg, owned by Mr. and Mrs. N. Swann of Chelsea, won 20 Bests in Show, six Hound Groups and 21 Challenge Certificates. He sired Ch. Swansford Estee, top longhaired bitch in England for 1974. —*Pearce*

Foreign Dogs Today

ENGLAND has long since outdistanced Germany and other countries on the continent of Europe in breeding, showing and exporting Dachshunds. The English got a head start in the 19th century by buying up some of Germany's best before the Germans had even begun to unify their breeding programs and set standards of perfection for their dogs. Americans followed in their raids on the great German kennels.

World War I brought everything to a standstill but the Germans recovered rather quickly. At the start of the War, they had dispersed their dogs and sent many of them out of the country to the benefit of Swedish, Dutch and Austrian breeders. But enough remained to start afresh.

Wartime hysteria regarding everything German in both the United States and England had virtually wiped out many good kennels and recovery was slower. Furthermore breeders from both countries were competing to buy the sparse stock of the Germans, so importation was slow and often costly.

Another reason for the decline of German imports is the insistence by the Germans on aggressive dispositions for their dogs to increase their hunting ability. American Dachshund owners want their dogs as show dogs or pets, sometimes both, and hunting in the United States, with every state having a different set of hunting regulations, is different than the German version where the rules are about the same throughout the country.

The picture of a Dachshund baying over the body of a dead stag is not one that appeals to American breeders and owners. They do not believe that a dog aggressive enough to chase and hold a stag or a boar, or fight twice its weight in underground wildlife, is going to adjust readily to suburban backyards or city apartments where encounters with other dogs and neighborhood pets presents the possibility of a fight and makes them difficult to handle in the show ring.

Perhaps there is a lesson to be learned from the fact that home raised pets of indifferent quality from the village of Gergweiss, ineligible for registration here, find a ready market from tourists, charmed with their dispositions, while

Ch. Cedavoch Vanity Fair, winner of the Mariner's Rose Bowl, 1973, awarded by the Dachshund Club Committee to the dog of the breed with the most outstanding show record for the year. Holder of the Scottish Best of Breed record for Dachshunds, all coats. Vanity Fair is owned by Mrs. Jean McNaughton of Ayrshire.

Ch. Rhinefields Diplomat, whelped 1966, top smooth Dachshund in England for 1968, 1969, 1970 and 1972, and top male of all hound breeds for 1972 and 1973. Diplomat is winner of 6 Bests in Show and sire of 5 champions. Bred and owned by Mr. and Mrs. John Gallop of Stafford.

fine German dogs from good kennels find a lesser market, despite the fact that export pedigrees are readily accepted by our own American Kennel Club for registration.

One also wonders whether or not this aggressive disposition is really necessary in a good hunting dog. A smooth miniature bitch, Ric Ran's Wee Waggie Maggie, recently became the first miniature Dachshund to make its Field Trial Championship. Maggie did it in two successive trials against anywhere from 20 to 30 standard Dachshunds. Obviously Maggie is a good hunter, but I can't imagine a dog with a name like that having a disposition like the Gib Hals Dachshunds bred by Paul Selchow, who felt that it was a sign of hunting fire and spirit when his dogs fought with each other in their kennels, sometimes to the death, as in the case of Gib Hals Olaf and Gib Hals Excellenz.

Austria, too, follows the German theory and its dogs are hunters first and show dogs second. In that country, natives and tourists hunt with such passion that any domestic animal other than hunting dogs are barred in some sections. In the small town of Obersterreich in the most sought after hunting region, the town's population is so dependent on hunters for their income that cats are banned and any feline appearing on the street can be shot, on sight, by anyone. Home owners, who want to cut down the mouse population in their homes, use miniature Dachshunds as mousers.

The friendship and cordial relationship between Canada and the United States extends to its Dachshund owners too. The ease with which dogs can be taken back and forth between the two countries makes it impractical to buy each others stock. Breeders have only to bring their dogs to the chosen sire or dam and, once the mating is accomplished, return home to await the results. There are, of course occasional outright purchases. Two of the best known, that have added to the quality of Canadian Dachshunds, are John H. Cook's Kleetal stock and that of Mrs. Pierce Onthank's Rose Farm Kennels. The Canadians also import as good English Dachshunds as those in the United States so there is no need for them to use our English imports. However, there is a great deal of competition at dog shows between American and Canadian breeders who go back and forth to shows in both countries with the same ease as they accomplish matings. What Canada does give Dachshund breeders here is judges. Canadian judges are as popular and sought after here as are the American judges who often officiate at Canadian shows. This exchange of judges cannot help but keep up the quality of dogs in both countries. American judges seem to have no difficulty in judging Dachshunds under the Canadian rules, where Dachshunds are judged in six varieties as in England — three in the standards and three in the miniatures.

Japan is the newest country to discover Dachshunds as show dogs. They look to the United States, England and Australia for their imports and are not

Eng. Ch. Limberlin Loud Laughter, standard smooth, pictured front and profile above, was winner of the Jackdaw Trophy for 1974. Owned by W. A. Hague of Yorkshire, whose Limberlin Kennels of smooth Dachshunds, standards and miniatures, has produced 21 champions since 1963, Loud Laughter represents a seventh generation of Limberlin breeding. Although a red dog, he was also winner of the Frieda II award "for the best black-and-tan Dachshund." Explains his owner: "Since the black and tans only won three CCs among them, it looks as though they decided I had better have this award, too."

Eng. Ch. Limberlin Americano, miniature smooth, distinguished winner and stud. Americano, who died in December 1974, was also owned by Mr. Hague. By mating a son and daughter of Americano, Mr. Hague produced Ch. Limberlin Golden Glory, the top English miniature for 1973. Mr. Hague gives this explanation of Americano's name: "I took his dam to be mated, but the chosen stud would not look at her, so I chose another. The sire was Ch. President of Minivale, and the resulting puppy was born July 4, 1972. His name had to be Americano."

190

yet prepared to meet competition on an international level. However, they seem to be on the right track. Mrs. Ramona (Van Court) Jones, in a recent conversation, told me that the Dachshunds she saw while on her judging assignment in Australia were among the best she had seen anywhere. American Dachshunds sold to Japanese have come from some of our best known kennels. The following letter (received in 1975) allows the Japanese to speak for themselves:

The Present Condition of Japanese Dachshunds

(By Mr. and Mrs. Nemoto. Translated by Junko Kimura.)

Japan Kennel Club was established in 1949, and in its 26 years' history, 76,448 Dachshunds have been registered. Among them, about 3,000 are the Miniature Dachshunds, including a wire, long-hair and smooth coat.

The registration totals of the last three years are as follows: In 1972 (April 1972–March 1973), 8,181 dogs were registered, and the Dachshund's ranking among all the registration with the Club was seventh (4.96% of the whole registration). In 1973 (April 1973–March 1974), 7,129 Dachshunds were registered and ranking was sixth or 4.67%. And in 1974 (April 1974–February 1975), 5,810 were registered. The monthly average, April 1974 through February 1975, was 528.2 dogs, so about 6,338 dogs are expected to be registered by the end of March, 1975.

There are seven member clubs in Japan at the present time, and four or five specialty shows are held annually around Japan. At these specialty shows, more than 100 dogs are always entered, and the record entry so far is 320 dogs (when Mrs. Ethel Bigler of Relgib Kennels judged here in November, 1973). Also, in November, 1974, we had an honour to have Mr. Maxwell Riddle as a judge at our specialty show, sponsored by one of the member clubs, Kanto Dachshund Club.

In the meantime, the Federal Association was established in 1974, and its specialty will be held annually by all the member clubs together.

The main current of the Japanese Dachshunds presently depends upon those which have been imported from the foreign countries, such as the U.S.A. and England. Especially, 80% of the Standard Dachshunds depends upon the American line. This tendency is also true with the Miniature Dachshunds in all coats, although about 10 wirehaired miniatures have been imported from England and they have been playing an important part.

The main line of the Japanese standard Dachshunds are Falcor of Heying Teckel, the son of Am. Ch. Falcon of Heying Teckel, and also Lime Light von Westphalen, as the first foundation dogs. Then, as the second stud dog, we had Von Relgib's Wizard, the son of the great Am. Ch. Herman VI. And recently, Von Relgib's Apollo of Dunkeldorf's Falcon's Favorite line, and his son, Von Relgib's Atlas, and Atchley's Shenandoah have been playing an active and an important role in Japan.

The following are the numbers of the imported dogs registered at Japan Kennel Club so far: from the U.S.A. — 119 dogs; England — 31 dogs; Germa-

Eng. Ch. Peredur Pimento, miniature wirehair, bred and owned by Mrs. R. D. Spong of South Wales. During a show career from December 1962 to November 1965, Pimento won 18 Challenge Certificates, a record that was unbroken for many years. Born as the result of a complete outcross mating, his ability to sire good, sound, healthy puppies when bred to his close relatives enabled his owner to fix his type in a very short time. He sired three champions, two of which were the result of mating him back to his dam, Orkneyinga Nereid.

Ch. Peredur Wicked Wangler, whelped 1970, a granddaughter of Pimento, and herself winner of 7 Challenge Certificates, 4 Bests of Breed including Crufts 1973, and Best in Show at the 1973 Miniature Dachshund Club's championship show.

ny — 26 dogs; Australia and other countries — 23 dogs. Among these, there are about 17 American Champions, such as Clayber's Rich Favour, Dixie-Dachs Fafner, Von Dachsheider's T-Bird, Markede Man About Town and None Such True Grit. There are also two German Champions, Cribs Von Der Warthebruck and Tobby Von Der Zeckenleiten. However, no champions have been imported to Japan from England.

The level of the Japanese miniature Dachshunds is no match as yet for those in either the United States or England. However, the number of fanciers has been growing over the last few years, and in 1974 they organized the Miniature Dachshund Members Club.

And happily, the quality of the standard Dachshunds, especially those with smooth coat, is rising year by year as a result of the long and endless efforts of the Japanese fanciers.

Regarding English dogs, Michael Triefus says it best. His opinion quoted in full here, came after his judging assignment at the San Diego Dachshund Specialty and more recent trips to shows in the United States. A number of American breeders share the criticisms of our dogs and our breeding practices that he expresses.

Since pictures speak louder than words, I've accompanied Mr. Triefus' critique with photographs assembled by him from among English Dachshund breeders. Through all the correspondence with Mr. Triefus which has occurred during the writing of this book, and the descriptions of their dogs by their owners, I sensed their great feeling for the breed — a feeling that I first became aware of on my visit to the Crufts' show in 1971. The English love their dogs, whether or not they are of show quality, and this love is transmitted to the children in their families. Dogs are looked upon as companions of people and are accepted everywhere. In this country dogs are banned in many places and a relatively few number of children are really educated in dog care. Many are afraid of dogs, and live to adulthood with this fear. Perhaps the improved communications between the dog owners in the two countries will in time remedy this situation.

Here is Mr. Triefus:

"It is not easy to make generalizations about differences of type or quality in a given breed in various countries. However, it does seem to me that there is some difference in type aimed for between, say, Germany and the Continent of Europe, England and America. In Germany and the Continent of Europe, they are clearly aiming for a smaller more active working dog then we are either in England or America. From the pictures published of winning Continental dogs it would appear that they want a less deep-chested animal, longer on the leg and more able, therefore, to run and go to ground than the show Dachshunds of either England or America.

In England I think we aim for a middle position between the German and American ideal; soundness and correct structure is the basic aim. My impres-

Ch. Delphik Debret, miniature longhair, winner of the Jackdaw Trophy—top winning Dachshund, all varieties—for two successive years. Owned by Mrs. H. Fielding of Blackpool.

Ch. Delphik Diplomat, another important winner from Mrs. Fielding's Delphik Kennels at Blackpool.

194

Ch. Prince Albert of Wendlitt, smooth miniature, winner of 41 Challenge Certificates and several Best in Show awards. Bred and owned by Mrs. Joan E. Littmoden of Dorset. Prince Albert is—on his dam's side—a grandson of Ch. Limberlin Americano, pictured elsewhere in this chapter. —Fall

Ch. Dandy Dan of Wendlitt, Prince Albert's sire. Dan represents three generations of home breeding at Mrs. Littmoden's Wendlitt Kennels. —Fall

Eng. Ch. Sunara Regal Artist, miniature longhaired Dachshund bitch, whelped June 18, 1972. Bred and owned by Mrs. Mary Fraser-Gibson of Swindon. Sunara Regal Artist has 6 Bests in Show, 10 Challenge Certificates and 9 Bests of Breed. —Fall

Ch. Runnel Petticoat, miniature smooth, winner of the Jackdaw Trophy for 1967, and the Arabis of Seale Cup (for best smooth miniature bitch) for 1967 and 1968. Petticoat, owned by Mrs. M. Gracey of Somerset, is the result of line breeding with four generations of Runnel bitches. —Fall

sion is that in America beauty rather than correctness is sought for, which is indeed a positive aim, as it goes for positive qualities rather than absence of faults. The danger, however, is that exaggerations can creep in, particularly those that militate against the dog carrying out its theoretical function as a sporting dog.

Although when I judged in San Diego my top winners were all of a size and type which I think would be generally equally appreciated in England, some other very striking dogs could be described as exaggerated in certain ways. I had this same impression also at a number of other shows I have attended in America. I have often heard it said, for example, that as in America it is rather easy to obtain the title of champion, greater store is set by winning or being placed in the Hound Group than would be the case, say, in England. In order to achieve this I have been told that only very large Dachshunds tend to get looked at in the Hound Group. There is, therefore, a natural tendency for the "Specials" Class to contain a number of very large dogs.

There also seems to be in America a desire to breed an ever longer and narrower head but here again I feel that though this may look pretty, it is not truly in accordance with the standard which is substantially the same in America, England and Germany. Excessive length and narrowness of muzzle surely makes for a weak jaw. I would certainly hate to think of some of the more extreme examples of this actually meeting a fox or a badger!

I also saw at various shows a number of dogs with an exaggerated depth of chest which really would make either prolonged running or going to ground very difficult.

As a rough generalization, therefore, I would say that the American Dachshund is on average bigger and better boned than the English one, also has a better head and possibly hindquarters, but that faulty shoulders are more prevalent in America. But the big cleavage of opinion as to what type to aim for is more between the German and European group of breeders on the one hand and both the English and American on the other.''

Diagram of Dachshund in Show Pose, Technical Terms, and Summary of Standard of Perfection

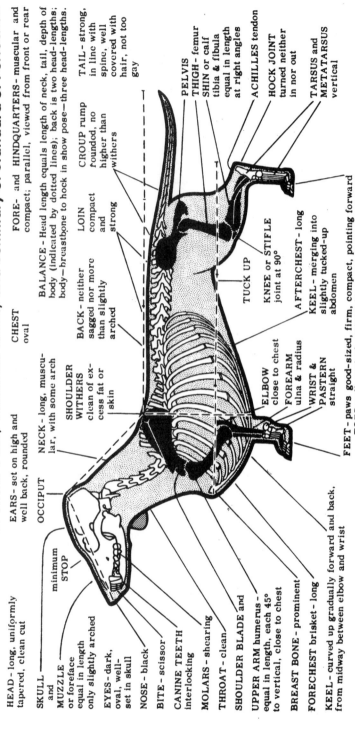

HEAD - long, uniformly tapered, clean cut

EARS - set on high and well back, rounded

CHEST oval

FORE- and HINDQUARTERS - muscular and compact; parallel, viewed from front or rear

BALANCE - Head length equals length of neck, tall, depth of body (indicated by dotted lines); back is two head-lengths; body—breastbone to hock in show pose—three head-lengths.

TAIL - strong, in line with spine, well covered with hair, not too gay

CROUP rump rounded, no higher than withers

LOIN compact and strong

BACK - neither sagged nor more than slightly arched

NECK - long, muscular, with some arch

SHOULDER WITHERS clean of excess fat or skin

PELVIS

THIGH - femur

SHIN or calf tibia & fibula equal in length at right angles

ACHILLES tendon

HOCK JOINT turned neither in nor out

TARSUS and METATARSUS vertical

OCCIPUT

minimum STOP

SKULL and MUZZLE or foreface equal in length only slightly arched

EYES - dark, oval, well-set in skull

NOSE - black

BITE - scissor

CANINE TEETH interlocking

MOLARS - shearing

THROAT - clean

SHOULDER BLADE and

UPPER ARM humerus - equal in length, each 45° to vertical, close to chest

BREAST BONE - prominent

FORECHEST brisket - long

KEEL - curved up gradually forward and back, from midway between elbow and wrist

ELBOW close to chest

FOREARM ulna & radius

WRIST & PASTERN straight

TUCK UP

KNEE or STIFLE joint at 90°

AFTERCHEST - long

KEEL - merging into slightly tucked-up abdomen

FEET - paws good-sized, firm, compact, pointing forward TOES well-arched. NAILS black, and kept short

This diagram, drawn originally for *The Pet Dachshund* by Laurence and Dorothy Horswell, has been widely distributed. Mr. Horswell had many copies made and gave them to individuals and clubs. It is still considered the most complete and accurate drawing of the breed.

A Judge Looks
at the Standard

by Jeannette W. Cross

EACH of the more than one hundred breeds that are accorded recognition by the American Kennel Club has a standard which is a verbal description of an ideal specimen of the breed. The purpose of a standard is to serve as a pattern or blueprint by which dogs are judged. If a dog were to meet in every detail the physical and temperamental attributes defined in the standard for its breed, it would be a perfect specimen. There has never been a perfect dog, although from time to time there have appeared dogs of such excellence that they came very close to the idealization. In the hands of ambitious (and highly solvent) owners such dogs usually achieve impressive show records.

Just as there exists great diversity of quality between the individual dogs within a breéd, there are also wide differences in the intelligibility of breed standards. Some are so vague as to be useless. One contains such terminology as to describe an ear as "filbert shaped." Another devotes not a single word to the breed's correct bite; in fact, does not even mention whether the dog should have any teeth at all. And this, mind you, is a breed that is supposedly capable of pursuing and bringing down wolves! But by and large, most breed standards are quite understandable and reasonably specific.

The Dachshund standard can be deservedly rated as one of the better guidelines to judging, as it is well written and characterized by the same Teutonic thoroughness that is found in the standard for German Shepherd Dogs. It is a sensible standard because it was written by sensible, practical men, who described the physical and mental attributes they knew a Dachshund had to embody in order to carry out its mission in life — the trailing of game and the pursuit of game into the underground dens and burrows. This is not to say that the Dachshund standard is so superb that memorization of it would transform absolutely anybody into an instant expert judge of Dachshunds. There are a few details which need a degree of clarification and one specification which is

199

absolutely misleading. Just as there has never been a perfect dog, there will probably never be a perfect breed standard.

In 1879, all the Dachshund clubs in Germany got together and bestowed upon themselves the splendiferous title, *Fachschaft Dachshunde Im Reichverband Für Das Deutsche Hundewesen.* Their purpose was to codify a standard for Dachshunds and this they did. The standard this group formulated remained unchanged until 1925 when some minor additions and subtractions were made at a meeting of the German Teckelklub held at Stuttgart. In 1935 a translation of this altered German standard was adopted by the Dachshund Club of America and was approved by the American Kennel Club.

In the original German standard, that is the one drawn up in 1879, the first word in the paragraph describing the Dachshund's general appearance was *gnomenhaft* which translates to "gnome-like." The changes made in 1925 removed this word as it was felt that it might give the impression that a Dachshund was as peculiar and misshapen as the gnomes who, according to the Brothers Grimm, lived in Germany's forests. Indeed, it is easy to understand how this word came to be used in the old standard. Those who have lived long and closely with Dachshunds will agree that a great many of them are whimsical of disposition, plus being possessed of an innate quaintness and a bent for elfin behavior. It is not difficult to imagine Dachshunds as residents of an Enchanted Forest consorting happily with unicorns, Valkyrie maidens, magic dragons and such like.

To return to the standard in current use in America, its major defect, in my opinion, is this portion of the description of the front feet *"Paws: full, broad in front, and a trifle inclined outwards."* In the first place, how much is a "trifle"? This line of the standard is simply ignored by judges and no Dachshund whose front feet point East and West has a chance of winning much in today's show ring. It would be more accurate if the statement were to read, "Paws: full, broad in front and should appear to turn neither in nor out." The reason for using the word "appear" is that there are some dogs whose front feet *do* point exactly straight ahead but *appear* to be pigeon-toed. This is often seen in English Foxhounds and in Beagles. There have been numerous attempts to change this misleading statement and there has always been opposition to such alteration.

The opponents to a change argue that a dog whose front feet point outward is a better digger than a straight-fronted dog. They are apparently unaware that the Fox Terrier, as expert an excavator as the canine world contains, is straight-fronted. Among wild animals there are several species which are diggers par excellence having straight front legs and feet. The eastern garden mole, an animated mining machine that can tunnel 15 feet in an hour, is actually pigeon-toed.

200

Porcelain statuette of a Dachshund holding a fox at bay, from the collection of Mrs. Jeannette W. Cross. Note the powerful thrust of the dog's hindquarters. —*Brander*

In her award-winning book *"Dogsteps—Illustrated Gait At A Glance,"* Rachel Page Elliott notes: "Function influences form. For example, (the Dachshund) is a variety of dog developed through selective breeding to ferret out farm pets from underground. The elbows became set above the line of the brisket in order to free the legs for digging, while the dog's weight came to rest on his chest. The long and gradual upward slant of the lower rib cage helps him to slide more easily over rocks and roots—a handy arrangement in case there is need for speedy retreat."

The paragraph which deals with the Dachshund's middle section (under the heading *TRUNK*) is for the most part self-explanatory. It might be a helpful addition if a dictum of Laurence Alden Horswell's were incorporated in this description. Mr. Horswell states, "Always remember that a Dachshund's length of body *must* be in his rib cage, not in his loin." Mr. Horswell was right, for it almost invariably occurs that a Dachshund short in rib cage and long in loin will have a poor topline.

The standard for Dachshunds gives no size or weight limitations except to state that to qualify as a Miniature a dog must weigh less than ten pounds when one year of age or older. This means that any Dachshund weighing ten pounds or more when he is twelve months of age is automatically a Standard. This is really a very loose qualification and it would be of benefit to the breed if a maximum weight limitation were imposed upon the Standards. Recent years have seen Dachshunds shown that I'm sure weighed as much as 35 pounds. This is approaching the weight of a Basset Hound. A good deal of agility is lost when a short-legged dog reaches this poundage.

Under the heading *QUALITIES* the standard says that the Dachshund should be *"clever, lively and courageous to the point of rashness."* The word "clever" is used here, I believe, as it is applied to horses — meaning physically adroit. A 35 pound Dachshund cannot be anything but clumsy and too big all over to do the type of hunting for which the breed was developed. Further along in the same section devoted to general qualities it mentions the breed's hunting spirit, good nose, loud tongue and *small* size (the italics are mine). So what should a Standard Dachshund weigh? I think about 24 pounds is a top weight for a mature male and 22 pounds is not too small. Bitches as petite as 16 to 18 pounds should not be considered undesirable. If a Standard Dachshund is faulted as being "too small" I think the best riposte is to ask the critic "Too small for what?" Certainly a Dachshund is never too small to be a good Dachshund, but he most assuredly *can* be too big.

In the early 1950s Ch. Hardway Welcome Stranger established a breed record when he finished his championship by winning Best in Show from the classes at the Old Dominion Kennel Club and then within the next month was Best in Show three more times at major Eastern events. He topped the 1953 Specialty and was Best of Breed at one of the last of the great Morris and Essex Kennel Club shows. Bred, owned and handled by Jeannette W. Cross.

Ch. Cinnabar Candy Man, the first dapple Dachshund to win Best in Show in America, and the first Longhaired dapple to win a Group. Owned by Barbara Keck and Alice Dildine; handled by Howard Nygood. Shown taking top honors at Suffolk County KC show in September 1973, under judge Jeannette Cross.

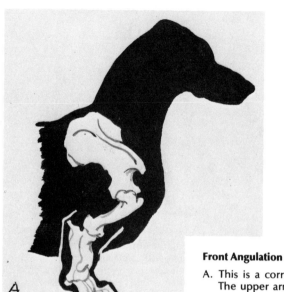

A

Front Angulation

A. This is a correctly angulated front.
The upper arm and shoulder blade
join at a 90° angle, and are approximately the same length.

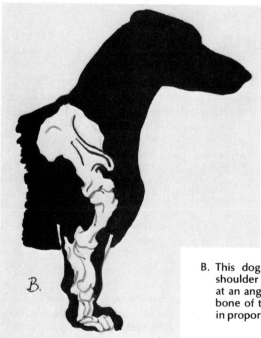

B.

B. This dog has a steep front. The
shoulder blade and upper arm join
at an angle wider than 90° and the
bone of the upper arm is too short
in proportion to the shoulder blade.

Official AKC Standard for the Dachshund

(Drawings by Kate O'Connell)

General Appearance—Low to ground, short-legged, long-bodied, but with compact figure and robust muscular development; with bold and confident carriage of the head and intelligent facial expression. In spite of his shortness of leg, in comparison with his length of trunk, he should appear neither crippled, awkward, cramped in his capacity for movement, nor slim and weasel-like.

Qualities—He should be clever, lively, and courageous to the point of rashness, persevering in his work both above and below ground; with all the senses well developed. His build and disposition qualify him especially for hunting game below ground. Added to this, his hunting spirit, good nose, loud tongue, and small size, render him especially suited for beating the bush. His figure and his fine nose give him an especial advantage over most other breeds of sporting dogs for trailing.

CONFORMATION OF BODY

Head—Viewed from above or from the side, it should taper uniformly to the tip of the nose, and should be clean-cut. The skull is only slightly arched, and should slope gradually without stop (the less stop the more typical) into the finely-formed slightly-arched muzzle (ram's nose). The bridge bones over the eyes should be strongly prominent. The nasal cartilage and tip of the nose are long and narrow; lips tightly stretched, well covering the lower jaw, but neither deep nor pointed; corner of the mouth not very marked. Nostrils well open. Jaws opening wide and hinged well back of the eyes, with strongly developed bones and teeth.

Teeth—Powerful canine teeth should fit closely together, and the outer side of the lower incisors should tightly touch the inner side of the upper. (Scissors bite.)

Eyes—Medium size, oval, situated at the sides, with a clean, energetic, though pleasant expression; not piercing. Color, lustrous dark reddish-brown to brownish-black for all coats and colors. Wall eyes in the case of dapple dogs are not a very bad fault, but are also not desirable.

Ears—Should be set near the top of the head, and not too far forward, long but not too long, beautifully rounded, not narrow, pointed, or folded. Their carriage should be animated, and the forward edge should just touch the cheek.

Neck—Fairly long, muscular, clean-cut, not showing any dewlap on the throat, slightly arched in the nape, extending in a graceful line into the shoulders, carried proudly but not stiffly.

Front—To endure the arduous exertion underground, the front must be correspondingly muscular, compact, deep, long and broad. Forequarters in detail:

Shoulder Blade—Long, broad, obliquely and firmly placed upon the fully developed thorax, furnished with hard and plastic muscles.

Upper Arm—Of the same length as the shoulder blade, and at right angles to the latter, strong of bone and hard of muscle, lying close to the ribs, capable of free movement.

Forearm—This is short in comparison to other breeds, slightly turned inwards; supplied with hard but plastic muscles on the front and outside, with tightly stretched tendons on the inside and at the back.

Joint between forearm and foot (wrists)—These are closer together than the shoulder joints, so that the front does not appear absolutely straight.

Paws—Full, broad in front, and a trifle inclined outwards; compact, with well-arched toes and tough pads.

Toes—There are five of these, though only four are in use. They should be close together, with a pronounced arch; provided on top with strong nails, and underneath with tough toe-pads. Dewclaws may be removed.

Trunk—The whole trunk should in general be long and fully muscled. The back, with sloping shoulders, and short, rigid pelvis, should lie in the straightest possible line between the withers and the very slightly arched loins, these latter being short, rigid, and broad.

Chest—The breastbone should be strong, and so prominent in front that on either side a depression (dimple) appears. When viewed from the front, the thorax should appear oval, and should extend downward to the mid-point of the forearm. The enclosing structure of ribs should appear full and oval, and when viewed from above or from the side, full-volumed, so as to allow by its ample capacity, complete development of heart and lungs. Well ribbed up, and gradually merging into the line of the abdomen. If the length is correct, and also the anatomy of the shoulder and upper arm, the front leg when viewed in profile should cover the lowest point of the breast line.

Abdomen—Slightly drawn up.

Hindquarters—The hindquarters viewed from behind should be of completely equal width.

Croup—Long, round, full, robustly muscled, but plastic, only slightly sinking toward the tail.

Pelvic Bones—Not too short, rather strongly developed, and moderately sloping.

206

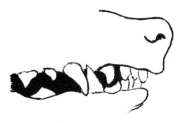

A.

Teeth

A. A correct scissors bite. Note that the front teeth overlap when the mouth is closed and that the inside surface of the upper front teeth is in contact with the outside surface of the lower front teeth.

B. This is an overshot mouth. When the mouth is closed the upper front teeth project out beyond the lower front teeth and are not touching them. A serious fault.

B.

C. This is an undershot jaw. The lower front teeth project out beyond the upper front teeth and when the mouth is closed the upper and lower front teeth will not contact one another. This is a serious fault.

C.

D. This is a pincers bite and is not as desirable as a scissors bite. The upper and lower front teeth touch at the edges instead of overlapping when the mouth is closed. The occlusion resembles the way in which the cutting edges of a wire-cutter meet. A minor fault.

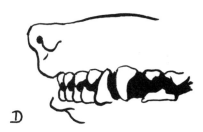

D

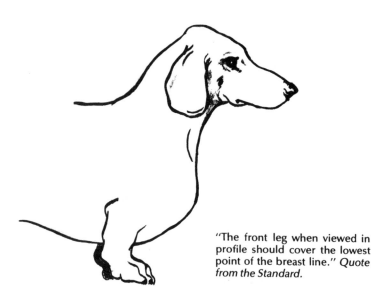

"The front leg when viewed in profile should cover the lowest point of the breast line." *Quote from the Standard.*

A faulty front. This dog is loose in the shoulders and elbows.

A bad front. The feet are turned outward.

Thigh Bone—Robust and of good length, set at right angles to the pelvic bones.

Hind Legs—Robust and well-muscled, with well-rounded buttocks.

Knee Joint—Broad and strong.

Calf Bone—In comparison with other breeds, short; it should be perpendicular to the thigh bone, and firmly muscled.

The bones at the base of the foot (tarsus) should present a flat appearance, with a strongly prominent hock and a broad tendon of Achilles.

The central foot bones (metatarsus) should be long, movable toward the calf bone, slightly bent toward the front, but perpendicular (as viewed from behind).

Hind Paws—Four compactly closed and beautifully arched toes, as in the case of the front paws. The whole foot should be posed equally on the ball and not merely on the toes; nails short.

Tail—Set in continuation of the spine, extending without very pronounced curvature, and should not be carried too gaily.

Note—Inasmuch as the Dachshund is a hunting dog, scars from honorable wounds shall not be considered a fault.

SPECIAL CHARACTERISTICS OF THE THREE COAT-VARIETIES

The Dachshund is bred with three varieties of coat: (1) Shorthaired (or Smooth); (2) Wirehaired; (3) Longhaired. All three varieties should conform to the characteristics already specified. The longhaired and shorthaired are old, well-fixed varieties, but into the wirehaired Dachshund, the blood of other breeds has been purposely introduced; nevertheless, in breeding him, the greatest stress must be placed upon conformity to the general Dachshund type. The following specifications are applicable separately to the three coat-varieties, respectively:

(1) SHORTHAIRED (or SMOOTH) DACHSHUND

Hair—Short, thick, smooth and shining; no bald patches. Special faults are: Too fine or thin hair, leathery ears, bald patches, too coarse or too thick hair in general.

Tail—Gradually tapered to a point, well but not too richly haired, long, sleek bristles on the underside are considered a patch of strong-growing hair, not a fault. A brush tail is a fault, as is also a partly or wholly hairless tail.

Color of Hair, Nose and Nails:

One-Colored Dachshund—This group includes red (often called tan), red-yellow, yellow, and brindle, with or without a shading of interspersed black hairs. Nevertheless a clean color is preferable, and red is to be considered more desirable than red-yellow or yellow. Dogs strongly shaded with interspersed black hairs belong to this class, and not to the other color groups. A small white spot is admissible, but not desirable. Nose and Nails—Black; brown is admissible, but not desirable.

209

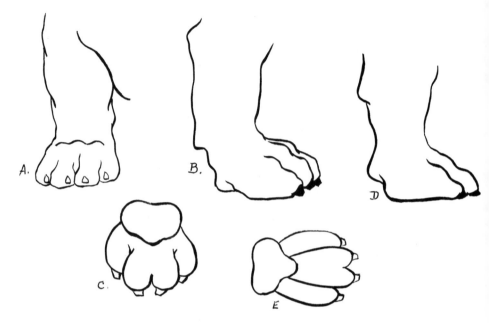

Front Legs and Feet

A. Front view of a well-knuckled-up foot and straight front leg.
B. Side view of a good front leg and correct compact foot.
C. Footprint of a proper front foot.
D. Undesirable long narrow foot. This type of foot is known as a hare foot as it is typical of animals of the rabbit family.
E. Footprint of a hare foot.

Two-Colored Dachshund—These comprise deep black, chocolate, gray (blue), and white; each with tan markings over the eyes, on the sides of the jaw and underlip, on the inner edge of the ear, front, breast, inside and behind the front legs, on the paws and around the anus, and from there to about one-third to one-half of the length of the tail on the under side. The most common two-colored Dachshund is usually called black-and-tan. A small white spot is admissible but not desirable. Absence, undue prominence or extreme lightness of tan markings is undesirable. Nose and Nails—In the case of black dogs, black; for chocolate, brown (the darker the better); for gray (blue) or white dogs, gray or even flesh color, but the last named color is not desirable; in the case of white dogs, black nose and nails are to be preferred.

Dappled Dachshund—The color of the dappled Dachshund is a clear brownish or grayish color, or even a white ground, with dark irregular patches of dark-gray, brown, red-yellow or black (large areas of one color not desirable). It is desirable that neither the light nor the dark color should predominate. Nose and Nails—As for One- and Two-Colored Dachshunds.

(2) WIREHAIRED DACHSHUND

The general appearance is the same as that of the shorthaired, but without being long in the legs, it is permissible for the body to be somewhat higher off the ground.

Hair—With the exception of jaw, eyebrows, and ears, the whole body is covered with a perfectly uniform tight, short, thick, rough, hard coat, but with finer, shorter hairs (undercoat) everywhere distributed between the coarser hairs, resembling the coat of the German Wirehaired Pointer. There should be a beard on the chin. The eyebrows are bushy. On the ears the hair is shorter than on the body; almost smooth, but in any case conforming to the rest of the coat. The general arrangement of the hair should be such that the wirehaired Dachshund, when seen from a distance should resemble the smooth-haired. Any sort of soft hair in the coat is faulty, whether short or long, or wherever found on the body; the same is true of long, curly, or wavy hair, or hair that sticks out irregularly in all directions; a flag tail is also objectionable.

Tail—Robust, as thickly haired as possible, gradually coming to a point, and without a tuft.

Color of Hair, Nose and Nails—All colors are admissible. White patches on the chest, though allowable, are not desirable.

(3) LONGHAIRED DACHSHUND

The distinctive characteristic differentiating this coat from the short-haired, or smooth-haired Dachshund is alone the rather long silky hair.

Hair—The soft, sleek, glistening, often slightly wavy hair should be longer under the neck, on the underside of the body, and especially on the ears and behind the legs, becoming there a pronounced feather; the hair should attain its greatest length on the underside of the tail. The hair should fall beyond the lower edge of the ear. Short hair on the ear, so-called "leather" ears, is not desirable. Too luxurious a coat causes the longhaired Dachshund to seem

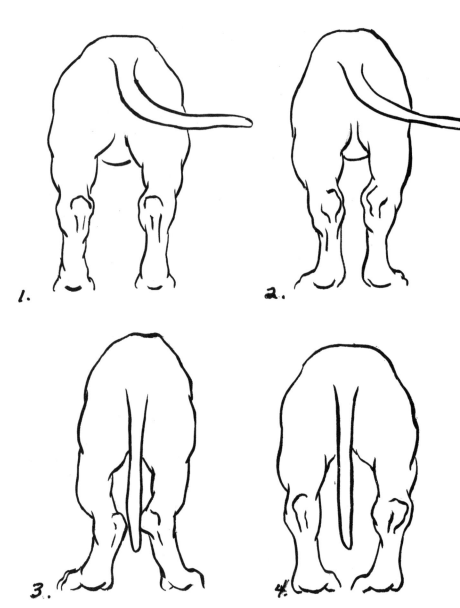

Rear Ends

1. Correct and sound rear end. The hocks are properly spaced apart and the legs are parallel from the hocks to the ground.
2. Faulty rear end. This dog is too narrow through the pelvic area and the hind legs are too close. The feet are pointing outward.
3. Very unsound rear end. This dog is cowhocked.
4. Another bad rear end. This dog is bandy-legged. The hocks are too wide apart and the feet are toeing in.

coarse, and masks the type. The coat should remind one of the Irish Setter, and should give the dog an elegant appearance. Too thick hair on the paws, so-called "mops," is inelegant, and renders the animal unfit for use. It is faulty for the dog to have equally long hair over all the body, if the coat is too curly, or too scrubby, or if a flag tail or overhanging hair on the ears are lacking; or if there is a very pronounced parting on the back, or a vigorous growth between the toes.

Tail—Carried gracefully in prolongation of the spine; the hair attains here its greatest length and forms a veritable flag.

Color of Hair, Nose and Nails—Exactly as for the smooth-haired Dachshund, except that the red-with-black (heavily sabled) color is permissible and is formally classed as a red.

MINIATURE DACHSHUNDS

Note—Miniature Dachshunds are bred in all three coats. Within the limits imposed, symmetrical adherence to the general Dachshund conformation, combined with smallness, and mental and physical vitality, should be the outstanding characteristics of Miniature Dachshunds. They have not been given separate classification but are a division of the Open Class for "under 10 pounds, and 12 months old or over."

GENERAL FAULTS

Serious Faults—Over- or undershot jaws, knuckling over, very loose shoulders.

Secondary Faults—A weak, long-legged, or dragging figure; body hanging between the shoulders; sluggish, clumsy, or waddling gait; toes turned inwards or too obliquely outwards; splayed paws; sunken back, roach (or carp) back; croup higher than withers; short-ribbed or too weak chest; excessively drawn-up flanks like those of a Greyhound; narrow, poorly-muscled hindquarters; weak loins; bad angulation in front or hindquarters; cowhocks; bowed legs; wall eyes, except for dappled dogs; bad coat.

Minor Faults—Ears wrongly set, sticking out, narrow or folded; too marked a stop; too pointed or weak a jaw; pincer teeth; too wide or too short a head; goggle eyes, wall eyes in the case of dappled dogs, insufficiently dark eyes in the case of all other coat-colors; dewlaps; short neck; swan neck; too fine or too thin hair; absence of, or too profuse or too light tan markings in the case of two-colored dogs.

Approved January 12, 1971

Two pictures of her owner showing Am. & Can. Ch. Fiddler's Hill Cinnamon Bun show what a difference your attire can make. At left, Katay Burg's dress provides a clear contrast for Cinnamon Bun in her win of Best in Show at Penticton and District KC (Canada) 1968 show. At right, Cinnamon Bun seems to melt into the background of Mrs. Burg's dark skirt.

Showing Your Dachshund

THE NAME given to competition among dogs is "Dog Show." Most exhibitors put the emphasis on "Dog" and take the "Show" for granted. This is a mistake, particularly for Dachshund exhibitors.

The judge sees two things when you and your dog enter the ring, the dog and its handler. In the larger breeds, the judge sees the dog first, then the handler. Breeds such as Irish Wolfhounds, Afghans and Borzoi are so dramatic in looks that they literally "fill the eye," with their striking appearance and stately, almost arrogant movement. Dachshunds, even the most impressive of the standards, are dwarfed by their handlers. It is the handler that the Dachshund judge sees first, and then, as he casts his eyes downward, the Dachshund. Your Dachshund needs help in his bid for the judge's attention in competition with his larger handler; the handler must make every effort to remain as unobtrusive as possible so that the judge's attention will be focused on the dog.

Let's look at the "Dog" part first. If you decide you want to show your puppy or young dog it is a good idea to get opinions as to the dog's show potential from the person or persons who own the dog's sire and dam. One person might own both or there could be two people involved. These are the people, beside yourself, who have most at stake when the dog makes its appearance, in the show ring. A winner not only adds prestige to the breeder's kennels, but also gives them assurance that their breeding practices are correct.

Next, get the opinion of a professional handler, preferably one showing Dachshunds among the dogs he or she is handling. A handler will not only see your dog on its own merits but in comparison with the Dachshunds that he knows will be its competitors at coming shows. Do expect to pay for this opinion. Handlers make their living, seven days a week, at dog shows or preparing for them and you will be taking up time which could be profitably spent elsewhere.

Next, form your own opinion by reading the standard, looking at Dachshunds at dog shows (leave your own dog home), and by getting a judge's eye view of your dog — by what I call the "mirror method." The idea is not original. It came to me after seeing ballet students practice before a mirrored wall, watching their own reflections to achieve the motions required.

Get two door mirrors, lightweight and inexpensive (about 14" x 4' is the usual size), and place them lengthwise on the floor facing each other, at opposite ends of the room. Then take your puppy or young dog, on lead (if he will walk on lead), or free — running toward or away from you — if he is untrained, and move him back and forth between the two mirrors.

Look at the reflection, which will give you what the judge will see when the dog comes toward him or moves away; looking down at the dog directly prevents your getting a good view of his movement. Then move him around the circumference of the room so that you see him moving in profile past the mirrors.

Now, in the corner of one of the mirrors tape two profile pictures: one of the Dachshund's bone structure, such as the drawing by Laurence Horswell shown elsewhere in this book, and the other of a top winning Dachshund in your dog's variety and size (standard or miniature). Stand the dog in profile before the mirror and compare him to the pictures. To bring out the bone structure, dip your finger in white tempera paint, (it washes off easily) and trace the bones on the side nearest the mirror, on his skin. You can feel them readily as your finger moves and you will have his skeleton painted on his skin.

Do the same thing with the dog posed facing the mirror and then with his rear toward it. If your opinion and those of the handler and breeders are in agreement, it's time to prepare for the Dachshund's show career: and yours.

The first thing you'll need to know are the rules. Get the booklet on rules and regulations for dog shows, the one for Obedience trials and the one for field trials from the American Kennel Club. (These booklets are available free upon request to The American Kennel Club, 51 Madison Avenue, New York, N.Y. 10010.) A surprising number of people in the show ring are not familiar with these. It makes sense not only to know the rules, but to know the different opportunities for winning that are available for Dachshunds. A dog who has finished his show career can still keep active and healthy by competition in Obedience and at field trials. So, if you enjoy the dog sport, you and your Dachshund can enjoy ten years or more of dog show activity. Don't worry about advancing age in your dog, so long as he's physically well. The first dog that my husband and I ever trained in Obedience was over ten years old.

It is not a case of old-dog-new-tricks. You do not really teach a dog anything he does not already know. You simply take the instincts and abilities with which he was born and adapt them to the situation. Before you enter an Obedience training class your dog has learned to sit without any help from you. All that happens is that he now learns to do it on command.

The same is true of tracking in Obedience or hunting rabbits at field trials; just accustom him to following human scent or that of rabbits, and let nature take its course.

Then subscribe to *Pure-bred Dogs — American Kennel Gazette*. (Address: 51 Madison Avenue, NYC 10010. Subscriptions are $10 a year for 12 monthly issues.) There are many other dog magazines and books which you will want to read. All of them are good but the Gazette is the official publication of the American Kennel Club, the sport's governing body, and its information is going to prove very valuable when you begin to enter your dog at licensed shows.

Another must on your subscription list is *The American Dachshund* (Address: 15011 Oak Creek Rd., El Cajon, Calif. 92021). Just as the Gazette will keep you posted in a general way on the world of dogs, *The American Dachshund* is the delineator of everything affecting the breed. Its articles, advice and information are things that no Dachshund exhibitor can afford to be without.

No dog show exhibitor should be without a copy of *The Complete Dog Book,* an impressive and complete work on dogs, containing the standard for every breed of dog shown in the United States. It is the official publication of the American Kennel Club and show committees are required to have a copy at the superintendent's desk as the final word for anything out of the ordinary that may arise at the show. Copies may be obtained from The American Kennel Club, 51 Madison Ave. NYC 10010. Cost $7.95 includes postage.

Continue to go to dog shows, still without your dog, but now go a step further. Don't mark your catalog at the ringside but wait until the judging is finished and the stewards have returned the judge's bag and his book to the superintendent's desk — then mark your catalog directly from the judging sheets which will be posted. This way you will be absolutely accurate — you will have not only the dogs entered and how they were placed, but the absentees as well. Count the number of Dachshunds shown in the dog classes and then those in the bitch classes. Do not count the absentees. The number of points won by the Winners Dog, Winners Bitch and Best of Winners is based on the number of Dachshunds actually in competition, not all those entered. Now to find how many points toward championship the winners dog and winners bitch won, turn to the front of the catalog to the page titled "American Kennel Club Scale of Points". You'll find an explanation of the point system on which championship points are awarded and also the number of Dachshunds required to be in competition to earn anywhere from one to five (the most possible points at any one show) points. Then figure out the number of points won by the dogs you saw in the ring. Sooner or later you will have to do this when your own dog wins, so practice now.

Don't leave the show grounds yet; you haven't yet taken full opportunity of the educational experience in showing dogs that your admission ticket provides. Go to a ring where short-legged dogs are being shown, Scotties, West Highland Whites, Sealyhams, Shih Tsu or Welsh Corgis. Watch the handlers, amateur and professional, and see how they handle the small-dog/large-handler problem. Remember those that looked best to you and those that were most successful. Then when you are at home, practice what you have learned in front of the mirrors, with your own dog. Before you leave the show grounds, pick up several premium lists, read them thoroughly and practice filling out the entry blanks. Unless the entry blank is filled out correctly, your entry will not be accepted by the show committee.

Since your dog cannot be shown until he is six months old you have plenty of time for this "paperwork". Even if he is old enough, say six months to a year old, don't enter him until you are familiar with dog show procedure. There is another reason to take your time. Puppies and young dogs need time to build up a natural immunity to infection and airborne viruses. No matter how many preventive innoculations the dog may have, they are not 100 percent proof against contagion. Match shows, which are smaller, informal versions of licensed shows, but carry no points toward championship, accept puppies from three months on — but the gain is so small and the risks so great that here too, we advise that you hold back your dog until he is at least ten months old. At that age you can more safely enter him at Match shows to familiarize him with dog show procedure and to test your own ability to show him.

Because your dog is not entered at Match shows and licensed shows it does not follow that you cannot be a participant. Join your local all-breed club and regional Dachshund Club. With your acquired knowledge of the rules, the point system and show ring procedure, offer your services as a steward. Since stewards are always in short supply, your help will be welcome, and as there are always two stewards to every ring, serving with an experienced steward will make the learning process easy. I can think of no better way to get a judge's point of view than standing beside him in the ring and listening to his comments. By the time your dog is ready for his first show you will already be experienced and "ringwise" as an exhibitor.

Meanwhile your dog is developing safely at home and you can help this along by practicing with him on lead. Use the mirrors to watch his gait and make it a practice to keep your legs and feet out of the picture. They are the worst possible background for your dog and their motion is a distraction from the dog's action. There are many ways to do this, but I have found that holding your arm straight out from the shoulder and letting the lead drop to the dog's neck from your hand keeps the dog at arm's length from your body.

A further help is to walk slightly ahead of or behind your dog, still an arm's length away, and when you stop, swing in front of him; he will look at you with an alert expression and at the same time, he will be blocked from any further forward motion by your body. Also he will be standing away from your legs and feet.

218

Almost all breed clubs and Dachshund clubs offer handling classes run by successful amateur or professional handlers. By all means, join one of these and get as much advice and help as you can. It also conditions your dog to moving around in the company of others.

Get him used to being handled, first by you and your family at home, then by friends, and finally by strangers and other people in your handling class. Go through the motions of examining him the way you have seen the judges do it. Be sure to accustom him to being placed on a table. Take care that the table stands firm, and has a non-slip surface. Dachshunds have great dignity and unless they are accustomed to handling they are apt to resent what they consider overfamiliarity by strangers, including the judge.

It is also a time for you to learn about grooming and trimming. Get advice from the dog's breeders, if they do their own and are currently competing, or take lessons from a handler.

Since you are not planning to show your Dachshund in the immediate future, a mistake in trimming will soon be covered by new growth. Things like nails, teeth and ears should be looked after regularly whether or not you intend to show your dog. Learn to do this yourself and save time, money and veterinary services by keeping your dog in prime condition at all times.

As your dog matures and the time approaches for his first show, do try to make it a Match show first, preferably an all-Dachshund one, with less dogs and less confusion then an all-breeds Match. Begin to accumulate the equipment you will need at the show. You already have his crate, and grooming tools (take them with you in a box for last-minute touch ups), several show leads (one is sure to be lost before the day is over), a dolly on which to place your crate in getting it and the dog to and from the parking lot to the show grounds, and a thermal picnic box with food and drink for you and your dog. Your previous tours of dog shows will have already prepared you for the long lines at food booths and drinking water facilities; avoid them by bringing your own supplies so that you and your dog will be relaxed and refreshed by the time you are ready to enter the ring. A word of caution — give the dog plenty of water but no food until after he has been shown. A hungry dog is a lot more active and alert than one who has a full stomach.

Talk to experienced exhibitors and look at the equipment handlers use so that you will be prepared for any eventuality at the show.

Now come the final preparations for the debut of you and your Dachshund into the show ring and here is where the "Show" part becomes very important. Put your best foot forward in a one color shoe, preferably a conservative color which does not take the attention away from your dog. Next consider your outfit; have more than one. Have one for a rainy day, too, and give some thought to its selection — plastic raincoat, hastily thrown over what you are wearing, could disturb your dog with its noise. The outfit or outfits should be of a solid-color or conservative striped, small plaid or small print material that

219

provides a background for your Dachshund when you kneel on the ground in a line-up or show him by himself on the table. It should provide a contrast, but not an overwhelming one.

Have a dress rehearsal in front of the mirrors before you make the final decision. A one piece dress or pantsuit for women is better than slacks and blouse or skirt and blouse. Men have an easier time. Most men's shops feature color-coordinated jackets and slacks in their sportswear department.

Exercise, to keep your Dachshund hard and fit, is frequently overdone. The popular belief that running is good for a dog is not necessarily correct. A little goes a long way. Dogs enjoy running, but keep the distances short and the number of times per day infrequent. Prolonged, violent running can stretch the muscles and tendons of puppies and growing dogs permanently out of shape. Even grown dogs are subject to these risks. A 50' x 100' plot of ground provides plenty of room for exercise with your dog. Lively children and frequent play help, too. Apartment house Dachshunds do well with just the run of the apartment and the daily trips to the street. If you feel your Dachshund needs more than this, walk up one flight of stairs before taking the elevator to your floor. There is a lot more money at stake in keeping race horses ready to run, yet these 1200 lb. speedsters are kept to top condition by a mile gallop in the morning and another mile or less during the race in the afternoon or evening. The rest of their time is spent in box stalls. If a horse can keep fit with this minimum amount of exercise, you don't need to be concerned about a 20-lb. Dachshund.

Finally, with a few victories at Match shows to bolster your own confidence and get your dog accustomed to the ring, you are ready to enter your first licensed show. If possible, make it a Dachshund specialty. First, you will be assured of a large enough entry to earn an award of three to five points if you win. Secondly, you'll have a larger number of good quality Dachshunds in competition than you would encounter in the Dachshund classes at an all-breed show. Third, a specialty show, while it has more entries in the breed and in the varieties, has fewer overall entries than an all-breed event. Finally, the judge is sure to be a Dachshund expert, selected by breeders and exhibitors who value his or her opinion. If you do well at the Specialty and meet other exhibitors who are encouraging, plan your all-breed entries.

Do show your Dachshund yourself at at least three shows. Then if you feel that you are no match for seasoned exhibitors, you might want to consider a handler's services. There is much to be said in favor of having a handler: expert handling, having expenses shared with other exhibitors, and weekly exposure to a number of good judges at a wide variety of dog shows. On the other hand, there is the fun of doing it yourself. You have the advantage over the professional handler in that you have just one dog 24 hours a day, 365 days a year to work with. No handler could afford to spend that much time on one dog. You can also choose your shows at a more leisurely pace, avoiding the less attractive ones with crowded conditions and inconvenient parking.

Note how much more effectively the dog in the lower picture is presented, thanks to the handler having managed to pose his dog clear of his own and other handlers' feet.

Never leave your dog unsupervised at a dog show. If you cannot bring a friend or a member of the family with you, arrange with a fellow exhibitor to share the supervision of his dogs and yours, or contact the show committee in advance and ask if there would be a 4-H youngster, or a boy or girl Scout who could help you. Handlers, too, will sometimes keep an eye on your crate if there is room to put it with theirs, but arrange ahead of time for this if you are planning on it. Someone carrying a tray could stumble over your crate and send scalding coffee down on your dog; children poke anything from fingers to dangerously sharp objects into a crate or feed the dog harmful things. There is no accounting for audience reaction. One man, after paying his admission fee to a show, took one look at the dogs neatly crated and waiting their turn, and decided that exhibitors were cruel people to confine the dogs in cages. He went around opening the crate doors as he passed. The show ground to a halt as the superintendent's staff rounded up the culprit and the exhibitors rounded up their dogs.

Ch. L and C's Gay Personality, UD, exhibiting his proficiency in the broad jump (top), the bar jump (center), and in retrieving over the high jump (below). Owned and trained by Larry Sorenson.

The Dachshund in Obedience

To THE SUCCESSFUL AMATEUR or professional Obedience trainer the task of training their first Dachshund presents the ultimate challenge. Unless they are familiar with the breed and its past history, they are in for a hard time. The usual methods which work so well with the Working breeds, the Non-Sporting dogs and the Toy breeds are just not right for Dachshund training. There is a reason for this. The Working, Non-Sporting and Toy breeds have had whatever hunting instincts they once possessed sublimated by many years of non-hunting activities. They feel that they are dependent on their owners for survival and tend to pay close attention to commands, feeling that, quite literally, their lives depend on it. The Dachshund, on the other hand, is fiercely independent, a superb hunter both above and below ground.

He feels quite capable of finding his own food, if necessary. Of course he could not live in our complex modern world without human care, but a Dachshund has no way of knowing this. His inherited instincts are what he depends on, a belief that often gets him into trouble, sometimes with almost fatal results. Harland and I learned this the hard way when we both made flying tackles in the mud of the Okeechobee Swamp to rescue our Dachshunds at the water's edge as they pursued an alligator into the muddy water.

In order to successfully train your Dachshund for Obedience trials or anything else, your first step is to have the dog so attached to you and so devoted, that he will *prefer* to do it your way rather than his own. It has always seemed to me that cat owners whose pets are even more independent than Dachshunds have achieved this technique superbly.

A cat will hunt all night and in the morning when the owner opens the door, there, on the doorstep is a dead mouse or another trophy of the hunt, uneaten, saved and deposited with pride and concern at the feet of a beloved owner. This is the attitude you want to cultivate in your Dachshund; not obedience to commands but cooperation with you in achieving whatever it is you want him to do and pride in fulfilling your wishes.

223

It is never a difficult task to win a dog's affection. A healthy, outgoing Dachshund puppy or adult dog already enjoys people. Being accepted as a new member of the family with as much attention as possible during his adjustment period is all that is needed.

However, during this period, avoid the necessity of correction or punishment. It is much easier to train a dog in good habits than to let him form bad ones and then retrain him. Just don't let him find out that when he is told to do something, it is possible to disobey you. For instance, if you want the dog to come to you, wait until you are positioned where he cannot avoid coming directly to you when you call him. If there is a chance that he might not come, a distraction or an alternate route, don't give him an order. Wait until you are in a position to pick him up and just lift him in your arms and put him where you want him to be.

If you don't want him to jump on the furniture, don't let him into the main part of the house unsupervised. You might even consider leaving a light leash on him when he is with you in the house and the minute he makes a move toward the chairs or the couch, step on it and just prevent him from finding out the comforts of upholstered furniture.

To leave any dog alone in a room or loose in the house while you are away is hazardous. With a dog as energetic, mischievous and curious as a Dachshund, it is disastrous. When you return, it is too late to scold him for the damage done. He will only understand he is being punished because the mess is there, not because he did it. Unless you catch him in the act, don't do anything. You will lose a good deal of his confidence in you if he feels, as he will, that you are treating him unjustly. He is apt to become stubborn and resentful.

Put him in a small room with his toys and nothing else available for chewing or in a wire crate, until you return.

A wire crate with a soft piece of old blanket instead of a dog bed is not only practical but economical, too. Unless the dog bed you buy in the pet shop is metal, the dog will chew it and the upholstered mattress that goes with it is apt to be filled with material harmful to a dog's stomach. Even if it is not ripped to pieces within a few days, it is hard to wash and even harder to dry.

The wire crate, whether or not you ever use it at a dog show, will have many uses other than a doggy bedroom. It can be a safe, comfortable place when travelling in the car and you will find yourself a welcome guest at motels if the clerks see that your dog is crated. At home it gets the dog out of the way quickly and comfortably when guests arrive who are afraid of dogs or uncomfortable with them or when the children invite friends allergic to dog hair to come over and play. Actually a crate is a modernized version of the cave in which the wild dog sought refuge. It is not at all difficult to get a Dachshund to accept it, particularly if there is enough blanket for him to burrow into. Left open, it provides instant security; closed, it confines him for short periods when he cannot, for some reason, be permitted the run of the house.

Many books have been written that outline step by step methods by which dogs can be trained to do almost anything. Dachshunds can hold their own when it comes to these accomplishments. Success with Dachshund training lies in the adaptation of these methods to suit the highly versatile, independent Dachshund. The late Blanche Saunders, first lady of Obedience training in America, said it best in the title of her book, *"Training You to Train Your Dog."*

With that, I'll tell you the saga of Larry Sorenson and his wife Cathy, who trained themselves first, then their Dachshund. Judging from the results, it is a good method.

According to Cathy, "Larry got into dogs through taking his Labrador Retriever through an Obedience class while he was in high school. The instructor, Bob Butz of Roseburg, Oregon, took him under his wing and Larry worked for him for three years until he graduated from school and went into the Navy." He and Cathy were married during his first assignment at San Diego. Larry's wedding present to his bride was a longhaired Dachshund puppy, "Missy", who later became Ch.L and C's Mischief Maker.

Getting "Missy's" championship was a snap compared to the try for her Companion Dog title. "She was a pill in the Obedience ring," says Cathy. "She always had a lot of fun flunking but she never did the same thing wrong twice." When she chose to do so, "Missy" was capable of good work. She got one score of 197½ (200 is a perfect score) and 196½ at another. She died early in 1975 before she had completed her third leg for the CD title. She left a handsome legacy behind. Bred in 1970 to Ch. Gay Lancer of Tauri, she produced: American and Canadian Champion L and C's Lancer's Image, a Specialty show Best of Breed and Hound Group winner; L and C's Tryann Surpasser, with only a major lacking for his championship; L and C's Jet Black Russian, just starting his show career; and L and C's Ch. Gay Personality, UD (Utility Dog).

In the meantime the Sorensons had been transferred to Oak Harbor, Washington, and had become active in dog clubs. For the past seven years they have conducted a 4-H dog group. Larry has been vice-president of the Cascade Dachshund Club and moved up to its presidency two years ago. He is also treasurer of the Whidbey Island all-breed kennel club and, in 1974, he became a professional handler. Cathy hopes to have her handler's license this year.

With this education in dogdom and their struggles with Missy in Obedience, the Sorensons were adequately prepared to take on the training of "Missy's" offspring, Ch. L and C's Gay Personality, or as he is known to Washingtonians, "Sunny."

In making his championship "Sunny" started and finished with majors, taking his first four points from the puppy class at the Seattle Kennel Club show under the late George Spradling, and finishing with another four-pointer at the Yakima Kennel Club show. He forged ahead taking a Best of Variety at the Cascade Dachshund Club Specialty and went on to take Best of Breed at another Specialty show. Then at the Vancouver Kennel Club show in 1974 he swept Best of Variety, the Hound Group, and Best in Show.

His Obedience career equalled his show record. Finishing his CD title in three shows with two firsts and a tie for fourth place, he finished his CDX (Companion Dog Excellent) title placing in the ribbons each time. He was just as successful in acquiring his UD title, with ribbons to show for every ring appearance. Shown in Canada, he acquired his Canadian Championship and finished his CD with a perfect score of 200 points. While in Canada he received the Dog World award for the dog making its CD title with scores of 195 or better.

When it comes to hunting, Cathy describes Sunny as a "pocket-sized retriever" on ducks and a skilled hunter of rabbits who "gives tongue" with the same vigor as his ancient forebears. The Sorensons look forward to his success in tracking, and in the meantime are enjoying his get which are on their way to championships.

"Sunny" is not the only champion longhaired Dachshund to have an outstanding Obedience career and also prove himself as sire of champions. Back in the late 1950s Dr. Betty Koss, a dentist living in Indianapolis, made one of her many trips abroad. As a breeder of smooth Dachshunds for about 15 years, she was surprised to see that in Germany the longhaired Dachshund was by far the most popular variety, while in America the longhair was virtually unknown in many parts of the country.

In searching for the reasons for this popularity, she became more and more interested in the variety. After visiting a number of kennels, she bought a male puppy, Gustav v. Steinwald from Heinrich Friedrich of Frankfort. Dr. Koss's associate (and co-owner of Gustav), Dolores Farley, took the gay little fellow to Obedience classes. He did so well that Dr. Koss and Miss Farley decided that they should enter him in an Obedience trial.

Gustav rewarded their efforts by finishing his CD in three shows with scores of 193½, 195½ and 196½ with Miss Farley handling. Ringsiders, watching the now mature Gustav in the Obedience ring, urged Dr. Koss and Miss Farley to enter him in breed. By 1961 he was not only a champion but had sired a number of promising offspring.

While Dr. Koss, with her knowledge of Dachshund conformation, recognized Gustav's potential as a show dog early, she had always been concerned with her dogs' dispositions and their response to discipline. Entering Gustav in Obedience *first* was her way of determining his disposition. Once that was proved, she could then proceed with his career as a show dog and producing sire.

It seems an interesting way, and a seldom-used one, of determining a dog's value as a sire who can pass on to his progeny both a good disposition and his own good looks. I'm sure there are others who have used this approach, but I can recall only one — The Seeing Eye, at Morristown, New Jersey.

Versatile Ch. L and C's Gay Personality, standard longhaired, is an all-breeds Best in Show winner, has the Utility Degree in Obedience, and competes in field trials. He is pictured in conformation win under judge Ethel Bigler, handled by his owner Larry Sorenson. —*Roberts*

"A pocket-sized retriever" is his owner's description of Gay Personality, shown here at work on a pigeon during a field training session.

I was an apprentice trainer there during World War II and among the many opportunities the job offered, was the sight of their top stud dog, a magnificent black German Shepherd Dog, line-bred from their own breeding kennels (Fortunate Fields). The institution's rule forbade the showing of the dog at dog shows but a number of Shepherd judges, including such authorities as Miss Marie Leary, Mrs. Madeline Baiter, Mr. and Mrs. Hugh Sloan and Mrs. Anne Carpenter, agreed that he could easily complete his championship. The authorities at the Seeing Eye were also well aware of his show potential and felt he should be kept at the kennel for breeding rather than be sent out as a guide dog.

However, before making a final decision, they put the dog through their routine guide dog training and tested him just like all their other dogs, on their own grounds and on the streets of Morristown.

When he passed the traffic tests with flying colors and proved steady and dependable in harness, they felt he was a wise choice and kept him for breeding.

The year 1961 was quite a monumental one for Dachshunds in Obedience. It was the first year that the Dachshund Club of America held Obedience trials in conjunction with its annual Specialty and it was the year that an Obedience-trained Dachshund won a standing ovation from the Sunday afternoon crowd at the International Kennel Club of Chicago's all-breed show.

The Dachshund Club of America's Specialty was held that year at Chicago on a Friday, just prior to the all-breed, two day Chicago classic. The Obedience judge was Harry Lowenbach. He found his highest scoring dog with 198½ points in Joseph and Hannelore Heller's longhaired Dachshund, Han-Jo's Alexander. The Hellers, from Minneapolis, could boast of a CD dam for their well-trained dog. She was Maxsohn's Desiree, CD. Second highest, with only a half point between them, was another longhair, Woden, owned by Betty E. Copeland of Little Silver, New Jersey. The dog that impressed judge Lowenbach most was one who failed to qualify. It was a wirehaired Dachshund, Holmdach's Most Happy Fella-W, owned by Jane and Marvin E. Paul of Springfield, Ohio. Mr. Lowenbach characterized his performance as "sparkling."

Most Happy Fella's ability to impress the judge was an inherited trait. His grandsire was American and Canadian Champion Fir Trees Coco, CD.

But it was a smooth Dachshund, Kleine Prinzessin Anastasia, CDX, owned by Mrs. Philip Kersch of Minneapolis that brought down the house at the Chicago show. Laurence Horswell was in the audience and describes the small red standard Doxie as "fairly frolicking through her paces." "Stacy" (the dog's call name) had earlier tied for first in Open Class B with a score of 199½, about as close to perfection as a dog can get without a perfect score of 200. She was then entered in the drill team exhibition, a tradition at Chicago, where Obedience-trained dogs are put through their paces in the Exhibition Hall's large main ring.

228

There were about twenty dogs entered, mostly large breeds, and the dogs walked around the ring single file, as if in an Obedience class. They were put through a series of exercises by a sort of judge-drillmaster. The crowd applauded ''Stacy'' on every exercise. It was when she was named winner that they rose to their feet to cheer.

Dachshund Obedience demonstrations were not a new thing for the Dachshund Club of America's membership. Nobody present at the DCA's Golden Anniversary Jubilee in 1945 can forget the one staged by Jack Baird. The participants were Kettlewire Fritz, CDX, owner-handled by Mrs. Beatrice E. Stamper and three veterans of World War II's K-9 Corps, handled by their trainer, Cpl. Harold Deitch. These were: Mr. and Mrs. John C. Chaffe's Zep v Waldbach, who served in the U.S.; Mrs. Richard Pell's Ch. Bertra v Hilldesheim; and Cpl. Deitch's own Herman of Lindakin. These last two had been successfully used for mine detection in Italy.

The first all-Dachshund Obedience Training Club was formed about 1965 by a group of Southern California breeders and Obedience enthusiasts. The Dachshund Obedience Club of Los Angeles continues strong to this day. However, most Obedience classes for Dachshunds have been sponsored by regional Dachshund clubs and the cost of the trainer and the training grounds paid for, at least partially, by the Club's treasury. Class members pay only a nominal fee.

Some of these found it necessary to include other breeds in the classes to help defray ever-increasing costs. I know of two such arrangements: classes sponsored by the Knickerbocker Dachshund Club and those of the Dachshund Association of Long Island, during the time when Mrs. William B. Hill Jr. was its president. There is a good case to be made as to how valuable the training results can be when the class is all Dachshunds and when it is a mixed bag. An all Dachshund class like the one in Los Angeles, sponsored by Dachshund breeders and trainers with an instructor knowledgable in the idiosyncrasies of Dachshunds should get excellent results. On the other hand, a class conducted by a trainer with experience in other breeds, and where the Dachshunds are worked along with a variety of other dogs, may be a good preparation for the Obedience ring where the dogs will encounter, at least one long sit and the long down, other breeds of dogs, and where the handlers will have a chance to compare their dogs' progress with that of potential competitors of other breeds. Apparently all systems work and Dachshunds from the East, West, North and South are holding their own in Obedience competition.

A good example of this is the story of Fritz von Morninseide owned by Herbert G. Renken of Corpus Christi, Texas. Back in 1960, Fritz, whose pedigree showed Marienlust in its background, made a perfect score, 200 points, in the Open B class and finished his UD title with a score of 198 in the Utility class at the same show — the Alamo Dog Obedience Club trials. Although Fritz was Mr. Renken's first Dachshund, he was not his first dog. Renken had owned and trained mongrels since boyhood and hunted with many of them. He once remarked, wistfully, that there were two things he would like to have, a Dachshund and a Cadillac. When his daughter, Allene, was old enough to earn her own money, she bought him a Dachshund. One out of two isn't bad.

In his effort to train Fritz in Obedience, Mr. Renken became a member of the Corpus Christi Kennel Club and chairman of the Corpus Christi Obedience Training Club. He confessed that Fritz was better in the Obedience ring than he was. His greatest problem, on entering a ring, was his own nervousness. He was so afraid that he would transmit this to his dog that he never once looked at him during the exercises. I can see it now; the man stalking woodenly around the ring, eyes straight ahead and the gay little dog at his heels, relaxed and happy, doing his job well and wondering what was wrong with his master. I had the same problem when I was showing a Whippet. I used the same strategy but it backfired. Hurt by what he considered my neglect, the Whippet sought consolation in the lap of an elderly lady who made encouraging sounds as we passed her. I wasn't even aware that I was alone in the ring until a burst of laughter from the ringside and the judge's command stopped me and on looking around I saw my dog watching me from ringside.

Charles Bonham, of Livermore, California, astonished his fellow hunters in Fresno County, during 1970, by taking to the fields with his two Obedience-trained Dachshunds, Mystery Maiden of Lotus Pond, CDX, a wirehaired and Amos of Lotus Pond, CDX, a longhaired. Mr. Bonham and his companions would hunt pheasant and quail in the long, grassy fields of a local ranch owner. The problem was not with the Dachshunds; they were satisfactory hunters but they carried their tails almost upright, like terriers while working, and these swift moving, feathery objects, the only visible sign of the Dachshunds in the tall grasses, were sometimes mistaken by Bonham's friends for running birds. The hunts were frequently enlivened by sharp cries from Mr. Bonham of "Don't shoot, that's my dog!"

One of the most spectacular achievements of Dachshunds and trainer occurred in 1974. In that year, Mrs. Eleanor B. Yetter of Lake County, Florida, and her smooth standard Dachshund, Berry III UDT, took highest scoring dog in trial at the Dachshund Club of America's Obedience trials. In 1973, he was the highest scoring Dachshund in the U.S. and the second highest scoring dog in the Hound breeds. Berry III has successfully passed eight tracking tests, a rare accomplishment for any dog. He was purchased from Peggy Westphal.

His predecessor, Berry Two, UDT, was bred by Mrs. Grace Burian. Another Dachshund, Karen, has been trained to help find lost persons. Mrs. Yetter's background is as impressive as her dogs' achievements. She has been working with and training dogs for nearly forty years. She is active with the

Lake County humane workers and law enforcement officials. Her German Shepherd Dog, Duke, is now in another Florida county helping law officers track down drugs.

It is not my purpose, in this chapter, to go into statistics and lists of individual accomplishments of Dachshunds and their owners in Obedience. This has long since been done by Barbara Nichols, Esthere Roberts and Ruth Morgan Sceva in their Obedience columns in *The American Dachshund*, which all of us who are interested in Obedience have enjoyed and which have provided much of the background for the material in this chapter. I have chosen the highlights of the sport to emphasize the importance of thorough preparation and knowledge of the Dachshund before undertaking its training and adapting the generally accepted methods of training to the Dachshund's unique personality. Having said that, I'll close with my favorite story about the Dachshund who reversed the whole process and trained the crew of the USS Oriskany to obey her.

Her name was Tripoli Schatzie, USN K-9 1/c, with three years of sea duty and one year of combat service. Schatzie covered the Pacific from Seattle to Korea, crossed the Equator, rounded the Horn, won the National Defense, Korean Service, China Service, United Nations ribbons and the Purple Heart, this last for injuries received in a gasoline fire during the Korean War.

Schatzie served her ship well. She had several litters of puppies, which, auctioned at raffles, brought in over $22,000 for charities. No dog but a Dachshund could have solved the problem of a shortlegged dog getting from deck to deck on a big carrier. Schatzie would just sit before the insurmountable obstacle in her way and look appealingly at the first passing sailor.

Ch. Theo vom Lindenbuhl, bred by Simon Barthel (Germany) and imported to America by Mrs. Joseph J. Donahue III, one of the early field trial enthusiasts.

A pair of miniature longhaired Dachshunds from the Primrose Patch Kennels of Mr. and Mrs. Peter Van Brunt strike a hunting pose with appropriate accessories. —*Shafer*

Tally Ho!

HUNTING WILD GAME with a shovel and a Dachshund may not sound very exciting to present day sportsmen but during the nineteenth century and earlier, it was considered an efficient way to keep rural areas free from fox, badger, otter, martin, weasel, ferret and small vermin.

Dachshunds were let loose to locate a hole or cave. Men followed with a pick and shovel. On locating the lair the Dachshund would enter it and work its way through the underground passages until it had cornered its prey. It would then hold it at bay, barking loudly. The men, above ground, followed the sounds of the Dachshund's bark and began digging at the point from which it came. When they had reached the prey, they dispatched it and brought out the Dachshund unless the little warrior had already scrambled out on his own.

Eventually this work became a sport and field trials for below the earth hunting were established. As the sport became more popular, more tests (including some held above the earth) and more rules were added. Natural conditions were not always available so artificial ones were made.

Dachshund field trials are still held today, in Germany and elsewhere on the continent of Europe and in the United States. There is one important difference between the American and European Dachshund trials; the Americans have thrown away the shovels and taken to the woods and fields with their Dachshunds for a day's sport with nobody hurt, not even the hunted.

For a look at nineteenth century hunting with Dachshunds and the conduct of field trials of that period we have the words of a German author who signs himself "R. Corneli." He wrote a book, *Der Dachshund*, published in Berlin in 1885. Corneli was an estate manager of a large hunting preserve owned by one of the German nobility. After the fashion of the day, the estate's owner is not named in the book.

Corneli was an avid hunter. He used dogs to help him locate game but he was not particularly interested in the various breeds. He only asked that the dogs do the work he required. It soon became apparent to him that some breeds worked better than others and he began to investigate the possibility of using just one breed for his hunting.

He found that there was no one breed that could hunt everything and cope with all kinds of territory; but he did find a combination of two breeds, working together, that gave him the results he sought. In the stilted, poetic language of his day, Corneli wrote, "Whoever today possesses a good Pointer and a Dachshund is substantially fitted to participate in all the wild arts."

"Working the earth," he wrote, "is the main business of the Dachshund. He is the only hound of our native breeds who is able to carry out a consistently good performance. Whether in rugged field, caving sand beds, cultivated farmlands or protective thickets, he always pursues a strong offensive to jump the enemy heartily and give indication of its presence to his master."

He appreciated the Dachshund's versatility both above and below the earth. He also liked the fact that the Dachshund would work alone, with another dog of his own or a different breed, or with a pack of dogs. He praised the work of Dachshunds with Otterhound packs and pooh-poohed the opinions of some foresters that the Dachshunds did not like to work in water. It was lack of training in water work, not lack of spirit, he said, that made the Dachshund reluctant to pursue game beyond the water's edge.

He liked to work upland game with a Dachshund but realized its limitations over large areas. So he used the Pointer and the Dachshund as a pair, the Pointer covering the large open spaces and the Dachshund flushing game from thickets and coverts. He also tells of its ability at tracking large game and following a blood trail. "Not even the tusks of the mighty boar discourages the small upstart." he wrote. "In all these tasks he shows the same ease, liveliness of spirit and endurance."

He also noted that the Dachshund was an excellent watchdog, persistent and smart in his assessment of strangers approaching his master.

"With the proper individual handling, he will be a successful and dependable dog. If he is badly handled, he is easily rebellious and unsuccessful — a sign of great dignity, honor and outstanding attainment," he said. It is probably as true an assessment of today's Dachshunds as those of past centuries.

Corneli valued Dachshunds as much for their loyalty and devotion as he did for their hunting ability. He recalls "a touching scene where the true companion of the hunt sits before his master who has been shot and in death as in life, will not leave him."

He tells of his own two Dachshunds, Daxl and Bergl. While hunting in the forest the dogs ranged out of sight. This was not alarming. It often happened and when game was located they invariably barked to let him know where they were. He waited to hear their voices but time went on and by nightfall, when no sound came, it was apparent that something had happened to the pair. For five days Corneli roamed the woods calling his dogs and leaving word with the woodcutters and foresters of his loss. On the fifth day a woodcutter approached him and told him of a small dog which could not be coaxed away from a stone which had rolled onto the forest floor.

234

Corneli followed him to the spot and there was a weak and exhausted Bergl. The dog greeted him effusively but immediately returned to the stone and began to dig furiously. Corneli and the woodcutter pried up the boulder. Below it was a hole, the entrance to a fox den and from it came the whining voice of Daxl. The dog had pursued the fox into the hole and the stone had rolled over the entrance sealing in both animals. "With a great deal of barking and manifestations of joy, the two friends greeted each other. The expressions of joy at their reunion was wonderful to behold," wrote Corneli.

Examining the den, Corneli found the head and skeleton of a full grown fox. Daxl had survived by killing it and eating it during his five day imprisonment. "Of the terrible battle for iife and death between Daxl and the fox, the traces were the bitten head and flanks of the dog. But the faithful Bergl had suffered too. He had starved for five days awaiting the return of his comrade. Truly a beautiful tribute to these animals."

Corneli observed that, with no hunting experience, Dachshunds could be taken to an area where game was plentiful and when turned loose would immediately begin to hunt, often giving tongue in the process. I have seen the same thing happen with modern dogs. In the late 1969s, at the Dachshund Club of New Jersey's field trial, a nine-year-old black and tan bitch entered in a class of 16 in the Open Bitch stake, placed fourth. She was Teckla von Teckelhof II, C.D. owned by Elizabeth W. McNeill of Manhattan. Teckla's only previous experience with rabbits had been casual encounters as she walked, on leash, through Central Park with her owner. Most of her exercise had been done walking the city streets with Mrs. McNeill.

From his experiences, Corneli concluded that Dachshunds were: "Not stunted misfits of another breed but a distinct type, a heritage from the dim past, which in their wild state pursued the same animals that they now continue to hunt since man has domesticated them." To substantiate his theory, Corneli pointed to the finding of short-legged, Dachshundlike animal skeletons in parts of South America and to drawings and carvings in Egyptian tombs showing short-legged, long-bodied dogs hunting with kings. This theory, believed by many at the time, has since been largely discounted by modern researchers but the belief still persists among some present day students of Dachshund lore.

The establishment of Dachshund field trials in Germany came about through the reorganization of the German Register in 1879–1882. It set standards for Dachshunds as to appearance and temperament. To best show their hunting abilities, the German Hunt Club, largely through the efforts of one of its members, Deputy Premier von der Bosch, Baron of Hirschfelt, established "open trials in the practical arts." The popularity of these trials spread through Europe. Corneli describes the International Hunt Show held at Cleves in Belgium.

The courses were set in the oak forests outside the city. They fanned out in radii from a central spot. The artificial burrows were cut in the heavy, greasy clay soil and covered with pieces of board. Rebound nets were placed at the end of each tunnel or burrow and the dog was to drive the animal, which had been previously placed in one of the burrows, out into the net where it was caught by the stewards and returned for use by the next dog. There were also blood trials where a freshly killed carcass was dragged along the ground and left concealed in a thicket. The Dachshund was expected to follow the trail and give tongue on finding the carcass. There were other above the ground tests on rabbits and other small game.

These tests, in Corneli's opinion, were of some value in setting standards for Dachshunds as hunters, but he felt that a good many able dogs did poorly because of the crowds and the artificial conditions. He tells of two dogs both awarded first place at Cleves: "Waldman, a yellowish, heavily built Dachshund who, in spite of his size, worked the narrow burrows with great persistence and drove the badger through the whole works without allowing him sojourn in any of the chambers; and Erdman, a black and yellow mottled Dachshund who drove the badger into the second chamber and held him at bay until the judges removed him." He was disappointed in the performance of two bitches, Ine and Erna. He had seen them work well but at the trials they were confused and frightened by the crowds and did poorly. Corneli felt the trial failed to bring out their true ability.

He was contemptuous of dog shows. This grading of dogs for form and beauty were, he said, ruining the breed. The show dogs were too soft, too large or low stationed and lacked the aggressive attitude of what he considered the true hunter. When confronted by a larger and more aggressive breed on the show grounds, they were more apt, he said, to seek refuge behind their owners than rush to attack with teeth bared ready to fight to the death. I think Corneli would have been pleased at a solution I saw at the Crufts show in England. It was a gamekeepers class and gamekeepers and professional hunters brought in their top dogs in various sporting breeds to be judged on condition and proven hunting ability. None of them would have placed in a breed class, but here they were, shown with pride by their owners, so that the public could see what a real hunting dog looked like.

Corneli and others like him declared that too much emphasis was being placed on looks and not enough on the dogs' ability to hunt. Many breeders agreed with him and the argument still goes on, not only in Germany but in other countries and with other breeds as well.

The German solution has been to make field trial awards a requirement for top honors in German and European dog shows. Germany, like most European countries, is a member of the FCI (*Fédération Cynologique Internationale*) with headquarters in Brussels, Belgium. Its members have a unified system of conducting dog shows and grouping the various breeds of dogs. It permits the country of origin to set breed standards for its native dogs and to make its own requirements for national and international championships. The Germans have made a field trial award, in addition to International Championships for Beauty (CACIB — *Certificats d'Aptitude au Championat de Beauté*) in two different countries under two different judges, a requirement for national and international Dachshund championships.

There are eleven different field trial awards that can be won. For work under the earth there are the following:

BhdFK (Bauhund-Fuchs-im Kunstbau), dog examined at an artificial fox hole.

BhdFN (Bauhund-Fuchs -im Naturbau), dog examined at a natural fox hole.

BhdDK (Bauhund -Dachs- im Kunstbau), dog examined at an artificial badger den.

BhdDN (Bauhund-Dachs- im Naturbau), dog examined at a natural badger den.

The next two are limited to Rabbit Dachshunds only:

KSsch1H (Kaninchenschleppe mit Herausziehen) Rabbit Dachshund examined at rabbit warren and dragging rabbit out.

KSprN (Kaninchensprenger Natur) Rabbit Dachshund flushing rabbit out of a natural warren.

For work above the earth, a Dachshund can receive:

Sp (Spurlaut) giving tongue at a live rabbit.

SchwhdK (Schweisshund auf der kuenstlichen Faehrte) following an artificial trail of natural blood.

SchwhdN (Schweisshund auf der Naturfaehrte) following wounded game on a natural trail. This test is rare for obvious reasons.

St. (Stoeberpruefung) finding game in thick underbrush, giving tongue and following. Three further obedience tests are also required for the St.

Vp (Vielseitigkeitspruefung) a complex series of tests of the dog's versatility as a hunter. It is considered the most important and prestigious of all trials and is earned mainly by expert hunters.

Besides the requirement of one or more of these titles as a condition for its championship, these field trial awards are listed in the dog's pedigree and underlined in red to emphasize their importance.

The position of the Dachshund Club of America reflects the thinking expressed by Corneli 100 years ago, namely that the Dachshund is a born hunter and that his skill at competitive field trials is largely dependent on the trainer's ability to bring out the best of an inherited hunting instinct. Since this acquired skill is not an inherited factor, only a trainer's improvement on nature, the DCA saw no reason to include it in the dog's pedigree or to make it a requirement of championship. They did, however, feel that those members who wanted to prove their dogs as hunters under competitive conditions, and who were willing to spend the time and effort to train them, should be provided with an opportunity to do so. In 1935, the Club sponsored its first Dachshund field trial at Lamington, N.J.

There had been Dachshund field trials in America prior to this. They were based on the German trials with artificial burrows, blood trails, above the earth tests and tests under natural conditions whenever possible. They were conducted by a group of Dachshund breeders who were also well-known sportsmen and women in other sporting endeavors. These people felt, like many German breeders, that Dachshunds were being spoiled by dog shows and the wide acceptance of the breed as house pets.

In 1933 this group incorporated under the name of The United States Dachshund Field Trial Club. Its seven charter members were George F. Steele, Mrs. H. Gordon Mullen, David T. Carlisle, Rudolph W. Ilgner, Mrs. C. Davies Tainter, Fred Vodegel and Mrs. Joseph J. O'Donohue, III.

They published a book early in 1935, listing their activities and accomplishments to that date. In the foreword, Morgan S. Reichner, then club president, wrote, "The purpose and aim of this organization is to keep alive the hardy courage and keen instinct of the Dachshund breed, spirited hunter in the old countries, but likely to be regarded as pets in this country. We propose to do this by encouraging and holding field trials for the breed, teaching those who are interested how to train their dogs, and offering information upon every subject connected with Dachshunds and their work."

In the same book, Mrs. O'Donohue wrote the club's brief history. She said, "It was because of a difference of opinion entertained by these people (the Club's seven charter members) that they broke away from the Dachshund Club of America, Inc., feeling that there was a need to develop, in America, the hunting qualities of the Dachshund, as well as to produce better dogs."

The club had some difficulties in its attempt to accomplish its first aim, to promote the Dachshund as a hunter.

The club's first board of directors, Rudolph W. Ilgner, G.F. Steele, Mrs. Norton Perkins and Fred Vodegel, imported two sets of digs and accessories from Germany. These were set into the ground, one in New Jersey and the other in Connecticut, for use by club members. Other members built digs on their own properties and all were made available to members for training. Rules for training and for conducting trials were translated from the German and adapted for use in America but only a few hardy supporters showed any

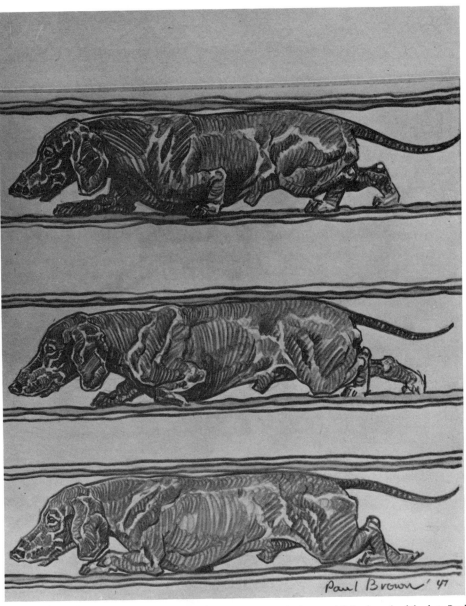

Dachshund working in an underground burrow. This never-before-published work of the late Paul Brown is from the collection of Mrs. Jeannette W. Cross. It illustrates both the skeletal and muscular action used by the Dachshund in its underground work.

real desire to continue training to the point where their dogs were ready for a full scale competitive trial.

Quite a few sports-minded people in the New York area joined out of curiosity, among them some important members of the Dachshund Club of America who kept their membership in both clubs. Most of them did not think it very sporting to send a dog down a hole to scare a caged young fox, rabbit or hamster half to death. Other members, like Harry T. Peters, Sr. (Master of the Meadowbrook Hounds in the days when the Duke of Windsor, then Prince of Wales, was often a member of the field) and Jay F. Carlisle (whose Wingan Kennels of Labrador Retrievers were making field trial history for their breed) found the going dull compared to the thrill of pursuing a fox by riding a spirited thoroughbred behind a pack of Foxhounds, or watching a Retriever complete a triple retrieve in the rough waters of Long Island Sound. So the club members held their private trials and hoped for an increase in trained hunting Dachshunds at a future date.

They had better luck with their secondary aim, breeding better Dachshunds. To encourage this they held their first specialty show in conjunction with the Ladies Kennel Club of America at Mineola, Long Island, in May of 1934. The prize list was a generous one for the time, $200. The entry was 44 dogs and the quality was indeed high.

Best of Breed was a black and tan smooth, a German import, Theo v Lindenbuhl of Ren Lak, owned by Mrs. O'Donohue. Born in 1931, Theo had been rated v — (*vorzuglich*) — which translates as "excellent" in English — at dog shows and field trials in his native land. He made his American debut at the 1933 Westminster show and promptly took Best of Winners. Another notable entry was a wirehaired bitch, Vodegel's Parmenia, Reserve Winners Bitch. Parmenia, a homebred from Fred Vodegel's kennels, had been shown earlier in the year at Westminster under James Trullinger. Trullinger, writing of his decision at the 1934 Westminster show, said of Parmenia, "She is one of the most outstanding wires I have ever seen. I am amazed to find she is only 11 months old. When she is fully developed, Parmenia will beat anything on the bench."

Then, as suddenly as it had started, the club ended. Weeks of digging in preparation for a trial, and the long periods of training just didn't seem worth the effort and most of the members just lost interest.

This sudden demise put the Dachshund Club of America in a quandary. Most of its members had no interest in field trials, but an important minority had broken away from the fold and organized and run field trials of a sort because of this indifference to the emphasis of Dachshunds as sporting hounds. To get them back, the DCA would have to hold field trials. But it was impossible to conduct them under the earth; it was just too much work. Some of the members felt that it was cruel and that the risk of cave-ins while the dogs were working underground was too much of a risk for their prize-winning dogs.

240

Finally they came up with a bloodless, above the earth trial which required the dogs to either find or be put on a fresh rabbit trail, follow it, give tongue and flush the rabbit into the open. Once this was accomplished the dog was picked up and the rabbit was free to pursue his own way. The dog's hunting instinct was established and nobody got hurt.

All that was required was a piece of land stocked with native rabbits, a committee (readily available from among those interested in holding the trials) to do the necessary paperwork, and the judges.

The idea was submitted and approved by the Dachshund Club of America's membership, which was quickly followed by American Kennel Club approval, and in September of 1935, the Dachshund Club of America's first Field Trial was off and running.

I remember taking my two longhaired Dachshunds to these trials during the '50s. The rules are still the same. There is an open all age stake for dogs, another for bitches and a third class for Field Trial champions only.

The dogs are divided in pairs and a schedule of starting times for each pair is established. At the start of the trial, each exhibitor is given a numbered armband and told the number of the dog that is to run the first series with him and the time at which he is scheduled to start. The two judges and the steward are followed by the first pair of dogs, on leash, with their handlers. The gallery and the other exhibitors, whose turns will come later, fan out and beat the bushes to rouse a rabbit to action.

Frequently a rabbit will pop up at some distance from the judges and the dogs, so the one who sights the rabbit calls out "Tally-ho" and stands at the spot where the rabbit appeared and vanished. The two dogs are rushed to the spot and unleashed. The dog that picks up the trail first, follows it with the most persistence, gives tongue and flushes out the rabbit, is the winner of that particular pair.

The second pair is then brought up and the process is repeated until all the pairs of dogs have been run. The winners of each of these pairs are then paired off again against each other for the second series and so it continues through the morning until the contest narrows down to a single pair. The winner here is the one to receive points toward a field championship. Points also go to the second and third place winners.

The process is repeated, after a remarkably hearty lunch, for the bitch stakes, and the grand finale is the championship stake where the really good hunters show their skill.

The chief workers during the 1935–1947 period were George McKay Schieffelin, Earl Cutler and, rather surprisingly, Mrs. Percy Hoopes, an actress-turned-sportswoman who bred Beagles and was interested in the idea of Dachshunds performing the same tasks as her little hunters.

Two trials were held during 1935. From then on there were three trials per year until 1941. For some unknown reason interest began to wane and the committee could mount only one trial per year. It proved to be the ultimate discouragement. With only a yearly chance toward the 25 points necessary for a championship and a steadily diminishing entry, the field trials lapsed after the 1947 trial and none were held from 1948 through 1950.

No one regretted this more than Laurence Horswell, information chairman for the Dachshund Club of America and a powerful voice on its board of directors. He felt that some action was necessary to remind judges and dog show exhibitors that the Dachshund's true purpose was as a hunting hound and no matter how much the breed triumphed in the show ring, the field trials should be revived as a way of proving its inherited hunting instincts.

Most of the club members were indifferent to the suggestion but there was a small but enthusiastic group prepared to undertake the revival. They were: the David Mullens, the George Wanners, Ernest Wood, the Charles W. Campbells, Mrs. Jeannette Cross (who had been active in the field trials since the 1930s), Fairfield Pope Day (a field trialer in Pointers and Setters who also had some good Dachshunds), the Allen Westphals, the Eric Holmbergs, Peter Monks, Dr. and Mrs. George Pickett, Ruth Gano and Mrs. Kay Buckmaster. There were others who lent moral support, if not active participation in the movement.

Strong opposition came from the club secretary, Mrs. William Burr Hill, Jr. Already familiarly known to Club members as "Gracie," she had a made a name for herself as a breeder of longhaired Dachshunds and had proved to be a capable and diplomatic officer of the club. Usually she and Horswell worked together as a team and it was strange to see them so divided on the field trial question.

As it turned out, Gracie's opposition was based on a childhood recollection of her older brothers' hunting prowess. "There was always something dead and bloody lying on the kitchen table" she once told me. She feared that encouragement of the trials might eventually result in underground work. Assured that the rules would not be changed, she withdrew her opposition and early arrivals at the 1951 trials found hot coffee and a breakfast awaiting them in the chill dawn of a November morning because Grace Hill and her committee had risen in the dark and made the long trip from Hicksville, Long Island, to Lamington to prepare it. While the trials were in progress, a gourmet feast of roasts and casseroles brought by Mrs. Hill and her committee simmered in the huge wood and coal stove. The DCA Field trial lunches became almost as much of a drawing card as the trials themselves.

With only one trial a year, the problem of gaining the 25 points necessary for championship seemed as remote as ever. Members of the New Jersey Dachshund Club with an assist from some of the Pennsylvania Dachshund Club members, decided that a second trial would be helpful and in April of 1967, they held their first field trial.

It was sponsored by the New Jersey Dachshund Club and the same group which supported the Dachshund Club of America's trials turned out to support the New Jersey Club's efforts. There have been nine trials to date, all well

242

supported. Some new names have been added (J. David Lambersons, David C. Feisner, Jr., Morris Greenblatt) and at the 1975 trial Mrs. Jeannette Cross was still listed among the exhibitors.

The Modern Scene

As early as 1965, Mrs. Cross saw the need for additional trials to hold the interest of newcomers and provide more opportunities for people to gain championships for their dogs. By 1971 she had convinced members of the Connecticut Yankee Dachshund Club that it was in the best interests of the breed to sponsor these trials and in May of that year the club held its first field trial on the grounds of the Naugatuck Valley Beagle Club. The date has since been changed to November and the grounds are now those of the Charter Oak Beagle Club at Durham, Conn. The New Jersey Dachshund Club originally used the Brady Camp at Lamington, the same grounds as those of the Dachshund Club of America, but found better conditions and more rabbits at the Central New Jersey Beagle Club grounds at Sergeantsville, N.J.

The great majority of field trial exhibitors are also breeders and exhibitors in the show ring, although not always with the same dogs. Thus the aims of the old United States Dachshund Field Trial club have been realized in a somewhat different way than its founders intended.

Special mention is due two of the many good judges who have officiated at the Dachshund field trials. Fred Huyler, who judged the 1935 trials and many others, was an authority on Beagles. As manager of the James Cox Brady estate at Lamington, he persuaded his employer to permit the trials to be held there, scouted the grounds to locate the places which held the largest rabbit population and held informal critiques after the trials which were an education to the exhibitors in training methods and the ways of wild life.

He was succeeded by Lloyd Bowers, another Beagle judge and breeder, who judged both the Dachshund Club of America and the New Jersey Dachshund Club trials. It was my privilege to judge one of the trials with Mr. Bowers. Like working with Fred Huyler, it was an education in both judging procedure and wild life management. George Wanner wrote me, "Lloyd Bowers helped me immeasurably from the very first and the Dachshund Club of America and the New Jersey Dachshund Club have a warm spot for Lloyd. Without his encouragement and training, it would have been much more difficult."

Probably the only German imports in recent years have been made by field trial enthusiasts, Dr. John Jeanneney and Herta Schofield. They have won their Field Trial Championships but have not been shown at dog shows. Perhaps they share Mr. and Mrs. George Goodspeed's opinion, that dog shows are just dull, compared to field trials and the Dachshund's hunting song.

This pack of hunting Dachshunds was owned by the late Mrs. Kent Leavitt of Millbrook, N.Y., a famous horsewoman who enjoyed maintaining her own pack of Dachshunds which she hunted regularly, and with which she sometimes gave exhibitions at hunt meets. Peggy Westphal gives this background on the pack's breeding: "The original was Pickle v Westphalen (Ch. Fleet of Gera ex Ch. Phalarope v Westphalen). She was bred to Ch. Limelight v Westphalen, who was subsequently sent to Japan where he became a champion. 'Limey' was by Ch. White Gables Ristocrat ex Phalarope. Some of the pups took their classes at the Dachshund Club of America specialty one year, right from the pack! Mrs. Leavitt had the pack trained to a fare-thee-well, and wow, did they hunt!"

The Goodspeeds are in a class by themselves in field trial competition. They entered their first Dachshund Field trial in 1952 and showed continually up to 1965. In 1965, the Greenfield Longhaired Dachshunds, from their kennels at Greenfield Hill, Fairfield, Connecticut, included eleven Dachshunds with points toward field trial championships, four that were Field Champions and one bench champion. Ch. Big Inch of Greenfield represented their one sortie into the world of dog shows. Once was enough.

Their breeding stock was a combination of German, English and the best of American show winners. Bianca von Gritgluck was brought home from Germany at the close of World War II, by their son. She was excellent quality, according to Mrs. Minna Dewell, a dog show judge and a neighbor of the Goodspeeds. Bianca was bred to Mrs. William B. Hill, Jr.'s, Ch. William de Sangpur; the Goodspeeds acquired another bitch, the English-bred Ch. Primrose Patch Pretzel Bit, who was, in turn, bred to Ch. Roderick von der Nidda and to Ch. Hussar von der Nidda. The Goodspeeds soon had their own pack of hunting Dachshunds to add to the week-end clamour of hunting dogs in action, as the Fairfield County Hunt's foxhounds and the Goodspeeds' pack of Dachshunds took to the woods and fields at the same time.

Mrs. Goodspeed contributed a short article "The Education of a Hunter" to *Popular Dogs Magazine* in its October 1965 issue. She concluded with this statement, "No special training is required for either handler or hound. All that a Dachshund needs, really, is rabbit country, a fresh tally-ho, and a chance to prove his natural skill." Corneli said the same thing more than one hundred years ago.

FIELD TRIAL CHAMPIONS

1936	Amsel v Holzgarten	George McKay Schieffelin
1938	Stine v Schwarlenbrook	Thomas H. Andrews
	Adolph v Ernst	Fred Ernst
1939	Amsels Truffles	George McKay Schieffelin
1940	Alfreda v Kargollheim	Gerald M. Livingston
1943	Vagabund v Paulinenberg	George C. White
1944	Truffles Trigamous Trixie	Earl Cutler
1956	Teufelin mit Honig	Mrs. George S. Goodspeed.
1957	Baskerville of Greenfield	Mrs. George S. Goodspeed
1958	Rock City Rickey	Paul J. Taylor
1959	Augusta of Willow Creek, CD	Mrs. Katharine Buckmaster
1961	Die Liebe Hussarin	Mrs. George S. Goodspeed
1963	Rock City Rocco	Paul J. Taylor
	Rock City Tess	Paul J. Taylor
1964	Cyrano's Plume of Greenfield	Mrs. George S. Goodspeed
1965	Red Mist of Da-Dor	Mrs. Dorothy M. Mullen
1967	Carla vom Rode (German import)	Dr. John Jeanneney
	Kookie of Da-Dor	Mrs. Dorothy M. Mullen
1968	Uta v Moosbach	Dr. John Jeanneney and James Swyler
1969	Quarta von der Lonsheide (German import)	Dr. John Jeanneney
	Baron von Haussen	George R. Magee.
1971	Klara v Wald Wind	Martha-Ann H. Lamberson.
	Holmdach's Constant Avenger	J. David Lamberson and Mrs. Elisabeth Holmberg.
	Ric-Rans Wee Waggie Maggie	Robert Stephenson.
1972	Bench Champion Nobles Carpetbagger	Nancy L. Nolan
	Helia v Wald Wind	Martha-Ann H. Lamberson
	Gabrielle v Wald Wind	Martha-Ann H. Lamberson
1973	Clary vom Moosbach	Dr. John Jeanneney
	Nantschi von der Rotmainquelle (German import)	Herta E Schofield
1975	Liesele von Wald Wind, CD	Martha-Ann H. Lamberson
	Magee's Little Haussen	George Magee
	Wald Wind's Constant Electra	Martha- Ann H. Lamberson.

Dachshund Racing

SIGHT HOUND RACING as an amateur sport is not new, but the inclusion of Dachshunds has turned it into a hilarious one. For a good many years coursing breeds have been stepping down from their benches at the Chicago International Kennel Club show and making their way to a tan-bark covered, two hundred yard straightaway in one section of the huge amphitheatre, to compete in a series of races, complete with starting boxes, an artificial lure and — just in case — muzzles for the excitable racers. The dogs, their owners and the audiences have loved it and various clubs throughout the country have formed racing groups and held exhibitions and race meets. Among these is the Eastern Coursing Club. From here on, Mrs. Jeannette W. Cross tells the story:

"The idea had its beginning in June, 1966 at the Greenwich Kennel Club's all-breed show in Connecticut where exhibition Afghan Hound races were presented for the first time on the Eastern seaboard. The Afghan racing was a smashing success. It had everything — glamour, comedy and excitement. The races were most professionally staged, with a fenced-in one hundred and eighty yard straightaway course, starting boxes, an authentic Whippet lure, walkie-talkies for the judges and officials and racing silks for the dogs to wear. Dachshund owners, watching the Afghans, felt a little wistful. 'Shucks', they were thinking, 'wouldn't it be fun if we could do something like this with our dogs?' Then came the cheering thought, 'Who says we can't?'

"The Eastern Coursing Club which was responsible for the racing at Greenwich, holds scheduled practice sessions. When the Coursing Club was approached by a representative of the Connecticut Yankee Dachshund Club about the possibility of some Dachshunds having a try-out at the Fall practice racing meets, a most cordial invitation was promptly offered.

"Before the first practice session took place, in September, there were serious doubts about whether the Doxies would follow the lure and race. The performance put on by the Dachshunds participating quickly settled that question. To the delight of their owners, they took to racing at once and loved it. The star athlete of the meet was Effie Allen's wirehaired bitch, 'Agnes'."

From then on, according to Mrs. Cross, Dachshunds frequently attended the practice racing meets. She describes a large, elaborate one held at the Edward Gerbers' farm at Millbrook, N.Y.

"Almost all of the coursing breeds were represented and no less than 26 Dachshunds were present and racing. Of all the breeds that raced that day, the Dachshunds had the greatest spectator appeal and won the most applause, cheers and laughter.

"Mrs. George Pickett's red smooth bitch, Sherry, was the leading lady at this event. A good time was had by all and it appears that the Eastern Dachshunds are really off and running."

By 1968, Dachshunds were racing on the West Coast. The hilarious performances put on by the galloping Dachshunds were the big hit of the enormous Golden Gate Kennel Club shows held at the Cow Palace in San Francisco in '68 and '69. In November of 1974, the Cascade Dachshund Club of Washington held its first exhibition of Dachshund racing for the Widbey Island Kennel Club.

The sport is on the increase and seems to offer an alternative to the Dachshund Field trials in areas where open land is limited, game scarce and dog owners unable to spend a whole day, from dawn to dusk, at a trial.

A Breeder-Exhibitor
Speaks Her Mind

M RS. ALAN WESTPHAL, Peggy to Dachshundists everywhere, is the owner of the famous von Westphalen Kennels at Bedford, New York. During her 20 years of raising dogs, Peggy has worked out theories of breeding and kenneling that are reflected in dogs that are happy and in robust condition, and in a record of some 200 homebred champions, plus many more sired by the kennel's outstanding stud dogs. All varieties are represented, and two of the older wirehaired and smooth champions have, between them, sired about 85 champions. The younger dogs include a several times Best in Show Dachshund and the top Best in Show winning American Cocker Spaniel of all time.

Peggy grew up in a pet-loving household. There were always plenty of dogs, but never a Dachshund. She acquired her first when her husband brought home a Dachshund puppy bitch as a surprise. It wasn't altogether a pleasant one. In fact, "I hated them," says Peggy, "I hadn't been exposed to them very much and thought they were strange-looking." Of course the puppy soon became a treasured pet, and proved her merit by winning Obedience titles and coming within two points of a field-trial championship.

One day Peggy was at a dog show for an Obedience trial. She wandered over to the Dachshund breed ring. "My dog didn't look like those dogs," she remembers, ". . . every beginner's story, I guess." Before long, she got to know some of the people breeding show quality Dachshunds. Foundation stock was purchased and von Westphalen was off and running. This was literally, all too true.

For Alan Westphal's business career has caused the family to make frequent moves, always accompanied by 15 to 30 dogs. The move to Bedford, about ten years ago, is probably the most enduring one.

Peggy is a firm believer in lots of attention for dogs and in the "no-run" system of kenneling. "I don't like putting dogs in runs," she explains. "They get bored and noisy and work up antagonisms running up and down their fences. Besides, the dogs are never handled if all you have to do is to open trap doors from stalls to runs." Her dogs are exercised in groups, in large enclosed areas, and for long periods of time.

The house and property are just fine for this type of set-up. The house has large, high ceilinged rooms, including a sun room at the back; three walls of windows, bright, warm and perfect for new puppies. The kennel addition was built directly off the sun room; two 9' x 12' rooms, the first for the older puppies and the farthest back for the adult dogs. Both rooms have cross ventilation and are heated through the house heating system, and air conditioned by window units. Floors are linoleum tile in the puppy nursery and in the older puppy room and cement in the adult dog's room. Walls are treated with epoxy paint.

All of the kennel dogs are individually housed in wire crates, with the new puppies in wood and wire mesh pens. The older puppy room has a shelf across one wall with storage cabinets above it. The adult kennel room has crates in two or three tiers. Bedding is shredded newspaper except for the adult dogs who have blankets, something that seems especially necessary for Dachshund contentment.

Except for young puppies, all the dogs are outside several hours a day. The doors from the two kennel rooms open onto adjacent pens, each 6' x 20' with a 4' chain link fence and an outer wooden stockade fence that screens the pens from the driveway. These face a narrow path, across which are four more pens used mostly for visiting bitches. The path opens into a half acre enclosed grass paddock to which the dogs always have access.

Dachshunds do best when kept busy. There is a lot to occupy them in these surroundings. They have each other to play with, land to investigate, holes to dig, moles to tunnel after. They are remarkably quiet. Either Peggy or an assistant is always around to put a quick stop to squabbles and to watch the kennel "pecking order." New homes are found for persistent bullies or the persistently bullied.

There is no question that personal attention for the dogs and "no-run" kenneling make for more work, but the routine is handled on a rotating schedule of meals, exercise and chores that starts early in the morning with the puppies' first feeding of the day, letting out the first group of dogs and putting fresh paper in the crates. It demands frequent daily contact with every dog. They love it and so does Peggy. This is what it is all about, she says.

Peggy has contributed some of her thoughts on Dachshunds for this chapter. Here, in her own words, are some observations on the differences in the varieties, with particular emphasis on the breeding of wirehairs:

Ch. Westphal's Just A Nip, dam of a number of champions, examples a good wire expression.

Ch. Westphal's Shillalah has a record of 6 BIS and 46 Groups, and is sire of 42 champions (as of December 1975.) —Wilson

Peggy Westphal showing Ch. Westphal's Shillalah to a 1968 win under judge Albert E. Van Court.—Shafer

Ch. Penny Candy v Westphalen, dam of champions. —*Wilson*

Ch. Kleetal's Raven Wing (pictured at 8 years of age), sire of 12 champions. Owned by Peggy Westphal. —*Tauskey*

Ch. Sheen v Westphalen.

252

Dachshunds are fun. They are a breed that has always been "way up there" in registrations and one can well understand why.

They are hardy, fun loving, intelligent creatures and Teutonically opinionated. They also put their genius to circumventing anything they choose not to do. They love their creature comforts, too.

When acquired as puppies, and raised with children, they are marvelous with kids. They are very inventive in their play and inexhaustible. But an older dog, suddenly confronted with toddlers, may not have such a charitable outlook.

At "Von Westphalen" we have mainly concentrated on our wires but we have also bred a lot of smooth and longhaired champions, both standards and miniatures.

There is a difference between all the varieties and, on top of that, there is a difference between the standards and the miniatures in their outlook on life. The longs are the more dulcet, the gentle ones. I assume there is something of a Spaniel cross behind them; just as our Spaniels, they melt. The smooths are something of an enigma. They can be very feisty, or gentle. Interestingly enough, the parody of the Doxie cartoon — the fat, waddling creature — isn't so. The show Dachshund (versus some of the overfed pets seen wheezing around) is lithe, elegant with a lot of muscle and vitality. Remember, they were originally bred to hunt badgers. Look at a badger (claws and teeth like a German Shepherd), and you'll see why the Dachshund is what he is. The good smooths are all muscle, all get up and go, and are very alert and inquisitive. The Dachshund standard states, "courage to the point of rashness."

Which brings us to the wire variety. They have had a terrier cross in days of yore, and it shows. They are more active, more outgoing, more vocal than the smooths and longs, and by far make the best pets in active households with children (the more the better).

Ten years ago everybody looking at our wire babies as pet puppies would ask, "Are they purebreds?" But that certainly isn't true today. Now we hear, "We really like those wires." It is a variety that has come up so far and so fast it boggles us.

The wires also make fantastic show dogs. They are imbued with their own love of life and self importance.

The "show type" wire runs two parallel courses. There is the extreme of what I call "evil" type — very harsh coated, almost a smooth. Sometimes they are mistaken for smooths until they are about six months old, when a few whisps of mandarin whiskers appear, some ear fringes, and some fur between the toes. At two or three years, they may be quite "wirey" in their whiskers and eyebrows and furnishings but they are, to me, never as appealing as the other type.

The second type just has more coat, and it has to be worked often minimally, but still needing "cleaning up." I am not suggesting in any way that a coat like thistledown, or dandelions about to expire, is the correct coat. As far as I am concerned, that's a very serious fault. The coat I'm speaking of is "double"; a shorter, more dense undercoat with longer guard hairs — yet there is enough to work with. The whiskers and eyebrows have a lot to do with expression.

We have bred both types, intertwining them. The very harsh-coated ones, bred to ditto, will eventually produce almost smooths. The others will deteriorate into soft coats. The old adage, never breed fault to fault to find a happy medium, holds here. The two types of coat are correct and temper each other. Our batting average is pretty good, although some litters can really be like Russian roulette, all over the lot.

Wires are, by unspoken and unwritten implication, allowed to be shorter and higher on the leg (the terrier influence?). However, we have found that if wires are bred to wires for too many unbroken generations, they tend to exaggerate these two aspects, plus getting "steeper" fore and aft, and their eyes get rounder. So every fourth generation we breed a wire to a smooth to get more length and a lower leg.

One has to fully realize the consequences of maybe a whole litter of smooth "wild boars" — wild boar being the most general wire color — and the disappointment of the litter being neither fish nor fowl. They can be shown (questionable at best) and they can be registered with the American Kennel Club, but they are ugly. However, some of our most famous wires have come from these "smooth" bitches bred back into a strong wire line (one having no smooth infusion for many generations).

Advice from a Geneticist
by Dr. C. William Nixon

Note: In writing this book, one of my objectives was to make the reader aware of problems within the breed, and to suggest ways in which these problems may be solved. As usual, someone else has already done this and done it better. That someone is Dr. C. William Nixon, geneticist, author, Dachshund judge and breeder. Two of his writings appear in this chapter. The first "Advice from a Geneticist" was written especially for this book. The second, "The Potential of a Breed as Seen by a Geneticist" was written in 1973 for the 35th Anniversary Issue of *The American Dachshund*. I found it so impressive that I asked Dr. Nixon to rewrite it for my readers. Both he and I found very little to change, and so, with some updating and minor changes by Dr. Nixon and our thanks to *The American Dachshund*, it is included here.

— *Lois Meistrell.*

THE COMPLETE GENETICS of Dachshunds encompasses so many facets that it would be virtually impossible for a writer to deal with all aspects in any detail within the confines of a single chapter. Therefore, we will resort here to various treatments of the different genetic factors — some will be dealt with in detail, some will be mentioned briefly, and still others will be keyed to the literature dealing particularly with that subject.

The first matter that one is confronted with involves the basic genetic principles underlying the subject. In this connection, a thorough understanding of the operation of these principles by the reader is clearly a necessity. However, this area is adequately covered by any one of several excellent textbooks of genetics presently available, and we will proceed on the assumption that the reader has at least some of this basic knowledge at hand. The second problem is that the area of inherited traits known to be present in the Dachshund is of such magnitude that it would be impossible to cover them all. However, these can be divided into categories, some of which can be dispensed with rather quickly. With these considerations in mind, we can proceed with our overview of genetics insofar as Dachshunds are concerned.

The first category of inherited factors in Dachshunds (and probably the one of most consequence) is that of genetic abnormalities. This, of course, includes all of the inherited diseases, deformities, etc.; in essence, those factors that are likely to be most damaging in some respect to the animal inheriting them. There are literally dozens of such inherited anomalies in dogs, and, fortunately, one can refer to other works for detailed discussions of most of them. An excellent book covering the subject is that of Burns and Fraser,[1] and a comprehensive bibliography has been compiled by Robinson[7] for the period to 1968 or thereabouts. *Table I* is a list of canine genetic anomalies, all of which are found in varying frequencies in Dachshunds.

Table I

Partial list of genetic anomalies found in Dachshunds:
1. Cleft palate
2. Cryptorchidism
3. Jaw and dentition anomalies
4. Epilepsy
5. Intervertebral disc protrusion
6. Merle syndrome
7. "Overshot" jaw
8. "Swimmers"
9. Crooked tail

"Slipped Disc" Syndrome

The most serious and widespread problem of all of these inherited abnormalities insofar as Dachshunds are concerned is that of intervertebral disc protrusion. The so-called "slipped disc" syndrome is of such importance that we will discuss it in some detail. The reader should bear in mind that the opinions expressed here in dealing with this subject are those of the author and come from his experience and observations over the past 25 years of Dachshund breeding. They may be correct or they may be incomplete and require additions and revisions as more is learned.

What are the facts about this disease? In this author's opinion, the disease is hereditary although its mode of inheritance is still uncertain, in part due to the late onset of the disease making a diagnosis of *all* pups in a litter (prior to breeding age) virtually impossible. The incidence of the disease in Dachshunds is far greater than any of the other breeds known to be afflicted (Beagles, Boxers, Cocker Spaniels, Pekingese, etc.). All coat varieties and sizes of Dachshunds appear to be involved, although the incidence in each category may be somewhat different. The necessarily limited breeding program of this author supports the hereditary nature of the disease and indicates with some certainty that the problem can be eliminated from a line with proper knowledge and genetic planning in the breeding program. This has been accomplished in both standard and miniature lines. Unfortunately, insufficient data resulting from a restricted breeding program would neither support a conclusive statement of fact nor warrant publication of causes and results at this time.

Misconceptions abound in regard to the disc problem. In this author's opinion, there is no relation of the incidence of disc disease to the basic structure considered normal in a Dachshund, that is, long and low to ground. Other breeds of similar structure do not necessarily exhibit the disease, and, within the Dachshund breed itself there is little or no correlation between body length or overall size to the disc problem. Our opinion is that a normal healthy young Dachshund should not be pampered. If it is prone to disc disease, it will certainly become manifest regardless of its habits. Of course, one must also realize that a Dachshund is not constructed for mountain climbing any more than a mountain goat is constructed for going to ground after game.

The unfortunate fact about the disc syndrome is that the animal does not ordinarily become noticeably afflicted until an approximate age of 2 to 5 years. This, of course, means that genetic damage has already occurred as a rule by the animal's having produced offspring which then carry the factor into a new generation. As early as 1970,[5] this author stated that the single most important finding that could be made in this connection would be a diagnostic method for detecting (in young dogs before breeding age) those animals that are predisposed to the disease, those that would almost certainly be afflicted by it by the time that they were two to five years of age. The necessary research to accomplish this should be done as quickly as possible. Indeed, in our opinion, it could have been accomplished long before the present time if adequate finances and brain power were applied correctly to the study of the basic *causes* of the problem instead of emphasizing the after-the-fact "cure" of the afflicted animal.

In the meantime, the breeder would be well-advised to refrain from breeding any and all dogs or their offspring if disc disease manifests itself at any age. Consultation and pedigree analysis by a knowledgable and *interested* geneticist (not necessarily a veterinarian) might then point the direction toward a successful breeding program that would exclude this dread disease. If one already has a line of Dachshunds unaffected by disc disease, exceedingly great care must be taken when using an "outside" stud dog in order to assure that the genetic potential to disc disease is not inadvertently brought into such a line.

In summary, although a start has been made on the scientific attack of disc disease, progress has been painfully slow. Meanwhile, breeders and especially pet owners are the ones who suffer both mentally and financially. The conquest of this most serious disease of Dachshunds should be of prime importance to all who are interested in the breed.

Size

The second category of inherited factors in Dachshunds is one of less serious consequence insofar as the animal is concerned. We refer here to the size of the animal, various coat types, colors, patterns, etc. All of these inherited traits, taken singly or in various combinations, are the building blocks for the varieties, types, etc. within the breed. The manifestations of these factors are not nearly so severe as those of the diseases already discussed. Indeed, this group of factors contributes to much of the interest the breed has for the fancier. Thus, we have those who could be termed miniature "freaks," dapple "freaks," etc.

For many years, the author has been closely associated with and has had an abiding interest in these factors as they are found in dogs as well as in other animals (hamsters, cats, etc.). He has authored approximately 12 scientific papers dealing with coat factors in hamsters, as well as a number of others as they concern Dachshunds. Most of the latter are to be found in *The American Dachshund* since 1956. Since the last paper on this subject in 1972, a new genetic factor for coat pattern has been found in Dachshunds and will be discussed here. Material on the more conventional colors and patterns will be reviewed and references given to original articles.

First, let us deal with the inheritance of size in Dachshunds. Clearly, size is determined in this breed, as it is in most animals that have been studied, by multiple genetic factors. This is disturbing to many breeders who expect simple "Mendelian" ratios for everything in genetics and that is not what one gets in dealing with size. Due to the influence of many inherited factors (the exact number is not known), a simple ratio is not forthcoming but instead we get a whole range of sizes when two animals of differing sizes are crossed. We need not get into the esoteric discussion of this, however, since the single important concern of the average Dachshund breeder is whether or not a specific dog will mature at under 10 lbs. (4.54 kg.) and therefore remain a miniature. In 1956, Nixon[2] published a study of normal growth in a series of Dachshunds. Over the years, several breeders have repeated portions of this work and have largely substantiated it. No exceptional cases have come to our attention. The main conclusion drawn from growth curves presented in the original paper was that it is possible to predict within a very narrow margin the mature weight of a Dachshund at 6 months of age. In addition, if one is familiar with and has established a growth *curve* for the dog's first 4 months, it is possible to predict at least grossly the mature weight from the *slope* of the curve. The mature weight cannot be predicted with any certainty from a single weight taken at 4 months.

Coat

If one excludes size (miniature vs. standard) in the Dachshund, the other variations of this breed are created by different combinations and manifestations of coat type, coat color, and coat patterning. Due to the fact that these are the most visible (and least detrimental to the animal) of all genetic traits, it is not surprising that they are often fixed upon as all-important in the creation of a beautiful animal, whereas, in truth, the most important factors required of such beauty in a specimen are those that govern its proper construction. However, these structural traits are not nearly so easy to work with genetically, and they are also not so easily observable and measurable for the non-professional. However, this is not true with coat color, pattern, or length — perhaps the first things that one notices and remembers about a particular dog. And in a general sense, these genetic factors (for coat type, color, and pattern) are all relatively simple to follow and to manipulate in their transmission from one generation to the next.

In a broad sense coat type appears to be inherited in simple "Mendelian" fashion and may be treated rather easily both here and in breeding practice. The genes for short hair operate as recessive to those of wirehair and as dominant to those of longhair. However, at a specific level, these factors are also influenced to varying degrees by modifying factors, also hereditary. Thus, a genetically long-coated Dachshund may exhibit almost any coat type from one closely resembling a smooth to one with great quantities of long hair; a genetically wire-coated Dachshund may be soft and fuzzy or else hard and wiry and the amount of coat may vary tremendously; the short-coated Dachshund may have hair in varying degrees of length and texture (short and bristly to long and soft). The modifying factors responsible for these variations are poorly understood at the present time, even though they are manageable by an experienced geneticist-breeder.

Color

Coat colors of highest frequency in the Dachshund population are red and black-and-tan, both basically self colorations. Beyond the general statement that red is dominant to black-and-tan, we will not discuss here the genetics of coat color inheritance of the common coat color factors but will assume that the reader is able to obtain such knowledge from the reference works. We will, instead, mention some of the lesser understood facets of coat color inheritance.

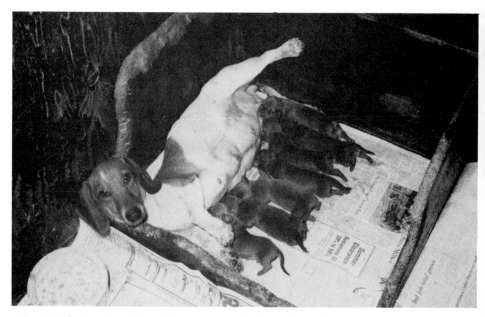

Nixon's Little Sunshine Girl, white and brown Dachshund, with her litter of 7 pups sired by a red miniature. Note that none of the pups is of the white and brown color, showing clearly that the white factor is a true recessive.

Laughlin's Topper Boy, a minature piebald Dachshund bred by Mr. and Mrs. F. Dewey Laughlin and now owned by Dr. Nixon. Piebald Dachshunds are extremely rare; only one other breeder has so far found them in her litters. She is Mrs. Maria Hayes, National City, California.

All coat colors and patterns vary considerably in shading and areas covered by the various colors in the coat, again the influence of modifying factors that are being inherited along with the more basic and familiar color and patterning factors. In a 1958 paper dealing with the color modifying factors in Dachshunds, Nixon, Stewart, and Eicholzer[3] came to two important conclusions. First, there are indeed modifying genetic factors present that influence red coloration (at least) of Dachshunds causing the color to vary enormously from dog to dog. These factors are in addition to, and independent of, the basic red or bicolor genes that determine the fundamental (or self) coloration of the dog. The second conclusion (which follows quite logically the first one) is that these modifying factors for color are carried and transmitted by *all* Dachshunds regardless of what self coloration they may be. Indeed, the same modifiers are likely responsible for variations in all of the self colors found in the breed. This means simply that modifying factors causing a particular shade of red in a red dog were inherited from *both* of that dog's parents even if one of the parents was a black-and-tan or some other color. It follows then that it is distinctly possible to produce a line of pure red Dachshunds of any shade desired (clear dark red is without any doubt the finest) that would breed true indefinitely once established. Color loss or dilution would not occur in such a line since all of the modifiers for color loss or further color enhancement would have been eliminated, and only the desired color modifiers would be present instead. The other self colors of Dachshunds (chocolate, blue, etc.) are less frequent and need not be discussed here except to say that they also vary in intensity and shade, much as any other color. Reasons for such variability are obvious in that they, too, are influenced by modifying factors, probably the same ones that modify the more ordinary colors of red and black-and tan.

Dapple or merle is a dominant factor for coat patterning and, as such, it can occur on any color of animal. A thorough treatment of dapple in Dachshunds was presented by this author in *The American Dachshund* in two companion papers[4][6] Little else need be added here except to say that, in the ensuing years since the publication of those papers, dapple Dachshunds have increased by leaps and bounds, and their overall quality has been greatly improved by careful and thoughtful breeding. Dapples now occur in considerable numbers in both standards and miniatures in all coat types and colors, and some of these are excellent specimens of the breed. It is encouraging to see what improvements can be made by a handful of persistent, dedicated, and knowledgable breeders.

The most recently discovered genetic factor affecting the coat of Dachshunds is another pattern factor, that of recessive (or piebald) white spotting. In many breeds of dogs, *e.g.* Beagle, Basset Hound, Fox Terrier, this is a standard coloration, but it has appeared only recently in Dachshunds. However, since it is a recessive factor, it must undoubtedly have spread through a large segment of the Dachshund population before it made its appearance as it now has. It is a real shocker for one to find pure white dogs with a few spots of color in a litter produced by two self-colored Dachshunds.

There are at least two logical explanations as to just how this new factor (for Dachshunds) came into the breed. It could have arisen as a spontaneous mutation within the breed, or it could have been introduced from another breed at some time in the past. It would be impossible to determine at this late date which route it took and exactly when it occurred. It is certain, however, that the occurrence was not a recent one, since a recessive gene must have the time and the generations to spread through a considerable number of dogs before two dogs that are carriers are, by chance, bred together and produce mutant offspring, in this case, piebald. (With close line-breeding or inbreeding, the time required for the appearance of a recessive factor could be somewhat shortened.) A carrier of recessive white spotting would be designated genetically as S/s^p and a piebald animal, s^p/s^p (The symbol "s^p" is used for piebald.) Clearly, when two piebald animals are bred together, they will produce 100% piebald. Please note that piebald white spotting (s^p) has no relation whatsoever to the dominant factor for dapple (M). Care should be taken not to confuse the two types of patterning.

Piebald appeared in a 1972 litter of smooth miniature Dachshunds bred by the late F. Dewey Laughlin and Mrs. Laughlin of Greensboro, N.C. The parents of this first litter (and succeeding similar litters) consisted of a red male and a black-and-tan female, both necessarily carriers of the s^p gene. There are no piebalds found in their immediate background. After Mr. Laughlin's death, Mrs. Laughlin transferred piebald animals to this author for further development and improvement. Utilizing this stock, it is now within the realm of possibility to produce not only tricolored Dachshunds but also the long sought after and elusive white (*not* albino) Dachshund with pigmented nose, etc.

It should be mentioned here that miniature longhaired Dachshunds of similar appearance have occurred in the kennel of Maria Hayes (National City, California). A picture of one of these dogs may be found in "*The Dachshund Variety,*" *3* (4): p. 21; Aug.–Sept., 1974. However, this author has not studied these animals nor their pedigrees in detail and can only report that their appearance in the photographs is similar to that of the miniature smooth ones in his possession.

Literature Cited

1. Burns, Marca and M. N. Fraser. *Genetics of the Dog,* J. B. Lippincott Co., Philadelphia, Pa. 1966.
2. Nixon, C. William. Growth studies in Dachshunds. *The American Dachshund, 17* (11): 4, 5, 18; July, 1956.
3. _____, R. C. Stewart, Jr., and A. W. Eicholzer. The inheritance of red color factors in Dachshunds. *The American Dachshund, 20* (1 and 3); 1958. (Also reprinted in the 20th Anniversary Supplement, *21* (Part 2, No. 1); Sept. 1959.
4. _____, and Barbara M. Murphy. Dapple Dachshunds — fact vs. fancy. *The American Dachshund, 32* (1): 4–8; Sept. 1970.

5. _____. The DCA disc project—its plans and hopes. *The American Dachshund, 32* (4): 8–9; Dec. 1970.
6. _____. Further notes on dappled Dachshunds. *The American Dachshund, 33* (9): 5–6; May, 1972.
7. Robinson, Roy. *Catalogue and Bibliography of Canine Genetic Anomalies*, CHART, 39 Queensway; West Wickham, Kent, England. 1968.

THE POTENTIAL OF A BREED
AS SEEN BY A GENETICIST

That progress in development and improvement of a breed ordinarily plods along at a snail's pace is fairly obvious to any keen observer. That it must do so is a ridiculous rationalization. What factors, then, are responsible for lack of progress, and what other factors could, if brought into operation, lead to a swifter overall improvement of a breed?

To begin, let us examine the usual status of a breed — any breed — of any valued animal (or plant), but particularly a breed of so-called purebred dogs. Among the several levels of activity among the breeders of said breed, we can identify everything from backyard pet breeder who is interested solely in the money to be made by exploiting the breed's current popularity, to the person who has a nice pet, would like to breed it once, and who knows or cares little about the breed as a whole, to the serious breeder who is ordinarily a lover of that particular breed and who works steadily over the years to effect its improvement. This last type usually possesses a good knowledge of the history and function of the breed, is aware of the standard of perfection, and tries to approach it through a rational breeding program, and perhaps shows the best specimens in competition. The three stereotypes are easily recognized, and, of course, there are all degrees of overlap between them. There are also all degrees from better to worse within each of the three categories. Furthermore, everyone fits into the scheme somewhere. The degree of breed improvement is partially dependent upon the proportion of these various groups to each other operating at a given time.

Breed improvement or lack of it is also influenced from another level, that of the parent organization and the final governing body, the registration agency. The importance of these groups cannot be underestimated, since their seriousness, progressiveness, and effectiveness directly influence their ability to *encourage* breeders in the constant but necessary quest for perfection. Such *encouragement* can only emanate from these organizations if they are functioning properly. At times, these bodies operate at somewhat less than peak performance due to such commonplace factors as party politics, lack of interest, lack of information, etc., all of which tend to place a blight upon all such organizations if not kept under constant surveillance.

Let us summarize at this point. Rate of progress in breed improvement is enhanced by the proportion of serious and knowledgable breeders working together with and being encouraged by governing bodies that are also serious and knowledgable and are thus also effective. The mutual respect coming out of such a working relationship is most important. Conversely (and obviously), rate of progress in breed improvement is slowed by a high proportion of non-serious, unenlightened, mercenary breeders working with (or against) governing bodies that are ineffective due, among other factors, to lack of interest and lack of knowledge of current problems. From this, it is an easy conclusion that, unless the breeders in the lower echelons can be somehow brought into the higher categories, any discussion of methods of breed improvement must be directed toward the serious breeder. It would simply be wasted on the others. Likewise, governing bodies must be responsive to suggestions and possibilities for breed improvement or all is lost. Therefore, from this point, the discussion will be directed toward that level where it will be understood and perhaps appreciated. The admonition "Shape up or ship out" is the advice to the others; either way the breed will be benefitted.

Since no one is ever perfect, it is axiomatic that the best and most serious breeders and governing bodies should be aware that there are various avenues that can facilitate and hasten breed improvement. The most promising of these at present is through the field of genetics. Since genetics is a most complex science and few breeders have the time or are interested in becoming proficient therein, the next best thing is to consult with a professional. It has become routine that breeders consult a professional, the veterinarian, in regard to health problems of their animals, and so it should be when it comes to matters of heredity and breed improvement as it may be influenced by heredity. The charge for services rendered by such a professional should be at the same level as that of a verterinarian or any other professional who may be consulted, since the field of genetics is by no means less complex.

It must be emphasized here that simple hereditary matters such as color and coat type inheritance can be handled by many tyros who are far from being qualified geneticists. The person who has mastered such simple rules of heredity to the point of handling them with ease often becomes a self-acclaimed expert in such matters. The problem here is that the simple factors of coat color, type, etc., are often of little importance. For instance, the color of an animal is of little consequence to that animal; whether it is deaf or has hip dysplasia on the other hand is exceedingly important. The more difficult areas, those of the inheritance of body size, length relationships of particular bones (proportional size), immunity to disease, head structure, lifespan, and the many hereditary diseases (deafness, blindness, hip dysplasia, disc protrusion, etc., etc.) will find these so-called experts retreating into the bushes.

It is well to realize, however, that little is known at present in some of these areas, whereas a great deal is known in others. The important point is that a professional geneticst should be able to understand the problem, find out what

Dr. C. William Nixon with Ch. Nixon's Forest Sprite.

is already known, and proceed with a sound scientific attack in an effort to solve it. Here, then, is where the breeder and the governing bodies of the breeds could avail themselves, either separately or together, of valuable means to improve a breed, whether it be to improve breed type with all its many subtleties, or whether it be to rid the breed of certain undesirable heritable factors. How often is this done?

In dealing with the genetics of living creatures, we know that mutations sometimes occur. In fact, that is how genetic variability comes about. For instance, all dogs or cats would be of the same color were it not for the coat color mutations that have occurred in each species over the years. It is reasonable to assume that mutations will continue to occur. Many of them are not beneficial to a breed but are clearly harmful and must be gotten rid of if the breed is not to regress. Other mutations may be beneficial or at least interesting.

As a specific example that such is the case, the cat fancy has recently been presented with an interesting dominant mutation causing the ears to fold down and the legs and tail to be somewhat shorter and thicker than normal. The mutation, first noted in Scotland, has been called Scottish folded ear. Resulting cats are interesting, attractive, and most appealing due to their appearance and excellent personality. It is a distinct possibility that every breed of cat can and will be produced with the folded ear trait. This, of course, presents certain problems to any cat governing body. How they approach such problems can

265

At left, Dr. Nixon's folded ear cat, Maude. At right, Maude's daughter, Maggie.

reveal much about the organizations themselves. The British clubs apparently have decided that folded ear is more of a deformity and should be ignored or eliminated. In truth, it is considerably less of a deformity than the tailless Manx cat, which they accept, or the bulldog type heads found in many dog breeds. Other examples could be cited of traits as serious or worse in their manifestation which are accepted as standard for a breed. However, Scottish folded ear cats have caught on and are becoming popular whenever they are known, and it will do little good to bury one's head in the sand, ostrich-style, and hope that it will go away. How will other cat governing bodies deal with this mutation? (See photograph of the author's folded ear cats, Maude and her daughter Maggie.) In the United States, at least three of the cat registration agencies accept the folded ear cat for registration.

If such a strange new form arose by mutation in a dog breed, would the breeder try to do something positive about it or would he simply get rid of the animal and deny that it ever occurred? In the event that he tried to pursue it, would he be assisted and advised by a sympathetic governing body or would he be accused of poor breeding practices? And finally, might not a geneticist be able to advise them both? One of the purposes of this lengthy discussion is to cause the reader to think a bit about all sorts of matters that are ordinarily pushed aside: about one's own breeding program — its success or lack of it; about the methods of operation of governing bodies — are they really going to the limits to help out or are they more of a hindrance, and if the latter why do we allow their continuation; about where improvement can be made in all of these areas; and about what further advice one may seek from the professionals — veterinarians, geneticists, biologists, psychologists, etc. Remember that there are vast unexplored areas in every breed where much improvement can be made rather quickly if *proper* practices are brought to bear. The warning flag is out to all — it says that if you don't do it, someone else will.

266

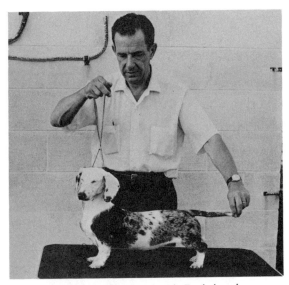
Phillip Bishop with dapple Dachshund.

Ch. Karlstadt's Mahareshi, bred-owned-and-handled by Barbara Murphy of Durham, N.H., winning at the 1969 Albany (Capital District) Dachshund Specialty under Dr. C. William Nixon. Mahareshi is the top producing dapple sire with 6 champions to his credit. —*Shafer*

268

For those who want a more sedentary pursuit with Dachshunds, there is Dachshund stamp collecting. The eleven foreign stamps pictured are from the collection of Morris Raskin of Newark, N. J. They are part of a collection shown in a series of articles titled "Stamp Hounding" published in *Dogs* magazine. Mr. Morris states: "I've been saving stamps since I was twelve years old and always enjoyed the hobby. About eight years ago I became interested in collecting stamps by topic instead of country. Because of my interest in dogs, having owned one most of my life, I selected them as my topic. The idea of combining the collection of stamps with my love of dogs was very appealing. However, there were no lists to use, and a lot of research went into finding the stamps that were needed. I constantly read the stamp papers and magazines, looking for information on dogs appearing on stamps. I have to prepare my own album pages, as there aren't any commercial albums covering the topic available." The Raskin family has a German Shepherd Dog and a white short-haired cat. A daughter appears to have inherited her father's love of animals, and is soon to graduate as a veterinarian from Purdue University.

Ch. Jager v Barcedor, longhaired, as a ten months old
puppy. Owned by Barton
Emanuel.

A smooth puppy from the
Westphal Kennels at Bed-
ford, N.Y.

Owning and Caring
For Your Dachshund

O WNING A DACHSHUND or any other breed of dog consti-
tutes an investment comparable to that for a major household appliance. Yet
while most families will shop and compare in purchasing such things as color
TV, microwave ovens, dishwashers and vacuum cleaners for price, upkeep
and the potential life of the machine, one out of a hundred will apply the same
sensible approach to acquiring a dog. Impulse buying, sentiment, emotional
reactions, and an almost total ignorance of the cost of keeping a dog during its
lifetime (an average of twelve years, with luck) are the usual reasons. Failure
to take a realistic look at dog ownership has meant disappointment for many
families and tragedy for many dogs. Humane Society shelters are filled with
dogs which, once acquired, proved too costly, too time-consuming, or both,
for their owners to keep. Only one-third of these ever find new homes; the
rest, unwanted, are destroyed. So for those of you who are about to buy your
first Dachshund, as well as for those who already own one, I've tried in this
chapter to give you a realistic picture of what life with your Dachshund en-
tails.

Most appliance manufacturers give a written guarantee for their machines,
as well as written directions for their use. Most Dachshund breeders will fur-
nish new owners with an American Kennel Club registration, a health certificate from their veterinarian and a medical record of the dog up to the time of
purchase — showing what innoculations, worming and any other veterinary
treatment it has received. They will also give you the feeding program which
the dog has been following up to the time of purchase.

Make Sure *You* Are Right for the Dachshund

However, they cannot be expected to foresee all eventualities, nor can they
be expected to be familiar with dog ordinances and regulations outside their

271

own community. So before you put your new Dachshund in the car and head for trouble, take the time to consider what you will have to invest in time and money in order to enjoy him or her for the rest of the dog's life.

First, take the dog to the veterinarian nearest you (better make an appointment in advance) and have him examine the dog as soon as possible after you bring it home. Some kennels will take the dog back if your veterinarian's opinion as to its general health does not agree with theirs. Others will not. So have it understood in writing before you take the dog. The kennels that do agree to take back the dog under the above circumstances usually set a time limit of not more than two days. There is good reason for their concern or outright refusal to take a dog back once it has left their kennel. They have no way of knowing what has happened to it. There might have been accidents, exposure to sudden changes in temperature, or contact with another dog already coming down with an infectious disease.

The maintenance of a Dachshund during its lifetime is cheap compared to the upkeep of many other breeds of approximately the same size and shape. Even the longcoated variety, unless you plan a show career for it, can be groomed at home. Such breeds as Dandie Dinmonts, West Highland Whites, Scottish Terriers and Sealyhams require almost professional expertise to keep them looking neat and well groomed.

Your Dachshund, once you bring it home, is your responsibility and it is important to find out what your community requires of you as a dog owner. Do prepare yourself by getting a copy of the rules and regulations from your town clerk. You may be startled at their number and at the harshness of the penalties for failure to comply with them.

Dog licenses and mandatory innoculations are usually a yearly requirement, at your expense. Others, which at first glance seem fairly easy, are regulations which require that a dog be kept on its owner's property, be kept on leash when on the public streets and in some areas, or require owners to clean up fecal matter deposited on the street by their dog and put it in a receptacle. Don't pass these over lightly with the thought, "Of course my husband and I and the children will walk the dog." Walking a dog three times a day, 365 days a year in all sorts of weather, is just not possible and you are kidding yourself if you think it is.

Housing Your Dog

Confining a dog to your own property is a lot easier said than done. A door left open inadvertently by children running in and out the house or a tradesman who leaves the gate open, etc., is an invitation to a Dachshund, with its curiosity and its built-in hunting instincts, to take off at full speed.

But take heart, there are answers. The most practical way, which solves both the daily walks and the property confinement, is to buy a portable wire enclosure. Most pet shops, hardware stores and mail order houses sell them in 4' × 4' × 3' panels, and a 4' × 8' enclosure placed conveniently near the back door where the dog can be let out, is large enough for a full grown Dachshund, and will last his lifetime and beyond. It can also be taken apart and carried on your car's rack when you go on vacation, and set up in a matter of minutes wherever you are staying. The cost is approximately $50 and it's worth it. The cheaper alternatives may be more costly in the long run.

Tying a dog, particularly a Dachshund, is very risky. The courageous little fellow feels that he is handicapped, and of course he is, when anything threatening comes along. A larger more aggressive dog, a child, waving something in its hand and running toward it, are all danger signals to the Dachshund. He has no alternative but to fight since he cannot escape. If you have ever tried to break up a dog fight, or had to deal with an irate neighbor whose child has been nipped (be it ever so slightly) by your Dachshund, you'll know what I mean. Even the types of chains that are designed to prevent a dog from becoming tangled leave your Dachshund at the mercy of anything or any person that approaches it. In time it will make the dog either vicious or timid. During World War II, when Dogs for Defense was experimenting in ways to train attack dogs, it was found that the quickest way to get a dog to attack was to march a column of people past it, shouting, waving sticks and generally behaving in a threatening manner. The dogs, tied to their kennels, had two reactions. Some were so frightened that they ran into their dog houses, whimpering pitifully and were no good for any further training. The majority of dogs leaped forward to the ends of their chains, snarling and barking in self-defense. They were no good either. They would attack all right, but they would go for anything, friend or foe and were so vicious that they were hard to handle in kennels.

Food is the easiest of your problems. Your Dachshund's breeder has probably given you the diet on which the dog was raised. If you are unable to get it, or wish to change it, do so gradually — not all at once. Even a good substitute diet can upset a dog's digestive system, if the change is sudden.

The shelves of your local supermarket have a wide variety of dog foods. Read the labels and find out what the manufacturer recommends as to the amount per day for a dog the size of your Dachshund and figure out the cost per meal. Many dog food companies have well-prepared booklets on the use of their products which can be obtained free. If you are confused by advertising claims, ask the nearest Dachshund owner whose dog appears healthy and in good shape. Another source of advice is a boarding kennel. They have to know how to feed dogs properly, including Dachshunds, or they couldn't stay in business.

The boarding kennel is another expense which sooner or later will confront you. At some time during the life of your Dachshund it will be necessary for you to close your house and leave the dog in the care of others until you return. Whether it is overnight or for a longer period, the boarding kennel is your best bet. There are some precautions you should take well in advance.

Find out what the rates are from a number of advertised boarding kennels; some charge less for small dogs, others have the same rate for all. Boarding kennels in cities and suburban areas tend to be higher priced than those in rural areas. Their taxes and expenses are usually higher, so it might be worthwhile if you are going to be away longer than a day or two, to drive out to a country kennel. Whatever your choice, inspect the kennel in advance. Don't stop at the reception room but ask to see the quarters where your dog will be kept. Overworked health officers seldom take time to inspect kennels unless there are complaints, so make sure that your Dachshund will spend his time in clean, comfortable surroundings.

The alternatives to leaving your dog under professional care run from dangerous to fatal. Leaving the dog alone in the house with a friend or neighbor to look in twice a day to feed and exercise him is risky. Your Dachshund, deserted by his family, may panic at being left alone in an empty house and chew everything in sight including the electric wiring, causing his own electrocution or a fire, or both. Leaving him alone in the cellar or garage with a supply of food and water for the duration of your absence will cause him to overeat, defecate all over the place, and here too, chew everything within reach including abrasive materials that could damage his stomach and intestines. It could be very expensive. Leaving him with a neighbor or friend puts them in an awkward position. They are not liable for accidents or the loss of your Dachshund, or for bites or violations of town ordinances, but you are — even if these things happened through their oversight or neglect.

The veterinarian is another expense as necessary for your Dachshund as the pediatrician is for your children. Ask him or her what the cost will be for the mandatory innoculations required by your town and what further preventative medication is recommended. Give the Dachshund's age and sex, and ask about the cost of spaying a female or neutering a male. You may think you do not want to do this, but later you may change your mind. In any case, it is not something that must be done immediately so you will have time to consider it carefully.

Selecting Your Dachshund

Decide first whether you want a miniature or a standard. If you have young children, the standard is your best bet. It will be better able to cope with active youngsters than the more delicate miniature. Other than that, the size and variety is simply a matter of preference for you and your family.

A puppy, whatever the sales price, is your most expensive choice. It will need more food, more often, more care and training and more veterinary services than an adult dog. It is also practically irresistible and there is great pleasure in watching it develop.

An adult dog, unless you want a show dog, will cost only slightly more than the puppy and you will have the advantage of seeing how it has developed and what its disposition is. Puppies can change almost overnight, physically and mentally, but a well-formed adult dog with a good disposition is not apt to change unless some major occurrence brings it about.

There is a reason for this apparent low price of grown stock at kennels. The dog may have been kept (rather than sold) as a potential winner or for breeding. When it failed to come up to exacting standards of the breeder, it was already out of the puppy stage, and its care and feed are a continuing expense, an expense which detracts from the kennels' investment in their show and breeding stock. To sell it at less than what it cost to raise, as a pet to a good home, relieves them of this expense.

I recall one kennel owner who liked to keep his kennel small; never more than ten dogs, including those being campaigned as dog shows, his breeding stock, and once a year a temporary increase by way of a litter of puppies. Once a dog or bitch finished its championship it was analyzed for future winnings in the Groups and Best in Show. If it did not have the potential, it was sold at the price of a well-bred puppy. The dog was already grown, leash broken (and usually housebroken, too) from its travels with a handler on dog show circuits, used to crowds and people, with a good disposition (it couldn't win if it bit the judge), and rated as a better than average specimen of the breed by a number of judges. That's what I'd call a real bargain. Perhaps you might be lucky enough to come across one like it.

The idea that a grown dog will not adapt readily to a new owner is just not true. There have been such things as "one man dogs," usually found among the Basque sheepherders who live alone except for the dog who works with them. But it is not true of most dogs. If dogs left in their care pined away for their owners, every boarding kennel and veterinary establishment would be out of business in a week.

Any Dachshund will be delighted to be the center of attention in the midst of his new family.

"Take the one that comes to you readily" is the advice given to most buyers when it comes to selecting your Dachshund. This is a good rule to follow if you have young children since a bold, outgoing dog will be happy in the rough and tumble play, noise and excitement that goes with children and their friends. However, if you have teenagers or an adult household, don't overlook the apparently timid dog, the one that hides in the corner and has to be coaxed out. There are, of course, dogs that are born shy but when it is a hereditary defect of temperament, there is apt to be more than one shy puppy in the litter. More likely, the timid dog is one that has been overwhelmed or bullied by the other puppies and, once removed from them, will turn out to be as pleasant and outgoing as the rest. If you are interested in the apparently timid pup, ask the breeder about it and get an opinion as to whether he or she thinks it will work out well with you and your family.

Male or Female

If you reject the female as a choice because of the twice-a-year nuisance when she comes in heat, think again. Spaying, which I recommend for a house pet, will take care of the problem once and for all. It will also provide you with a better watchdog since the female will be content at home all year round.

No question, a bitch in heat presents problems. During her heat periods she is as anxious to get to the males which will gather around your house, as they are to get at her. Wait 'til you get the bill for repairs to your lawn and shrubs from the males that come for miles around, or figure out what it will cost to board her at a kennel for three weeks twice a year. And there is, of course the very great probability that at some point she will be bred by a mongrel or cross-bred in spite of your watchfulness. The resultant pregnancy and disposal of a litter of unwanted puppies will be expensive and a sad experience.

Don't think you can avoid such problems by choosing a male instead. It will be almost impossible to keep him at home when there is a female in heat, either in the neighborhood or a stray, which he and other dogs will follow, only to get lost, far from home, when the pursuit is over. Here too, your best bet is to have the male neutered so that he, like the female will be content at home and worth his weight in gold as an alert watchdog. If he should accidentally breed a female or if you should mate him, forget about his house manners. Once bred, he will lift his leg on anything and will mount anything from the sofa pillows to your children's legs in frustration when he is not bred frequently as are stud dogs at kennels.

Breeding: For the average Dachshund owner there is just one word re breeding, "Don't." If you hope, by breeding to get another Dachshund just like the one you own, the chances are but one to 100 that you will succeed. It takes considerable know-how, plus a first hand knowledge, to determine which bloodlines produce which type of dog with what temperament. This book is full of stories about successful breeders who, on way to their success, failed many times to breed the kind of Dachshund they wanted.

Your best hope for getting another Dachshund with the qualities you so admire in your own dog is to go back to the same breeder or buy another dog with a similar pedigree.

There are other practical considerations. You are not going to have just one pup but anywhere from five to seven, which will require as much care as your newborn baby — even more, because there will be more than one.

"Doesn't the mother take care of them?" you ask. Yes, up to a point. She will nurse them usually (some are not good mothers) and keep them clean while they are nursing, but once they are on solid food it becomes your job to keep both the pups and their surroundings clean. Of course you still have to feed the mother, special food and more often, all during pregnancy and afterwards. Also, there is the veterinary bill for both mother and pups; they will need three inoculations each by the time they are eight weeks old.

When it comes to disposal of the puppies you're apt to have a hard time even if you plan to give them away. The friends who have been saying "if you ever breed her, I want one of the puppies," will have changed their minds by the time the pups arrive. And to try and sell them is like opening a small grocery store with a supermarket next door; your small classified ad in the local paper must compete with the display advertising and enticing claims put out by pet shops and the year-round advertising by Dachshund breeders in dog magazines that reach the really serious buyers who expect to pay a high price for a good Dachshund. Do talk to breeders and read some books on the subject before you undertake something that is going to cost you a lot of time and money. There are, of course, agreements regarding breeding which some kennel owners make with the buyer at the time of the sale, but think carefully about this before you agree. Find out what responsibility regarding care and sales the breeder is willing to assume in exchange for the use of your bitch for breeding purposes, or your male as a stud dog.

DAY TO DAY CARE

Few Dachshund owners realize the importance of grooming their dogs on a daily basis. Grooming makes the Dachshund look better and keeps him clean. This means less housework for the owner since dirt and loose hair are not tracked into the house. It is also a preventive measure to keep your dog and your rugs and upholstery free from ticks and fleas which a low-slung Dachshund can pick up in a five minute walk around the neighborhood, particularly if you let him roam in open fields or in parks frequented by other dogs. Daily brushing and inspection will keep the skin healthy and help you spot minor cuts and scratches before they become infected.

Dachshunds and most other dogs hate to be groomed but when it is gently done every day they will come to accept it, if not with pleasure at least with calmness and resignation.

The best way to insure this cooperative attitude is to do your grooming a little at a time. Don't attempt to get it all over with at once. A prolonged session tires a dog and makes him even more restless and harder to hold than when you first started.

Both puppies and adult Dachshunds are apprehensive when their owners begin poking around and lifting up their ears and feet. To overcome this I usually start by holding the dog in my lap and doing some gentle brushing. I don't really try to do a thorough job, but just try to get him used to the sensation, and to reassure him that he is not going to be hurt. From there I progress to a firm table at what is, for me, a convenient height. It has a rubber mat on it to prevent the dog from slipping and a good overhead light so that I can see what I'm doing.

Dogs seem to object least to brushing, so this is a good place to start. In the Smooth variety a rubber brush worked first against the growth of the hair and then with it, will provide a pleasant massage, loosen the dead hairs and surface dust and stimulate the natural oils in the skin, giving the coat a shiny, glossy look. In Wirehairs with close, hard coats, the same method may be used with the addition of a fine-toothed flea comb for his whiskers and eyebrows. (Be very careful in working around the eyes.)

In the soft-coated wirehairs, and of course in the longhaired variety, you will need more equipment and more time. The slicker brush, a standby for professional groomers, is not for the novice or amateur who is working on his own Dachshund. It does not get through to the undercoat and while the surface appears well brushed, tangles and mats build up underneath. Use, instead, a pin brush. It has longer and more widely separated teeth and penetrates deeper into the coat without scratching the skin. Brush the coat in sections and get the Dachshund to lie first on one side and then on the other so that you can work better and the dog does not become tired.

If you find mats and tangles, separate them gently with your fingers, a few hairs at a time, and then brush, in small sections, until you have them thoroughly combed out. If the mats are thick, a few drops of oil or of one of the commercial tangle removers placed on the mats and allowed to soak in for a few minutes will make the job easier. You will also need a pair of blunt-ended small scissors to trim the hair that grows between the toes and extends downward and outward from the soles of the feet, giving the dog's feet an untidy appearance and accumulating dirt and mud. Trim the hair so that the dog's feet appear neat and well-rounded.

As a final touch, run a medium toothed comb through the coat to make sure it is clear of tangles. A good buy is the metal comb that is half fine toothed and half medium. It can serve as a flea comb too.

Never wash your longhaired or heavily coated wirehair before grooming. The soap and water will make the tangles worse and set the mats more firmly. Bathing should be the very last step in the grooming process and if the dog is groomed daily, it is not necessary very often.

The longhairs have a special problem. The heavy growth of hair under the tail and on the rear legs often traps the bowel movement so that it remains in the hair rather than falling to the ground. To prevent this, we'll make use of the blunt scissors. Lift up the tail with one hand, and with the other, scissor the underside of the tail from the base outward about an inch. Do the same with the hair around the anus. Trim an area of about one inch around the opening, trimming close to the skin, so that there is room for him to defecate without the interference of hair. Roll the dog on his back and do the same with his genital organs. These fine soft hairs are the first to tangle and mat and unless they are either scissored away or kept combed, they will mat and pull on the dog's skin when he walks, making every step painful.

One of the most neglected areas in grooming a Dachshund are the ears. The pendulous flaps which cover the Dachshund's ears tend to retain moisture, foreign substances and promote the build-up of ear wax within the ear canal. This is not true in dogs whose ears stand erect, where better circulation of air is provided by the large unhampered opening, although they too need their ears cleaned and inspected.

To inspect and clean the Dachshund's ears, turn back the flap so that the inner ear is exposed and take a soft cotton ball (not Q-tips or their equivalent) moistened with baby oil. Gently push it into the ear and twist it around to clean the surface. If it comes out clean, shake a little dry boric acid powder into the ear and let the dog shake his head to toss out the excess. This will act as a preventative and a disinfectant. If there is a wax build-up, there will be an odor plus the yellowish stain on the cotton ball; and if ear mites are present, they will show up as little black specks on the cotton. If the ball comes out with a reddish stain and caked reddish particles, it is time to take your Dachshund to the veterinarian for a thorough cleaning and medication of the ear canal. Once this is done, follow his instructions until the ear is again clean. For wax build-up and ear mites that are not too advanced, there are a number of ear oils for dogs sold by pet shops that do a good job.

Nails are another badly neglected area in grooming, mainly because most owners do not know how to take care of them properly. The dog is apt to make it even more difficult by backing away and jerking his feet from you the minute you touch them. Here again, reassurance is the first step. Take the dog in your lap, roll him on his back and pick up one foot. Gently run a file over the nail, barely touching it. Like the start of brushing, you want him to find out that it is not going to hurt. As he becomes used to it, press down more on the file so it gives off a scraping noise and actually does file away some of the nail.

Once he will hold still for this, you can proceed to really file the nails. Do one foot a day at first, and work up to the use of the table instead of your lap. As the nails get shorter and need less filing, you can progress to all four feet in one day.

There are three ways of doing a dog's nails: with special scissors that cut off the ends, with electric sanders that file very quickly, or with a hand file. The hand file is the safest to use on a Dachshund.

In breeds that have white nails, the nerve ends (or the "quick") can be readily seen. They show pink, while the rest of the nail that grows beyond them is translucent white. With these dogs, you can see where to cut. So, if the dog will accept the noise of the electric sander, you can file quickly by this method, although the sander tends to heat up the nail if held too long in one spot.

Dachshund nails, on the other hand, are either black or brown, and it is impossible to tell where the nerve ends are located. If the nails are badly overgrown, one can take an educated guess and scissor off the tips. But from there on, the hand file should be used. With the file you control the speed and pressure by hand. You will be able to tell when you are getting near the nerve when the file no longer moves readily over the hard surface but becomes harder to push across a softened surface and does not give off the usual scraping sound.

I consider the use of scissors or electric sander in trimming nails to be unwise choices for the home groomer. Scissors can inadvertently cut a nerve and cause it to bleed. The electric sander will often frighten a dog by its noise, or cause an over-bold dog to try to touch it with his nose out of curiosity. If a Dachshund's nose is not scraped by the fast whirling disc, his ear tips may be, since they tend to fall forward into the machine. In the case of dogs of the

Nail Trimming. The method illustrated here is to take a sharp file and stroke the nail downwards in the direction of the arrow (as in Figure 24) until it assumes the shape in Figure 25, the shaded portion being the part removed. A three-cornered file should then be used on the underside, just missing the quick (as in Figure 26.) The operation is then complete; the dog running about quickly wears the nail to the proper shape.

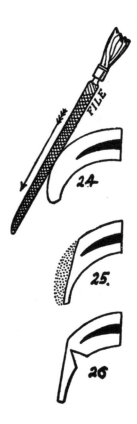

longhaired variety particularly, the hair can be caught almost instantly and tightly wound into the machine in seconds. Any of these will be painful experiences for the Dachshund, and will make it harder than ever to do his nails properly.

Short nails are of vital importance in a long-backed breed like the Dachshund. Even slightly overgrown nails can cause the feet to turn outward and very long ones can cause the feet to twist as he moves. In either case, bad posture which leads to back problems in later years, is the result. So, with nails, "do it yourself" and don't put it off until your visit to a groomer or the veterinarian.

Teeth represent another area which needs constant inspection and care. Puppies are born with "milk teeth" that fall out and are replaced by the permanent set of teeth. The milk teeth, 28 in all, begin to push through the gums a few days after birth and are all in by the time the dog is a month to six weeks old. These teeth are very sharp and since puppies grab everything in their teeth (including your hands), they scratch and draw blood easily. Also, if you own the mother as well as the pups, she will be more reluctant to nurse them since the teeth will scratch her, too.

There is a way to overcome this and at the same time get an early start on doing your dog's teeth. File them. They are not permanent teeth, and will drop out by the time the dog is about four months old, so you are doing no damage and making life easier for yourself, your family and the nursing Dachshund mother. Don't go to extremes, just file off the sharp points.

Normally, the milk teeth begin to fall out at about four months, but it doesn't always happen this way. Sometimes the permanent teeth are hampered or pushed into a wrong angle by some of the milk teeth that have failed to drop out on their own. Don't try to remove these leftover milk teeth yourself; take the dog to a veterinarian. The roots of the teeth are curved rather than straight and you can do permanent damage to a dog's jaw by improper extraction. The permanent teeth are 42 in number, 20 in the upper jaw and 22 in the lower.

Clean them, in adult Dachshunds, by taking a moist cloth or a soft bristle tooth brush dipped in warm water and baking soda. Rub gently first the upper and then the lower set. Watch for signs of tartar buildup, a brownish crust that forms at the gum line, which must be scraped off if the gums and teeth are to be kept healthy. To do it at home you will need a dental scaler with right and left angles. Begin with the upper teeth and scrape downward from the gum line. Repeat with the lower teeth, scraping upward. The dogs actually hate this more than any other phase of grooming, so, unless you have accustomed them to work on their teeth from puppyhood, you may want to give up and take them to the veterinarian for a monthly session.

There are a number of commercial products that keep a dog's breath sweet smelling and at the same time destroy bacteria and slow down the formation of tartar. I use a product called "Happy Breath" but I'm sure in the competitive world of dog suppliers there are other equally effective products.

Many Dachshund owners are not even aware of the presence of anal glands in their dogs. Every dog, including Dachshunds, has a pair of these glands located, one on each side, just below the opening of the anus. Their use is controversial. Some believe that the glands are left over from the dog's primitive ancestor and once functioned, like a skunk's, to repel enemies. Other believe they are there to help in the bowel movement, and that the secretion they discharge acts as a lubricant.

Sometimes the anal glands function normally for the dog's entire lifetime. More often they tend to become clogged. The accumulation of this bad smelling mass in the glands, irritates the anal canal and the dog tries to relieve himself by licking at his rear, or sliding across the floor on his rear end (a symptom often mistaken by owners as a sign of worms) or by biting at his tail. If neglected, this mass hardens and forms an abscess, which is very painful, and the dog becomes listless, his appetite decreases and he is constipated. The skin around the anus may bulge over the glands.

If you suspect trouble with these glands it is not difficult to expel the accumulation by squeezing. It is not very pleasant, but it is something that has to be done. Here's how to do it. With the dog on the table, take a good-sized piece of cotton in your hand and cover the anus with it. The stuff will spurt out when you squeeze, so place the cotton where it will absorb it. Hold the tail up with one hand and with the other take your thumb and index finger, protected by the cotton, one over each gland, and press gently in an upward and outward motion. Do it very gently; usually the liquid will spurt out at the slightest pressure. If it has been accumulated for some time, it will come out in a semi-solid form like paste out of a tube.

The color of this secretion is normally a brownish yellow but if you notice specks of blood or pus in the discharge take the dog to a veterinarian. This means there is infection and the dog will need antibiotics, by direct injection into the glands, to combat it.

There is a really awful smell to the whole business so be prepared to wash the dog's rear immediately after with warm soapy water. Rinse and dry thoroughly, and for your own sake, spray the room with your favorite room deodorant.

Bathing the dog should be done only after he has been groomed. Use a mild shampoo and, for around the head, a no-tears baby shampoo. Depending on the Dachshund's size you can use either the kitchen sink or the bathtub. Have everything ready before you start. Plenty of clean towels, your grooming table near the sink or tub, and your hair dryer ready to be plugged in. Plug the Dachshund's ears with cotton balls that have been smeared with vaseline.

Put a rubber mat in the sink or tub so that he does not slip and attach a spray hose to the faucet. Run the water at a warm (but not hot) temperature and place the Dachshund in the tub. Wet him all over and then apply the shampoo, beginning at the rear and working forward to the neck and chest. Leave the head until last. Massage the soap with your finger tips and work up a good lather. Still leaving the head dry, rinse the dog's body thoroughly. In the long-hairs it is well to give two soapings to get the hair absolutely clean, but with all varieties, be sure that the soap is completely rinsed off so that the water runs clear.

Now for the head. Wet it with a sponge or washcloth and apply the no-tears soap, and rinse. Squeeze out the excess moisture and quickly wrap the dog in a dry towel and transfer him to the table. Towel him as dry as possible and then take more fresh dry towels to keep him warm and start the hair dryer. Remove cotton from the ears and make sure the ear flaps are dry. A Dachshund of the longhaired variety looks absolutely beautiful if you brush him while the dryer is on. Brush the hair in the direction you want it to lie. As the dampened hair dries it fluffs and hastens the drying.

A word about the dog's eyes. A daily use of an opthalmic solution such as Eye-brite, or Clear Eyes, keeps them free of irritation.

Where you walk your dog will also affect his health and well-being. Sidewalks in hot weather can be torture for a dog. A sandy beach in the heat of the day can be just as painful. Because he is so low to the ground, the heat reaches the body as well as the feet. Do try to exercise your city dog during the cooler periods of the day or, if it is absolutely essential to take him out, put on boots, which are usually reserved for cold weather to protect the feet from the salt solution used by departments of sanitation to melt ice.

Country fields can be just as injurious. Our own Dachshunds survived our first Florida circuit thanks to a friendly tip from one of the handlers. We learned to never walk them anywhere but on the cement sidewalks without covering the grass or dry ground with newspaper. There are weeds that drop tiny round seeds with spiked burrs. One step on them and the dog is lame for days. Do think about the outdoor environment before you take your dog for a walk.

Dogs do not always take kindly to this concern. During the Easter season of 1976, Betty McNeill and I drove to Lincoln Park, New Jersey, to visit Laurence Horswell at a nursing home. We took Betty's two Dachshunds with us since on a previous visit he had so enjoyed them. The temperature had broken all records and earlier in the day the thermometer outside Betty's apartment had registered 108 degrees.

On our arrival we walked the dogs toward the entrance on the cool lawn avoiding the cement walks. The two Dachsies, city-bred, strained at their leashes until they reached the familiar cement sidewalk and then relaxed and walked on loose leads to the entrance.

Worth waiting for!

A Last Word

We've tried to give you a realistic picture of the cost of keeping your Dachshund safe, well and happy. It is not all that expensive, but it usually turns out to be more than the average person believes it to be.

But the rewards of Dachshund owning are many, too. You don't just have my word on this — look at the thousands upon thousands of Dachshund owners in the United States. If people didn't enjoy owning them, the breed wouldn't be so high in the registration totals.

Importantly, don't rush getting your dog. If you feel you cannot undertake a Dachshund right now, wait — as did the Mehrers, the Horswells, and more recently the James Muses — all of whose stories are told elsewhere in this book. Wait until you are in a position to care for your Dachshund properly.

BIBLIOGRAPHY

ALL OWNERS of pure-bred dogs will benefit themselves and their dogs by enriching their knowledge of bree
and of canine care, training, breeding, psychology and other important aspects of dog management. The follo
ing list of books covers further reading recommended by judges, veterinarians, breeders, trainers and other authoriti
Books may be obtained at the finer book stores and pet shops, or through Howell Book House Inc., publishe
New York.

BREED BOOKS

AFGHAN HOUND, Complete	Miller & Gilbert
AIREDALE, New Complete	Edwards
AKITA, Complete	Linderman & Funk
ALASKAN MALAMUTE, Complete	Riddle & Seeley
BASSET HOUND, Complete	Braun
BLOODHOUND, Complete	Brey & Reed
BOXER, Complete	Denlinger
BRITTANY SPANIEL, Complete	Riddle
BULLDOG, New Complete	Hanes
BULL TERRIER, New Complete	Eberhard
CAIRN TERRIER, Complete	Marvin
CHESAPEAKE BAY RETRIEVER, Complete	Cherry
CHIHUAHUA, Complete	Noted Authorities
COCKER SPANIEL, New	Kraeuchi
COLLIE, New	Official Publication of the Collie Club of America
DACHSHUND, The New	Meistrell
DALMATIAN, The	Treen
DOBERMAN PINSCHER, New	Walker
ENGLISH SETTER, New Complete	Tuck, Howell & Graef
ENGLISH SPRINGER SPANIEL, New	Goodall & Gasow
FOX TERRIER, New	Nedell
GERMAN SHEPHERD DOG, New Complete	Bennett
GERMAN SHORTHAIRED POINTER, New	Maxwell
GOLDEN RETRIEVER, New Complete	Fischer
GORDON SETTER, Complete	Look
GREAT DANE, New Complete	Noted Authorities
GREAT DANE, The—Dogdom's Apollo	Draper
GREAT PYRENEES, Complete	Strang & Giffin
IRISH SETTER, New Complete	Eldredge & Vanacore
IRISH WOLFHOUND, Complete	Starbuck
JACK RUSSELL TERRIER, Complete	Plummer
KEESHOND, New Complete	Cash
LABRADOR RETRIEVER, Complete	Warwick
LHASA APSO, Complete	Herbel
MASTIFF, History and Management of the	Baxter & Hoffman
MINIATURE SCHNAUZER, Complete	Eskrigge
NEWFOUNDLAND, New Complete	Chern
NORWEGIAN ELKHOUND, New Complete	Wallo
OLD ENGLISH SHEEPDOG, Complete	Mandeville
PEKINGESE, Quigley Book of	Quigley
PEMBROKE WELSH CORGI, Complete	Sargent & Harper
POODLE, New	Irick
POODLE CLIPPING AND GROOMING BOOK, Complete	Kalstone
ROTTWEILER, Complete	Freeman
SAMOYED, New Complete	Ward
SCOTTISH TERRIER, New Complete	Marvin
SHETLAND SHEEPDOG, The New	Riddle
SHIH TZU, Joy of Owning	Seranne
SHIH TZU, The (English)	Dadds
SIBERIAN HUSKY, Complete	Demidoff
TERRIERS, The Book of All	Marvin
WEIMARANER, Guide to the	Burgoin
WEST HIGHLAND WHITE TERRIER, Complete	Marvin
WHIPPET, Complete	Pegram
YORKSHIRE TERRIER, Complete	Gordon & Bennett

BREEDING

ART OF BREEDING BETTER DOGS, New	Onstott
BREEDING YOUR OWN SHOW DOG	Seranne
HOW TO BREED DOGS	Whitney
HOW PUPPIES ARE BORN	Prine
INHERITANCE OF COAT COLOR IN DOGS	Little

CARE AND TRAINING

COUNSELING DOG OWNERS, Evans Guide for	Eva
DOG OBEDIENCE, Complete Book of	Saunde
NOVICE, OPEN AND UTILITY COURSES	Saunde
DOG CARE AND TRAINING FOR BOYS AND GIRLS	Saunde
DOG NUTRITION, Collins Guide to	Colli
DOG TRAINING FOR KIDS	Benjam
DOG TRAINING, Koehler Method of	Koeh
DOG TRAINING Made Easy	Tuck
GO FIND! Training Your Dog to Track	Da
GUARD DOG TRAINING, Koehler Method of	Koeh
MOTHER KNOWS BEST—The Natural Way to Train Your Dog	Benjam
OPEN OBEDIENCE FOR RING, HOME AND FIELD, Koehler Method of	Koeh
STONE GUIDE TO DOG GROOMING FOR ALL BREEDS	Sto
SUCCESSFUL DOG TRAINING, The Pearsall Guide to	Pears
TEACHING DOG OBEDIENCE CLASSES—Manual for Instructors	Volhard & Fish
TOY DOGS, Kalstone Guide to Grooming All	Kalsto
TRAINING THE RETRIEVER	Kers
TRAINING TRACKING DOGS, Koehler Method of	Koeh
TRAINING YOUR DOG—Step by Step Manual	Volhard & Fish
TRAINING YOUR DOG TO WIN OBEDIENCE TITLES	Mors
TRAIN YOUR OWN GUN DOG, How to	Good
UTILITY DOG TRAINING, Koehler Method of	Koeh
VETERINARY HANDBOOK, Dog Owner's Home	Carlson & Gif

GENERAL

AMERICAN KENNEL CLUB 1884-1984—A Source Book	American Kennel Clu
CANINE TERMINOLOGY	Spi
COMPLETE DOG BOOK, The	Official Publication American Kennel Clu
DOG IN ACTION, The	Ly
DOG BEHAVIOR, New Knowledge of	Pfaffenberg
DOG JUDGE'S HANDBOOK	Tietj
DOG PEOPLE ARE CRAZY	Ridd
DOG PSYCHOLOGY	Whitn
DOGSTEPS, The New	Elli
DOG TRICKS	Haggerty & Benjam
EYES THAT LEAD—Story of Guide Dogs for the Blind	Tuck
FRIEND TO FRIEND—Dogs That Help Mankind	Schwar
FROM RICHES TO BITCHES	Shattu
HAPPY DOG/HAPPY OWNER	Sieg
IN STITCHES OVER BITCHES	Shattu
JUNIOR SHOWMANSHIP HANDBOOK	Brown & Mas
OUR PUPPY'S BABY BOOK (blue or pink)	
SUCCESSFUL DOG SHOWING, Forsyth Guide to	Forsy
TRIM, GROOM & SHOW YOUR DOG, How to	Saunde
WHY DOES YOUR DOG DO THAT?	Bergm
WILD DOGS in Life and Legend	Ridd
WORLD OF SLED DOGS, From Siberia to Sport Racing	Copping